Sketches of Landscapes

Sketches of Landscapes

Philosophy by Example

Avrum Stroll

A Bradford Book

The MIT Press

Cambridge, Massachusetts

London, England

This book was set in Sabon on Ventura Publisher by Wellington Graphics, South Boston, and was printed and bound in the United States of America.

First printing, 1998.

Library of Congress Cataloging-in-Publication Data

Stroll, Avrum, 1921–
    Sketches of landscapes : philosophy by example / Avrum Stroll.
        p.   cm.
    "A Bradford book."
    Includes bibliographical references and index.
    ISBN 0-262-19391-4 (alk. paper)
    1. Philosophy. 2. Description (Philosophy) I. Title.
B105.D4S77 1997
191—dc21   97-18852
                                                              CIP

For Mary

Contents

Preface

I was somewhat uneasy about choosing "Sketches of Landscapes" as part of the title of this book. It is a well-known consequence of the computer revolution that librarians sometimes catalog disquisitions on the prisoner's dilemma as criminal psychology and treatises on game theory as sporting activities. I feared this study might be classified as horticulture or landscape architecture. Instead, it is, of course, a work in philosophy, yet its connection with gardening may not be wholly remote. Like Wittgenstein's later philosophy, it is dedicated to "clearing up the ground of language" on which certain kinds of "houses of cards" stand. I hope, however, that it does more: that it makes positive and constructive contributions to this ancient subject.

I found the phrase "Sketches of Landscapes" attractive in itself, and it fits my approach as well. It is taken from the Preface to Wittgenstein's *Philosophical Investigations*. There in a famous paragraph he wrote the following:

After several unsuccessful attempts to weld my results together into such a whole, I realized that I should never succeed. The best that I could write would never be more than philosophical remarks; my thoughts were soon crippled if I tried to force them on in any single direction against their natural inclination. And this was, of course, connected with the very nature of the investigation. For this compels us to travel over a wide field of thought criss-cross in every direc-

tion. The philosophical remarks in this book are, as it were,
a number of sketches of landscapes which were made in the
course of these long and involved journeyings.

In these essays the reader will find sketches of various
philosophical landscapes. They deal with major problems
of metaphysics and epistemology: scepticism, meaning and
reference, representative versus direct realism in perception, holism, and the use of names in fiction. Like Wittgenstein, I felt that what I had to say about these issues fell
short of the book-length treatment each deserved. Yet the
topics are connected by a particular methodological approach. This, as the rest of the title indicates, I call "philosophy by example." Each of these problems is analyzed
from this perspective. It thus provides the connective tissue
that binds these sketches together. Still, the method is not
the message. It is the substantive results that ultimately
matter, and these will be found in the chapters that follow.

Nevertheless, because the method is crucial, it may be
useful for me to give a brief account of it, while emphasizing that it is best understood and appreciated in its detailed
applications to problems. Like most philosophies, it has
both positive and negative features.

On the positive side, it espouses a descriptive approach. It accepts the ancient tradition, deriving from the
Greeks, that one of the fundamental tasks of philosophy is
to give an accurate account of the world's various ingredients, including its inanimate and animate features. But it
contends that because these features are inexhaustibly
complex, no single, overarching theory or conceptual
model can provide such an account. Instead, it emphasizes
the plurality of specific cases, episodes, scenarios, and
contexts. The approach is thus piecemeal, and follows
Wittgenstein in finding and inventing intermediate cases
(*Zwischengliedern*). In stressing the importance of examples, it runs counter to one of the most powerful and

seductive ways of thinking about the world, the Platonic tradition, which denigrates examples in the search for essences. To be sure, the search for common properties is not limited to Platonists. An empiricist such as Hilary Putnam is committed to a similar quest with respect to natural kinds. As we shall see in the chapter "Reflections on Water," my approach arrives at wholly different results from his.

From a negative perspective, my piecemeal, example-oriented approach disavows any sort of all-encompassing philosophy. It rejects the thesis that the essence of philosophy is argument or justification; it rejects all forms of philosophical monism, such as idealism or materialism, including eliminative materialism; it rejects all dichotomies that purport to give exhaustive and exclusive classifications of reality, such as Plato's use of the appearance and reality distinction; and it rejects the doctrine that science and science alone is the key to understanding the world. It favors pluralism on the ground that this is how the world is, and without denying the importance of science, it describes alternative, philosophically autonomous ways of comprehending reality. These positive and negative aspects will appear with almost equal emphasis in the essays to follow.

Acknowledgments

In the five years and the several revisions it took me to write this book, I was enormously helped by a large number of persons: philosophers, graduate and undergraduate students, and friends with a literary bent. I especially wish to thank Henry Alexander of the University of Oregon, who read through the first two drafts of the manuscript, supererogatory acts beyond any question, and whose critical and constructive comments were indispensable to the final version. Former colleagues Zeno Vendler and Robert Rowan each went through the whole manuscript at least once, and their comments too were perceptive and beneficial. My thanks go out to Marianne McDonald, Georgios Anagnostopoulos, Paul Churchland, John Searle, Michael Mendelson, Eero Byckling, John Smythies, Rosaria Egidi, Marco Borioni, and Guido Frongia. In different ways, each of them provided invaluable assistance.

I am especially grateful to Professor Caroline Bruzelius, a distinguished medieval art historian, and Director of the American Academy in Rome, and to Pina Pasquantonio, Assistant Director, for their kindness and hospitality. Much of the final version of the manuscript was written while I was a visiting scholar at the Academy on two occasions, in 1994 and 1995, and without the cooperation and assistance of Caroline and Pina this work might never have been written at all. Finally, my debt to my wife, Mary, is the largest of all. Taking time away from her research and writing about twelfth-century papal politics, she subjected the many arguments in this book to intensive critical scrutiny. Her standards of clarity and precision have been a model to me. But this is only one of the respects in which she made this work possible.

Sketches of Landscapes

Scepticism Undone

In this chapter my focus will be on scepticism and how it is possible to meet its powerful challenges. There are many forms of scepticism, some of which professedly do not advance arguments. Since they presumably are not systems of beliefs or doctrines, I shall set them aside here. But there is an argumentative tradition that is at least as important, and it is this set of doctrines that I shall refer to when I speak of "scepticism." This tradition is parasitic on a kind of philosophy it calls "dogmatic," and its aim is, and has been, to show that dogmatists are mistaken in believing that knowledge and/or certainty are attainable by human beings. Interestingly enough, scepticism and its dogmatic opponents share certain deep beliefs: that epistemology is dedicated to the justification of knowledge claims; that justification consists in argumentation, i.e., in providing reasons (grounds, evidence) in support of such claims; that in the justificatory process some of these premises function as criteria; and that such criteria must be satisfied if any claim to know that p is true. While accepting these principles, sceptics also deny that there are any criteria whose satisfaction will guarantee that p is known to be true.

As mentioned in the Preface, I reject these principles and the sceptical challenge to them. I hold, for example, that criteria may not exist where assertions of true knowledge are made, and that even where criteria do exist, they are sometimes relevant to the determination of knowledge claims and sometimes not. I regard the dichotomy that one must either be a dogmatist or sceptic as spurious, and I further deny that every defense of knowledge and certainty must follow a justificatory pattern. I am thus neither a dogmatist nor a sceptic.

It is essential that scepticism and dogmatism be accurately characterized if one is to avoid tilting at windmills. I will therefore begin with a little history, using Richard Popkin's definitive study of scepticism as a main text.[1]

ONE

Popkin has taught us some valuable lessons about the history of modern philosophy, and especially about the important role that scepticism plays in that history. Before Popkin's seminal writings on the influence of Sextus Empiricus on Bayle, Montaigne, and Hume, many historians regarded scepticism as an eccentric aberration in the steady movement toward a better understanding of the nature of knowledge. What Popkin has shown is that scepticism is central to that process and one of its main driving forces. Benson Mates concurs:

Due largely to the work of Richard Popkin and his students and associates, it is now clear that the rediscovery and publication of these works in the sixteenth and seventeenth centuries led directly to the skepticism of Montaigne, Gassendi, Descartes, Bayle, and other major figures, and eventually to the preoccupation of modern philosophy, right down to the present, with attempts to refute or otherwise combat philosophical skepticism.[2]

According to Popkin scepticism operates by accepting certain basic assumptions (or principles or conceptual models) of its so-called "dogmatic opponents," rather than rejecting them from the outset, and then proceeds to show that they have sceptical implications. Scepticism is thus one outcome that a deeper exploration of such assumptions, principles, or models may produce. Hume is an exemplar of the point. Starting from an acceptance of Newtonian science as providing a model of knowledge, he is driven reluctantly to sceptical conclusions about the fundamental tenets, such as the principle of induction, upon which any science is based.

It is no accident, then, as seen from Popkin's perspective, that in the central domains of philosophy, wherever knowledge claims have been seriously advanced, sceptical challenge has marched in tandem with dogmatic assertion. This is true in moral theory, in philosophy of religion, in philosophy of mind, in epistemology, and now even in the philosophy of language—witness the sceptical implications that Kripke has drawn from Wittgenstein's account in the *Investigations* of what it is to follow a rule.[3] Popkin's further point is that the needlelike thrusts of the sceptic have not only had a deflationary effect but have also exercised a positive influence as well, forcing theorists to reformulate and to rework their conceptions of knowledge and/or certainty in order to make them resistant to such challenges. In this way the sceptic has given impetus to the forward movement of philosophy since the Renaissance.

In the early part of the twentieth century, for example, both Moore and Wittgenstein were caught up in this dynamic development. Moore's late, famous papers, such as "A Defense of Common Sense" (1925), "Proof of an External World" (1939), "Four Forms of Scepticism" (1940), and "Certainty" (1941), and Wittgenstein's last written work, *On Certainty* (posthumously published in 1969), are explicit attempts to defend the capacity of humans to attain knowledge and certitude. Even more recently there has been a torrent of books and articles emphasizing the continuing importance of scepticism: Peter Klein's *Certainty: A Refutation of Scepticism* (1981), Barry Stroud's *The Significance of Philosophical Scepticism* (1984), P. F. Strawson's *Skepticism and Naturalism: Some Varieties* (1985), Thomas Nagel's *The View from Nowhere* (1986), Marjorie Clay and Keith Lehrer's *Knowledge and Scepticism* (1989), Cristina Baccillieri's *L'Erba È Veramente Verde? Wittgenstein e le Modalita della Certezza* (1993), my *Moore and Wittgenstein on Certainty* (1994), and Benson Mates's *The Skeptic Way* (1996).

Because of its symbiotic function, scepticism has historically taken a variety of different forms, most of them engendered in response to new developments in science and science-oriented theories of knowledge. Accordingly, it is subject to multifarious classificatory schemes reflecting various contrasts and distinctions. One of the oldest, most familiar, and still among the most useful of these taxonomies distinguishes radical from mitigated forms of scepticism. And within this division finer discriminations can be drawn among forms of radical scepticism, such as Pyrrhonic and Academic scepticism, as both Popkin and Mates make clear.

Without trying to explore this rich and complex distinction in any depth, I can say that what unites both categories, that is, what allows historians to subsume them under the rubric "scepticism," is their common attitude that knowledge and certainty are unattainable. By contrast, what divides them is a disagreement about whether any reliable information about the world is possible. Radical sceptics, such as the Pyrrhonists that Popkin describes, affirm that any supposed advance toward knowledge is illusory. Moderate sceptics are of the opposite conviction, holding that some beliefs have more evidential warrant than others, though none can be established with certainty.

Sometimes both attitudes are to be found in the same philosopher. Hume is a good example. The radical scepticism found in the chapter "Of scepticism with regard to the senses" in the *Treatise of Human Nature* drives him to the position that we have neither demonstrative nor probable grounds for believing in the existence of an external world. In that work he also develops a parallel, radically sceptical argument with respect to the principle of induction. Though we believe these principles, and indeed could not live or function without assuming they are true, he avers that there is absolutely no evidence whatsoever in support of such belief. Yet elsewhere in the *Treatise*, e.g., in discussing probability, he asserts that some inferences about the external world, and some about the future, are more probable and have more evidential support than others. In these latter cases his scepticism is of a mitigated sort.

It is also important to stress that both forms of scepticism presuppose the same conception of knowledge, a conception, as Popkin indicates, that is also espoused by their dogmatic opponents. This conception rules out any claim to the effect that a high degree of probability could be a case of knowledge. It has three facets: first, if A knows that p, p is true; second, if A knows that p, it is impossible for A to be mistaken; and third, if A knows that p, A must have "suitable" grounds, a justification, for the claim to know. The last two facets are controversial and have been subject to intensive scholarly debate. For example, with respect to the latter, Gettier's counterexamples show that one can be justified in believing that p without knowing that p.[4] And apart from Gettier's countercases, there is widespread disagreement about how to characterize such notions as "suitable grounds" and "justification."

The idea that if A knows that p it is impossible for A to be mistaken about p is a key element in the sceptical challenge. As the radical or mitigated sceptic views the matter, it is not necessary to show in any given case that A, who is asserting a knowledge claim, is *in fact* mistaken. All that needs to be pointed out is that *it is possible* for A to be mistaken, for if that is so, it follows from this conception of knowledge that the dogmatist also accepts that A cannot know that p is true.

This inference gives rise to the issue of whether any form of justification, such as evidential backing, is ever airtight. Once this possibility is surfaced, the sceptic is in a position, via such arguments as the dream and demon hypotheses, to challenge the contention that any species of evidence is conclusive. If it is always possible that statements describing the evidence are true while the derived conclusion p is false, one can never know that p is true. One might give a true description of what one is sensing, say a fire burning in a fireplace, while in fact one is hallucinating such an event. Historically, the sceptics have developed a panoply of arguments emphasizing the gap between the evidential base and the conclusion upon which it rests—a gap that allows for doubt about the conclusion. Curiously enough, although Gettier is not a sceptic, his contention that true belief is not a sufficient condition for knowledge follows the same pattern of argumentation. The strategy also has parallels in formal logic, where to show that an argument is invalid, one need not show that its premises are false but only that it is possible for them to be true and the conclusion false. In the same way, it is sufficient for the sceptic to show that true premises do not guarantee the truth of a knowledge claim based on them.

I illustrate the point with an actual historical example. In "Certainty" Moore claimed that he knew that he was not dreaming because (at the moment of speaking) he knew he was standing up. The sceptical response to this argument was not to make a counterclaim, i.e., to deny that at the moment he was speaking, Moore was standing up.

Rather, it was to point out that since Moore *might* have been dreaming at the moment in question, he could not know that he was standing up. This rebuttal thus turns on the notion that if *A* can possibly be mistaken, *A* cannot know that *p*.

This mode of argumentation is quite powerful. If no grounds for any claim to know are conclusive, then even if *p* is true and even if *A* correctly believes that *p* is true, it does not follow that *A* knows that *p*.

This strategy has two important implications for the historian's understanding of modern philosophy. First, as Popkin makes plain, the sceptic is not contending that the concept of knowledge per se is unintelligible or senseless; quite the contrary. Instead, sceptics concur with their dogmatic adversaries that they both are referring to the only correct conception of knowledge. Both the sceptic and the dogmatist would thus disagree with Quine, for example, who tends to think of knowledge as that body of information discovered and utilized by science at any given moment in history. Such information is only probable, since future developments in science may require that it be revised or even abandoned. But this for the sceptic and the dogmatist alike is too weak a conception. Thus what the sceptic and the dogmatist are arguing about is not the meaning of "knowledge" but whether there are any instances to which the concept applies.

Second, the fact that both the dogmatist and the sceptic espouse an identical conception of knowledge is, from an historical perspective, highly significant. What it portends for the historian is that the dispute between the two is genuine. Their disagreement is not to be described as one of those familiar cases in philosophy where, because the disputants are working with different conceptions, they are advancing views that do not really contradict or oppose one another, even though, from a terminological perspective, they seem to. By accepting the same conception, these adversaries have advanced beyond definitional difference to genuine disagreement about whether there exist cases of knowledge. This has been the historical situation since the seventeenth century.

TWO

The fact that this is so brings me to the main point of this chapter, namely, an examination of two famous sceptical arguments: the problem of the criterion and Descartes's dream hypothesis. I shall show via a piecemeal, context-orientated analysis that both can be undermined. Let us begin with the first of these.

Robert Amico's *The Problem of the Criterion* contains an excellent discussion of the history of this problem, as well as his solution to it. His solution is that what he calls "metaepistemic skepticism" is self-refuting because the conditions laid down by the sceptic are in principle impossible to meet. He asserts that settlement of the dispute is possible only if agreement on the metastandard for acceptable justification is reached by the disputants, and he outlines an approach where both disputants would agree to an acceptable metastandard that would justify their first-order knowledge claims. His solution is ingenious, and yet it is unacceptable, for it attacks the problem in the wrong place. In effect, Amico has bought into the conceptual model upon which the sceptic's strategy rests, namely, that one must always justify knowledge claims and must invoke criteria in order to do so. Amico fails to see that such presuppositions can be rejected without the need to develop a countertheory, for any countertheory will in turn have its critics, and those critical countertheories their own critics, and so on; and in the end nothing will have been decided. To make these objections more specific and eventually to show how the argument can be defeated, let us see how Amico sets up the problem. I will quote him at length to avoid any misrepresentation of his position:

Wonder brings questions, and these questions constitute a natural beginning to philosophy. Yet beginnings can be difficult and elusive, at least if we take the philosophical skeptic seriously. The skeptic would have us believe that we cannot begin at all, and this claim is the challenge posed by "the problem of the criterion." Before we can know just how seriously to take this skeptical claim, we must come to understand clearly the problem of the criterion.

Suppose you had a basket of apples and you wanted to sort out the good apples from the bad apples. It seems that you would need a criterion or standard by which you could sort them, either a criterion for recognizing good apples or a criterion for recognizing bad apples. But how could you ever tell whether your criterion for sorting apples was a good criterion, one that really selected out all and only the good ones or all and only the bad ones? It seems that in order to tell whether or not you have a good criterion, you need to know already which apples are good and which are bad; then you could test proposed criteria by their fidelity to this knowledge. But if you do not already know which apples are good and which are bad, how can you ever hope to sort them out correctly? And if you already know which are good and which are bad, by what criterion did you learn this?

This analogy is a paraphrase of Roderick Chisholm's explanation of the problem of the criterion, which itself was inspired by Descartes's reply to the seventh set of objections. Chisholm claims that if we substitute beliefs for apples, we encounter the problem of the criterion—how do we decide which beliefs are "good" (actual cases of knowledge) and which beliefs are "bad" (not knowledge at all)? In the case of apples, there is no real difficulty because we already know the criteria for their goodness—firm, juicy, no worm holes or bruises, and so on; but in the case of beliefs we do not. What is the correct criterion, method, or standard for picking out good beliefs or bad ones? It seems as if we need such a criterion or method for sorting out our beliefs. But how will we know whether or not we have the correct criterion, unless we already know some actual instances of good beliefs or bad ones so that we can check our proposed criterion against these known cases? So if we do not already know which beliefs are good ones and which are bad, how can we ever hope to sort them out correctly? How can we ever hope even to begin in epistemology?[5]

Before discussing these passages, let me quote Chisholm. He writes as follows:

To know whether things really are as they seem to be, we must have a *procedure* for distinguishing appearances that are true from appearances that are false. But to know whether our procedure is a good procedure, we have to know whether it really *succeeds* in distinguishing appearances that are true from appearances that are false. And we cannot know whether it does really succeed unless we already know which appearances are *true* and which ones are *false*. And so we are caught in a circle.[6]

In this citation, Chisholm speaks not about beliefs but about appearances; nonetheless it is possible to construe his remarks as referring to beliefs about appearances. In any case, as Amico correctly indicates, Chisholm in many other places explains that the problem is about belief. Let us accept this as so. That the problem catches us "in a circle" is one reason why it has been called "the wheel argument" or "diallelus." Commentators historically have interpreted the argument in at least two different ways as concluding (1) that there exist no criteria for distinguishing "good" from "bad" beliefs, or (2) that criteria exist but will never succeed in helping us make such discriminations. Chisholm's claim that "we are caught in a circle" buttresses the second interpretation, since it presupposes that there are criteria whose application will lead to vicious circularity.

Amico and Chisholm reflect the tradition by espousing both interpretations. When Amico writes, "It seems that we need such a criterion or method for sorting out our beliefs," the context indicates that he is presupposing that no such criteria exist. This would be a case of interpretation (1). When he goes on to say, "But how will we know whether or not we have the correct criterion," he seems to presuppose that criteria exist but that they will fail to help us sort out good from bad beliefs. This is interpretation (2). That Amico and Chisholm, like many of their early modern predecessors, adopt both interpretations is puzzling, since the two interpretations seem incompatible with one another. The former denies that there are criteria, and the latter asserts the opposite. Perhaps the argument cannot be given a consistent formulation. But I will not pursue this issue, since it is philosophically less interesting than the claims made in (1) and (2). It is also worth mentioning that a vast literature supports interpretation (2) in a way that differs from Chisholm's notion that we are caught in a circle. According to this literature, the argument contends that to know that A is a good criterion for selecting beliefs, we require another criterion B that will select A as a good criterion, but then we will need another criterion C for deciding that B is a good criterion, and so on ad absurdum. According to Popkin, this is Montaigne's position. It sustains interpretation (2) by holding that the attempt to apply criteria leads to an infinite regress. These two construals of the argument have something in common: they conclude, though for diverse reasons, that no knowledge claim can be justified. In arriving at this result, they both assume that every knowledge claim must be justifiable.

The Cartesian dream hypothesis resembles the wheel argument in certain ways and differs from it in others. It also presupposes that knowledge claims require justification and that criteria based on sense experience exist for adjudicating such claims. The thrust of the dream hypothesis is that the application of such criteria will never guarantee knowledge. So in effect, Descartes concurs with interpretation (2) of the criterion argument in holding that criteria exist but that such criteria can be satisfied without producing knowledge. Of course, apart from these affinities, the wheel argument and the dream hypothesis are basically dissimilar arguments and are generally subject to differing assessments. But since my main concern here is to show that interpretations (1) and (2) are both mistaken, it would be repetitive to discuss both arguments with respect to each consideration. Accordingly, I will defer consideration of interpretation (2) until I turn to the dream hypothesis later in this chapter, and I will confine my analysis of the wheel argument to interpretation (1) that there exist no criteria for discriminating good from bad beliefs. I shall show that the thesis is false and accordingly that the problem of the criterion is a misnomer, for it turns out to be no problem at all.

THREE

Let us look carefully at what Amico says, and in particular at how he formulates the problem. He begins with an analogy, the sorting of apples. His point is that we lack criteria for sorting apples and by analogy also for sorting beliefs. But as he continues to describe the problem of sorting apples, he admits, "In the case of apples . . . we already know the criteria for their goodness—firm, juicy, no worm holes or bruises, and so on." He then adds "but in the case of beliefs, we do not." If we do have criteria for sorting apples, how can this case be assimilated to that of sorting beliefs? Clearly it cannot, and Amico's analogy is self-defeating.

Moreover, if Amico concedes this much, how can he contend that we do not have criteria for sorting beliefs? It is just as plain as in the case of apples that we do. Good beliefs are true, are buttressed by evidence, have a high degree of probability, and so forth. Truth and strong evidential support are criteria for discriminating good from bad beliefs. The correct conclusion to draw from Amico's presentation is that the analogy is well taken after all. There exist criteria for sorting both apples and beliefs. Similar remarks apply to Chisholm's version of the wheel argument. We can surely distinguish, at least some of the time, true from false appearances. Artificial flowers may look like real flowers, and in certain circumstances (uncertain light, bad eyesight on the part of a percipient, very good imitations) it may be difficult to distinguish one from the other. But in general, it is not. There are criteria for making such discriminations. Since Amico and Chisholm give accurate renderings of how the wheel argument has traditionally been formulated, I see no reason to accept its conclusion that we lack criteria for distinguishing good from bad beliefs.

My purpose here, however, is not merely to discredit the wheel argument or even the notion that we lack criteria with respect to knowledge claims. It is rather to stress that behind the wheel argument lie synoptic philosophical presuppositions, and these are the deepest sources of conceptual perplexity. In this particular case, we are given a factitious dilemma: we must either accept that there are no criteria or that even if there are, they are inevitably abortive in allowing us to distinguish good from bad beliefs. By disagreeing with this synoptic cast, philosophy by example provides both a corrective to such distorting conceptual models and provides an alternative to them, namely, an accurate, piecemeal account of the world. The fact of the matter is that where knowledge claims are advanced, we sometimes lack criteria and sometimes do not. It is also true that even where we have criteria, they may or may not be needed for such discriminations. It depends on the situation and other contextual factors. What is false, as the wheel argument presupposes, is that we always have or need criteria in such cases, and that every knowledge claim requires justification via their satisfaction. I will describe two cases that illustrate these points. I begin with an example where one can make a knowledgeable judgment without using criteria.

A decorator has been asked to decide between two shades of blue for a couch. She looks at two swatches and says, "They are certainly different. One is much darker than the other. I think the darker one would be more suitable." The statement "One is much darker than the other" is true. She now knows something she did not know before looking at the samples. She did not arrive at this judgment by invoking criteria. She can just see that the two shades are different. Seeing is not a criterion in this situation, though it makes the judgment possible in a way in which touching, smelling, or hearing would not. We can see why it is not a criterion if we look at the second case.

I am in a foreign country, Italy. I meet a stranger who wishes to exchange Lire for U.S. dollars. Are the bills he is holding counterfeit? I have been given instructions before traveling about how to identify Italian counterfeit money. Legitimate bills held against a light will reveal a figure of Dante; fake currency will not. In addition, legitimate money will have a thread pattern that cannot be reproduced by counterfeiters. So I hold these particular bills against the light and see that they satisfy the criteria for authenticity. In this circumstance, I have, need, and use criteria.

The case thus both resembles and differs from the preceding. In the previous example the decorator looked at samples in order to arrive at a true belief about the shades of a color. I said that seeing was not a criterion in that situation, and we can see why by comparing it with the new case. In looking at the bills against a bright light, one is able see a picture of Dante and a specific thread pattern. The presence of the picture and the thread pattern are the criteria for the judgment that the bills are genuine. Looking was not itself the criterion; it made the application of criteria possible. It thus functioned in a presuppositional relationship to those criteria. It was the invocation of the criteria that made the judgment of legitimacy possible. In the previous case, seeing a difference between the shades made a judgment possible without the intervention of criteria. But seeing was not itself a criterion.

I could continue to adduce other cases, even cases where seeing is a criterion. Some of these would be "intermediate" cases in Wittgenstein's sense. But I assume that piling up further illustrations is not necessary to support the point in question, namely that the assumptions upon which the wheel argument rests are unsound. Because this is so, I conclude that the wheel argument does not generate a real problem. In particular, it does not require a theoretical solution of the kind that Amico and Chisholm wish to find.

FOUR

Before turning to the dream hypothesis itself, I wish to consider an ingenious strategy for dealing with scepticism that, with a few caveats, can be attributed to Moore in some of the papers I referred to earlier, such as "A Defense of Common Sense," "Proof of an External World," and "Certainty." Moore never explicitly states that this is his strategy, so I am glossing what he does say. But there is textual evidence in support of this construal. Since I have discussed the matter elsewhere,[7] I will assume the interpretation is a reasonable one. This interpretation gives us some reason for believing that Moore has identified a flaw in the wheel argument. Moore's approach is both clever and persuasive, and yet, for reasons to be explained below, I think it is ultimately unsuccessful. Still, let us see why his approach should be taken seriously.

In his later epistemological papers Moore is well aware that in the problem of the criterion the sceptic is demanding a type of justification that the appeal to sense experience cannot satisfy. It cannot satisfy it, according to Moore, for the reason the sceptic gives in the dream hypothesis: one might be dreaming and thus might be mistaken about what the senses on any particular occasion reveal about external reality. Moore states that to give such a justification would require that he prove he is not dreaming at some particular time, but Moore says he cannot prove this and does not think that such a proof can be given. Yet he insists that he knows he is not dreaming. He is thus drawing a distinction between knowing that p and proving that p. He also goes on to affirm that he cannot explain *how* he knows that he is not dreaming. This last remark is significant. Moore's response is tantamount to refusing to play the sceptic's game. He is thus, in effect, denying that one must provide a justification whenever one asserts p or asserts that one knows p. To the extent that he holds such a view, his position is in accord with mine. But as we shall see, Moore stops short of espousing a deeper deflationary strategy that philosophy by example suggests. Still, let us follow his reasoning in opposing the criterial argument.

From Moore's perspective, the sceptical scenario can be developed only if someone is willing to answer what seems like a perfectly reasonable question, namely "How do you know what you claim to know?" But in refusing to explain how he knows that p, Moore blocks the sceptical strategy at its source: his strategy prevents any reductio, including the need to appeal to criteria, from getting off the ground.

I interpret this maneuver on Moore's part to be more than a confession of incompetence, sheer obstinacy, or a kind of Johnsonian kicking of stones. On the contrary, I see it as a thoughtful decision. What I am calling Moore's strategy is his deliberate rejection of the criterial game. But this refusal is not willful; it rests upon a supposition that Moore believes is true, namely that one can know something without knowing how one knows. In short, we can interpret Moore as thinking that the sceptic's criterial argument rests upon the principle that one is never justified in making a knowledge claim unless one has and can adduce grounds in its support. Moore's tactic in dealing with scepticism amounts to rejecting this principle. From the standpoint of the Western epistemological tradition, Moore's presumption is quite extraordinary. Most philosophers would reject it (and indeed have rejected it) out of hand.

Wittgenstein, an arch antisceptic, and his sceptical antagonists both believe that one cannot *legitimately* assert one knows that p without being able to explain how one knows. We can thus again see that these opposing parties agree, as against Moore and me, that any legitimate knowledge claim must satisfy criteria. There is, to be sure, some disagreement within these divergent camps about what criteria are, e.g., whether they are reasons, grounds, sense experience, and so forth. But let us set this issue aside. That Wittgenstein disagrees with Moore is plain. In *On Certainty,* with Moore in mind, he writes the following:

It would not be enough to assure someone that I know what is going on at a certain place—without giving him grounds that satisfy him that I am in a position to know.[8]

In these cases, then, one says "I know" and mentions how one knows, or at least one can do so.[9]

From these quotations we can see that Wittgenstein and the sceptic concur that the issue of justification is of central concern in epistemology. If *A* were to assert, "I know that Smith is now in his office" and is asked "How do you know that he is?" then according to Wittgenstein and the sceptic, *A* must provide justificatory support for the statement. But for the sceptic, though not for Wittgenstein, *A* faces a dilemma in such a case. If *A* appeals to sense experience as the basis for his claim, his reasoning can be shown via the dream hypothesis to lead to sceptical conclusions. But if he cannot give any reasons whatever, others are justified in doubting that he knows what he claims to know. Either horn leaves him in the position of not being able to persuade an auditor that he knows that *p*.

Now Moore's response to this sceptical analysis was, in effect, to challenge the second horn of the dilemma. He did this—as I read him—by challenging the assumption upon which that horn rests, namely, that one is never justified in asserting that one knows without providing support for that assertion. Moore states, on the contrary, that he is in just that position. He knows with certainty that the earth exists, that it is very old, and that this is his hand. Admittedly, he is unable to say how he knows. But that fact, he argues, does not invalidate his contention that he does know these propositions to be true. Moore seems to have a point here. Suppose we have a close friend whom we see every day. We see him again today. How do we know that it is the same person? We certainly do not have to check. It is surely incorrect to say "From experience." What experience assures us *now* that it is the same person? What experience assures us that the earth exists? As we consider such examples, Moore's remarks seem less unconvincing than they did at first. If he is right, the sceptic's insistent demand for such reasons is not *always* in order. What is true is that justification is *sometimes* required for knowledge claims and sometimes not. It is the synoptic nature of the sceptic's demand that can and should be rejected.

A case can thus be made that Moore has found a chink in the sceptic's armor. On this construal, he has shown that the flow of reasoning that generates the wheel argument can be interrupted, or better yet, blocked, by denying the propriety of the sceptic's questions "How do you know that this is a true appearance?" and "How do you know that this is a good belief?" Because Moore offers no criterion—such as seeing, hearing, or touching—for his assertion that he knows many propositions to be "good" ones, such as that the earth is very old and that the earth exists, the sceptic cannot initiate the kind of challenge that the dogmatic tradition has found so compelling.

Moore's move is clever: it immediately changes the momentum of the debate by putting the onus on the sceptics. Either they must concede Moore's point that he does know some propositions without appealing to criteria, or they must put themselves in the position of being de facto dogmatists, i.e., of claiming to know that Moore does not know what he claims to know. Either alternative amounts to a victory for Moore and a defeat for the sceptic.

Let us find further support for Moore's notion that there are cases where a person can know something without being able to say how. Moore, of course, does not provide such examples, but it is easy to construct them. Here are two:

A has absolute pitch and therefore can identify any musical note with complete accuracy. Suppose that in an appropriate context *A* states that a certain note is B flat.

Suppose that someone else asks *A* how he knows this. *A* might well answer, "I don't know how I know—I just do. It's a gift I have. I can't give you any reason. Whenever a note is played, I can invariably identify it. That's all I can say." No appeal to criteria is being made in this case.

The second example is similar. There are idiot savants who can infallibly add large numbers. When questioned, they generally cannot explain how they obtain the answers they do. It is just an aptitude they have.

These examples support Moore's position. Moreover, in both cases the answers are capable of independent confirmation. If, under appropriate test conditions, the individual is always successful in identifying various notes, an independent observer would conclude that the person knows which notes are being sounded. Similar remarks apply to the idiot savant.

From these examples it thus seems that Moore is right and the sceptic is wrong. There are occasions on which *A* can know that *p* without knowing how he knows, and therefore without invoking criteria. Since the sceptic's argument presupposes that criteria are always needed, it would seem that Moore has indeed refuted the sceptic.

Why, then, do I say that Moore's solution will not do? It is susceptible to three powerful—and, I believe, decisive—objections that Wittgenstein and radical sceptics have made or might make to Moore's approach. To appreciate their power, we should recall the nature of the sceptic's challenge. The challenge is to determine *in an objective* way whether a person who claims to know something really does. It is thus designed to elicit a response that any rational person will find compelling. What the sceptic is demanding is a rationale, a justification, for one's claim to know. So if a person refuses to give such a justification, he is not meeting the challenge. He is not playing the rational objective game.

The first objection to Moore's strategy turns on this point. Moore supposes that for some propositions, his knowing that *p* is itself a justification for his asserting that *p*. Indeed, he seems to suppose that there could be no better justification of *p* than someone's knowing that *p* is true. This suggests that there can be a "silent or private justification." This is how Wittgenstein interprets Moore:

> Moore says he *knows* that the earth existed long before his birth. And put like that it seems to be a personal statement about him, even if it is in addition a statement about the world. Now it is philosophically uninteresting whether Moore knows this or that, but it is interesting that, and how, it can be known."[10]

Let us agree that Moore knows that *p*. Wittgenstein and the sceptic would deny that such knowledge is the same as a justification. On this point, which is a matter of logic, they are clearly right. It is impossible in principle to have a private or silent justification. A justification is a public performance. It requires explaining "that, and how," *p* can be known. The need for a justification arises from the mutual interaction of human beings, and this is why it cannot be merely private. Moreover, what counts as a justification is *defined* by the rules that arise from such interactions. Since Moore has given no reasons and refuses to answer the question, he is not playing in accordance with those rules and therefore, by definition, is not giving a justification. But if he is not, his tactics do not come to grips with the challenge that the obsessive doubter has posed.

Second, both the sceptic and Wittgenstein would point out that the examples I have developed in support of Moore's position are misleadingly selective. They would argue as follows: Idiot savants and persons with perfect pitch have special talents, and the situations in which they exercise those talents are also special. In contrast, the scenario about *A*, an ordinary person and his situation, is typical. *A*'s assertion that Smith is now in his office arises from the normal interaction *A* has with others. His claim is buttressed by his remark that he has just seen Smith there. It is this sort of justification that persons ordinarily provide when challenged to prove that they know that *p*. Wittgenstein and the sceptic thus claim they are describing an ordinary human being in an ordinary situation.

They would also ask, "How would the manager have reacted if *A* had said that he knows that Smith is in the building but doesn't know how he knows?" The remark would be bewildering. When an idiot savant claims to know the correct sum and adds that he does not know how he knows, his remark is not bewildering. This shows, they would contend, that there is something unusual about his case. Idiot savants and persons with perfect pitch are special persons with special powers, and they are treated differently by ordinary persons. They are not standard examples. But Moore's case is not like theirs. Moore is not a special person who exercises special powers in claiming to know that the earth is very old. He is an ordinary person, presumably in an ordinary situation, presumably reporting what he knows. But his case is not really ordinary; it is not like *A*'s. For if he were to utter his comments in standard situations, they would be bewildering. Therefore, Moore's case is neither special nor ordinary, and because this is so, the examples of idiot savants and persons with perfect pitch do not apply to, and hence do not support, his position.

Finally, there is an even more powerful sceptical objection, namely that Moore's strategy ultimately begs the question. It presupposes that there are independent tests to confirm that a person can accurately identify various sounds. These tests justify *others* in asserting that the person knows what he claims to know on those occasions. But there is a difficulty here. The tests in this sort of case take for granted the validity of sense experience. They assume that the individual and those verifying his responses have been exposed to the same external stimuli. The procedure thus presupposes that there is an external world, that the participants have auditory access to it, and that on those occasions the participants are not dreaming that those events are taking place. But this is to presuppose what is open to sceptical doubt: that the visual and auditory experiences the participants are apprehending are connected to external happenings.

The same considerations apply to the office scenario. To confirm that A has seen Smith, one must suppose that A was not dreaming and that the visual experience he had on that occasion was veridical. But that supposition is precisely what the dream hypothesis challenges. In short, that sense experience provides grounds for justification cannot be assumed to be correct *but indeed is just the point at issue.* So A's attempt to justify his claim that Smith is now in his office, on the basis of his sense impressions, begs the question. What the sceptic is stressing, then, is that there can be no independent verification based on sense experience that is not viciously circular. Moore's objection to the second horn of the sceptic's dilemma is thus ineffectual. Since there is no possibility for a nontendentious justification of A's claim—and this is the typical situation— then A would be reduced, as Moore was, to asserting without supporting reasons that he knows that *p*.

Therefore, according to the sceptic, Moore ultimately finishes where he started. To defeat the sceptic, he must still prove he is not dreaming, and must do so to show that independent tests, which depend upon the senses, are reliable. But since he has admitted he cannot prove he is not dreaming, he cannot justify his claim to know that p by an appeal to sense experience. The sceptical position has thus not been undermined.

Yet, as I have indicated above, Moore's intuitions were correct. One can sensibly assert knowledge claims without giving grounds in their support. But, of course, my contention that Moore is correct presupposes that one can know on certain occasions that one is not dreaming. The dream hypothesis challenges this presupposition. Can the challenge be met? I shall show that it can.

FIVE

To make my response compelling, I wish to begin with some additional comments about my example-oriented approach to philosophical theorizing. I gave a partial account of it at the beginning of the chapter, but now more needs to be said about its deflationary and constructive strategies. I will emphasize the former in dealing with the dream hypothesis. From this perspective, it is theories that lead to spurious oppositions, to paradox, and to useless quests to justify what needs no justification, such as our everyday knowledge about so-called "external objects." Scepticism, in its argumentative versions, consists of such theories. In synoptic forms they cast doubt upon the existence of knowledge and certainty. The dream hypothesis is perhaps the most celebrated of all such sceptical arguments. To show how it can be neutralized, I start by mentioning the kinds of bogus dichotomies that philosophical theorizing engenders.

From the time of the Greeks to the present, theorizing has produced such dichotomies. Consider Plato's line of argumentation (with variations, to be sure) in the *Republic* and the *Phaedo*. According to Plato, there are two sorts of existences: one seen, the other unseen. What is real is unseen, what is seen is an appearance. This generated the doctrine that the reality/appearance distinction is both exclusive and exhaustive. It follows that if x is an appearance, x is not real, and if x is real, x is not an appearance. Driven by theory, Plato expanded the dichotomy in increasingly less compelling ways. He contended that one can have knowledge only of what is real—a puzzling assertion on the face of it. We can certainly know that a bent stick in water is an illusion or that a flower that appears to be real is made of paper.

But why did he hold that anything apprehended through the senses must be an appearance? He seems to have been led to this implausible thesis by assuming that whatever we sense must appear to us and then inferring from this fact that the senses produce only appearances. That appearances are in general to be construed as entities, or that they can be reified, is a well-known error, and Plato may well have been among the first to have committed it. This sequence of theses led him to the famous principle that to obtain knowledge, one must transcend sense experience. Working with still another exiguous contrast, namely that all the information we possess must come either from the senses or from reason, he concluded that it was only through the exercise of reason that one could apprehend reality. This whole doctrine is sometimes called Plato's rationalism.

The Platonic interpretation of the distinction between appearance and reality has persisted until today in innumerable variations. We can discern resonances of it in Chisholm's formulation of the wheel argument. There it takes the form of an opposition between true and false appearances. In the first half of the twentieth century it frequently appeared as the contrast between material objects and sense-data, the former being real and the latter being appearances. But the dichotomy, as so construed, is spurious, as Austin demonstrated in *Sense and Sensibilia.* Austin pointed out that if the dichotomy were legitimate, anything unreal would be an appearance. Since false teeth are not real teeth, they must be appearances, which is absurd. An artificial leg is not a real leg, yet it is not a sense-datum either.

Austin's point was not that the distinction between appearance and reality per se is illegitimate. On the contrary, it has useful and sensible applications in ordinary life. A person could appear to be tired and yet not really be tired, or could not appear to be tired and yet really be tired. And, of course, one could also appear to be tired and really be tired, or not be tired and not appear to be so. In these latter cases, there is a coincidence and not an opposition between appearance and reality. There is thus nothing wrong with the distinction as it is employed in daily life; it is rather the philosophical construal of it as both exclusive and exhaustive that is illicit.

In making these various points, Austin was not constructing a theory, was not making a scientific statement, and was not mandating how the world must be. He was simply describing how it is. His descriptivism was both an antidote and an alternative to bad philosophizing. In this chapter I have been advancing a similar thesis with respect to scepticism.

As two types of infelicities, bogus dichotomies and philosophical paradoxes should be distinguished from one another. It is not infrequent, of course, that they play interdigitating roles in a theory. I am using "paradox" in its literal sense, namely, to mean that which runs counter to the received opinion or to common sense. An ordinary person reading a philosopher like Bishop Berkeley, who claimed that "we eat and drink ideas," would recognize that something had gone wrong.

That person might say, "But that is perfectly ridiculous. We eat meat and drink water, but certainly not ideas." Berkeley's response to this might well have been, "But what you are calling meat and water are just heaps of ideas. I agree with you that we eat and drink what you are calling 'meat' and 'water', but what you fail to recognize is that in so doing, we are eating and drinking ideas. Moreover, a person too is a bundle of ideas; hence, there is nothing puzzling about an idea eating ideas."

The person of common sense is not able to meet these rejoinders. To do so, he or she would have to show that meat, water, and human beings are not congeries of ideas, and this would require either the development of a full-blown counter philosophical doctrine (the sort of thing a realist like Moore undertook to supply in "Proof of an External World") or the deconstructive approaches that Austin, Wittgenstein, and I favor.[11] The ordinary person lacks the training to do either.

Let us pursue the example a bit further from a deflationary perspective. A vast range of moves is possible here, but we can illustrate the deflationary technique with a simple one. It is obvious that the word "idea" has been given a special, extended employment by Berkeley. The question becomes, "What use does it have, then?" In reflecting on this question, one comes to realize that, as he uses the term, everything referred to is an idea. Thoughts, shadows, dogs, planets, and running water are all ideas. Therefore, nothing is being picked out or excluded by the expression. Berkeley has taken a word used by common folk to discriminate special features in their experience and has preempted it from having any discriminatory function at all.

By meaning everything, the word has come to mean nothing. This is clearly paradoxical. His theory was expressly designed to deepen and make more accurate the common man's picture of reality. Yet by rendering impotent the language in which the theory is couched, it fails to affect the commonsense picture at all. His attempt to re-form common sense is thus nugatory. This is a good example of how synoptic theorizing can result in a dead end. In stressing this consequence, I am showing that bad philosophizing need not be opposed by another theory; it should simply be exposed for what it is.

The deflationary approach can be applied to sceptical arguments. It supports the idea that common sense needs no justification. Many philosophers, from Kant to Stroud,[12] have argued that it does. But I think their responses were premature and gave more credit to radical scepticism than it deserves. I will now illustrate this thesis with respect to the Cartesian dream hypothesis, which Kant and Stroud have found so compelling. How good is it, after all? I say, "Not very." It can be rejected on at least three grounds. The moral to be drawn, if my analysis is correct, is not that philosophers need to justify common sense against sceptical challenges, but rather that such challenges that appear prima facie implausible invariably are. The correct response is not to advance another theory, as Kant assumed, or even to provide a countervailing argument, as Moore attempted in "Proof of an External World," but to explain why one is not necessary. I reject the argument, then, for the following three reasons:

Reason 1

First, in formulating the argument, Descartes makes several statements that undermine the very point it purports to establish, namely that we cannot differentiate waking from dream experiences. In the first of these he has this to say:

How often has it happened to me that in the night I dreamt that I found myself in this particular place, that I was dressed and seated near the fire, whilst in reality I was lying undressed in bed.[13]

That he can say that in reality he was lying undressed in bed implies that he then knew that he was lying there undressed, and this implies, of course, that he then knew that he was awake, contrary to what he says.

His second statement contains a similar slip. He writes this:

> But in thinking over this I remind myself that on many occasions I have in sleep been deceived by similar illusions, and that in dwelling carefully on this reflection I see so manifestly that there are no certain indications by which we may clearly distinguish wakefulness from sleep that I am lost in astonishment.[14]

Here the mistake is even more obvious. In using the expressions "I remind myself that on many occasions I have in sleep been deceived by similar illusions" and "I see so manifestly," Descartes is presupposing that when he reminds himself of how he has been deceived and when he can see so manifestly, he is at that moment awake and knows that he is. Once again, the thrust of the dream hypothesis has been undercut in its very formulation.

The argument also presupposes that certain sorts of sense experiences are criteria. What it denies is that the satisfaction of such criteria will guarantee the possession of knowledge. When Descartes refers to "indications" in the preceding passage, he is alluding to what in modern parlance would be called "criteria." He states that because such indications are not certain, one cannot distinguish waking from dream experiences. But this is a nonsequitur. There may be all sorts of things to which the notion of indications or criteria is not applicable, yet one has no difficulty in distinguishing one such thing from another. I do not possess *any* "indications," certain or otherwise, for distinguishing the color yellow from the color purple. Yet

I have no trouble making such a discrimination. Indeed, I have no idea what such indications or criteria could be, or what sort of thing one could appeal to, in judging that the colors differ. In this context I neither need nor use criteria or indications. I can just see that the colors are different. There are likewise no indications for determining *in general* that one is awake. If such a question might arise, it will arise in a particular situation, perhaps when someone emerges from an anesthetic. If in that circumstance there is need for criteria to make such a determination, they will apply only to that specific situation.

Reason 2

In the same sentence Descartes says something that forms the basis of my second criticism of the hypothesis and the supposed scepticism that results from it. He says, "In dwelling carefully on this reflection I see so manifestly that there are no certain indications by which we may clearly distinguish wakefulness from sleep." What Descartes fails to realize is that to *dwell carefully*, one must be awake. For "dwelling carefully" means to linger over in thought, to deliberate, ponder, and assess a particular consideration. This is not something that one typically does in dreaming. Dreams are not normally subject to one's control or voli- tion. In dreaming, we do not "dwell carefully." Instead, dreams force themselves upon one, as it were. The point I am making here can be generalized into a second criticism of scepticism as follows:

The dream hypothesis can be formulated briefly in a sentence or two. Presumably the sceptic wishes to express his challenge with the words "Isn't it possible that I am now dreaming?" or "For all I know, I may be dreaming at this moment." Now in certain circumstances, one who employs these words may be using them to say something that is sensible and true. Someone may have just won a lottery and may be indicating his pleasure and surprise by saying "Isn't it possible that I am dreaming—dreaming that I won all this?" In such circumstances, the speaker does not intend to say that he may be asleep and dreaming. He uses those words in a nonliteral way to express his astonishment. He might have used a different idiom, such as "I am amazed." An auditor would understand that the speaker's words "Isn't it possible I am dreaming?" were not being used literally in that context. The auditor certainly would not take the speaker to be saying that he might now be asleep. These are the typical adjustments human beings make in communicating with and understanding others.

Now, are there circumstances in which a speaker could use those words literally, that is, to mean at the moment of speaking he might be dreaming and therefore might not be awake? The answer to this question is "No." The reason is that if one meant those words literally, the utterance would be self-defeating. It would violate certain communal conditions that define meaningful intercourse. We all learn from experience when to give credence to the words a person utters, and such experience tells us that when a person utters words while asleep, he not only does not intend them in the usual way but does not intend them at all. The sceptic is, of course, a member of the human linguistic community and accepts its linguistic practices. His mistake is to think his utterance is in accord with those practices when it is not. For even to formulate his challenge, the sceptic must be awake and must know that he is. For his words to be used literally, the sceptic must be aware of what he is saying, must intend to mean his words in a specific way, and both of these conditions entail that he must be awake when he utters them.

But if the sceptic were dreaming and hence were not awake, those conditions would not be satisfied. Therefore, any speaker who uttered those words while asleep would not intend anything by them. The moral is, If the sceptic's utterance were literally meaningful, that would entail that he was awake when he uttered it and that he knew he was, and thus the hypothesis that he might be dreaming and hence asleep is self-refuting. I can formulate the objection as a dilemma. If the sceptic is asleep, he cannot mean anything by the words he utters. If he does mean something by the words he utters, he cannot be asleep. On either alternative, nothing that needs refuting has been said by the sceptic. The plain man does not have to develop a countertheory. He can just go on believing what is true, namely that he can sometimes distinguish his waking from his nonwaking experiences.

Reason 3

We come to my third reason for rejecting the dream hypothesis. Though it was Descartes who formulated the difficulty, it purports to be a general conundrum. It is not simply Descartes who cannot distinguish whether he is awake or sleeping, but presumably every human being is thus incapacitated. The argument would have no philosophical import if it turned out that only Descartes suffered from this particular liability. But a set of insuperable problems emerges if the argument is generalized in this way. To my knowledge, no one has previously pointed out these difficulties.

The dream hypothesis presupposes that everyone dreams, and indeed, it presupposes that proponents of the argument know that this is so. But how could they know this? Take a particular case, that of Mr. Smith. If they do know that Smith has had dreams, they are able to determine when Smith is asleep and when he is not. But they could not do so if they themselves were asleep. Hence, in assuming that the argument holds generally, they are presupposing that they themselves are awake on some occasions and know that they are. The very generality that the argument requires thus constitutes a ground for the rejection of its conclusion.

Finally, suppose a certain person has never had a dream. What then happens to the dream hypothesis? If one has never had a dream, one has never had any internal experiences that he cannot distinguish from waking experiences. But if that is so, then he has no trouble distinguishing those occasions when he is awake from those occasions when he is asleep. He doesn't have to compare experiences. He doesn't need those "indications" that Descartes mentions. He just wakes up every morning and realizes that he has been asleep. These objections show that we don't need to justify our commonsense beliefs about the so-called external world. It is sufficient to show that the arguments that question these beliefs lack cogency.

SIX

I shall conclude the chapter by accentuating the positive, as promised. This constructive aspect of my approach will differ from anything that science or an overarching theory, such as Kant's transcendental idealism or Quine's naturalized epistemology, tells us about the world. On the preceding analysis we can dismiss the challenges to the existence of knowledge that the foregoing sceptical arguments pose. My positive account therefore begins by concurring with transcendentalists and naturalists that we have knowledge of the world and that much of it derives from perception. The question is whether there is a synoptic philosophical theory that is fine-grained enough to account for the diversity of what we know. I deny that there is, and will illustrate the difference between a synoptic approach and a context-oriented approach with the following example.

In the early part of the twentieth century philosophers generated theories of perception that were very attractive. One of these culminated in the thesis that if a perceiver is looking at an opaque object from a particular standpoint and at a given moment, the most the observer can see of that object is a facing part of its surface.

The argument they adduced in support of this thesis was powerful. It began by holding that every opaque object has an exterior, and that its exterior is its surface. It continued as follows. Since the object is opaque, one cannot see its reverse side or its interior, and accordingly there are parts of it, including parts of its reverse surface, that are invisible at the moment of perception and from the position the observer occupies. What one can see, then, is at most that part of its exterior that faces the observer, and that, by definition, is part of its surface. The argument concluded that under the stipulated conditions, the most one can see of *any* opaque object is part of its surface.

All sorts of powerful conclusions were drawn from this putative perceptual fact. To some writers (including some contemporaries, such as Benson Mates[15]) it seemed that surfaces stood between the observer and the whole object, blocking at least part of it, and this "fact" was interpreted as having sceptical implications. Given the opacity of the object and the perceptual situation as I have described it, Mates inferred that one could not know what the back surface or the back side of the object looked like. He thus concluded that any judgment about those areas of objects transcended the available evidence and opened the door to sceptical doubt. This is another variant of the notion that sense experience cannot guarantee the reliability of judgments about so-called external objects. But the argument, *in this general form,* is fallacious. Once again, we do not need to mount a counterargument to this position. It is sufficient to show that the argument, when carefully examined, does not go through.

The examples of opaque objects that philosophers advancing this theory invoked were constrained in topological and spatial variety. Such things as billiard balls, tomatoes, dice, inkwells, tables, persons, and planets constituted the limited range of examples used to support this sceptical conclusion. It just seemed obviously true that under the conditions stipulated one cannot see the back surface of a spherical object like a tomato, and since it clearly has a surface, it surely follows that the most one can see of the object is the facing part of its surface.

But with a simple change of examples, the theory and its sceptical conclusion collapse. Tennis courts, putting greens, roads, and mirrors are opaque, yet, depending on the contextual circumstances, all of their surfaces can be seen. One watching a tennis match from a good seat can see the whole surface of the court. But if one's seat is behind a post, one may be blocked from seeing all of it. The whole surface of a large body of water, such as Lake Victoria, which is about 200 miles long, cannot be seen by a person standing at ground level on its southern shore, but this is not because one cannot see its reverse surface. Not being spherical, it has no reverse surface. One cannot see all of its surface because it is so long that it dips below the horizon due to the curvature of the earth. But no part of its surface blocks any other part, as one could ascertain from a high-flying airplane. From that height, all of its surface can easily be seen. Under typical weather conditions and when seen from a high altitude, Lake Victoria is opaque, so under these conditions one can see all of the surface of an opaque object.

Any holistic theory must thus take account of the differences between opaque objects having various topological characteristics, between objects that are spheres, cubes, rhomboids, rectangles (such as tomatoes, dice, etc.), and between them and those entities I call "stretches," i.e., such things as putting greens, tennis courts, sheets, lakes, and roads. These are differences we find in the real world. When we add to these differences other contextual constraints—for example, that many objects we look at are moving, that they may or may not have surfaces even though they are opaque, that the observer may also be in motion, that light playing on objects takes many different forms, that particulate matter in the atmosphere produces a host of differing effects, that the observer's visual acuity and his distance from the object condition what he sees—it becomes impossible to accept a theory that claims there is single thing, such as a surface or part of a surface, that is invariably seen in each of these cases. A context-sensitive description of the vast range of perceptual situations is able to take account of these multifarious factors in ways that no all-encompassing theory can. It is thus the right way to do epistemology. It is, as such, a powerful alternative to the all-encompassing theories, including the sceptical ones, that we have been considering.

I have shown in the preceding analysis of the dream hypothesis that my philosopy-by-example approach does not require new forms of model building. With its deflationary strategies, it simply undermines bad arguments, leaving us less perplexed than we were before, and in its constructive phases it replaces theorizing with an example-oriented account of the world. That such an account is not only feasible but indeed exists is a good reason for thinking that philosophical scepticism is and always has been a paper tiger.

ONE

As far back as our written records go, the poets have spoken about water: recall some of the great sea episodes in Homer's *Odyssey,* in Virgil's *Aeneid,* and in Shakespeare's *Tempest* by way of example. Water has also been a favorite subject of painters: from the pounding waves of the early Turner to Monet's calm ponds on which water lilies float. The first Western philosopher about whom there is any reliable evidence was Thales, a Greek who lived in Asia Minor. Thales was obsessed by water; indeed, he argued that everything is made of water. This seems to be the earliest theory about the fundamental nature of the universe that we have. Some scientists have recently asserted that human beings are composed 98 percent of water. If they are right, Thales missed the correct answer, at least in the human case, by only 2 percent. Of course, his immediate successors did not think he was right at all. As they pointed out, the theory failed to explain how anything like sand could be dry and yet be wholly composed of water. They concluded that the theory didn't hold water—a negative judgment that is surely correct. Their technique of providing counterexamples was a precursor to the deflationary strategy I described in the previous chapter. It revealed how wildly wrong theorizing can go in its attempt to provide a synoptic account of a pluralistic world.

But even though Thales may have been wrong (and by more than 2 percent) there seems to be no doubt that as an intelligent and perceptive person, he knew what water was, just as Homer, Virgil, Shakespeare, and Turner did. But what was it that these philosophers, writers, and painters thought water was when they wrote about it or in their various other ways depicted it? A reasonable answer is the following:

Water is a transparent, tasteless, odorless liquid that constitutes rain, oceans, and lakes and that can freeze into ice and boil into steam. It is a liquid fundamental to life, animal and vegetable alike, and just for humans alone it has myriad uses: washing, drinking, mixing with powder, and so on.

I will call such features as being odorless, tasteless, transparent, and liquid, *phenomenal properties*. The term will thus refer to characteristics that ordinary persons can observe without instruments, as distinct, say, from the microcomposition of water, which is not visible to the naked eye. Not having any science, or at least any science at the sophisticated level that we have today, Thales, Virgil, and Shakespeare knew nothing about the molecular structure of water. For them, water was thus defined in terms of its phenomenal or observable properties, namely as a uniquely useful tasteless and odorless liquid. Now most of us who are not scientists think of water in just this way. If a foreigner learning English wishes to know what the word "water" means, a good dictionary would describe water in roughly the way that Thales thought of it. As far as I know, every human language would define its equivalent for the word "water" in the same way.

It should therefore come as something of a surprise to find that some distinguished contemporary philosophers, among them Hilary Putnam and Saul Kripke, contend that Thales, Virgil, Shakespeare, and indeed the rest of us, including the makers of most dictionaries, are just plain wrong in thinking that water is to be identified with its phenomenal properties or that the word "water" means the familiar substance having such properties. In a moment I will describe what they take water to be and also what they think the word "water" means.

Putnam and Kripke have reached their conclusions by means of a clever argument which turns on recent findings in the theories of meaning and reference. In Section 3 below, I will lay out this argument, showing why it is plausible and why it has had such a powerful impact. But later I will try to prove that the argument is fallacious and that ordinary folk like us are right in thinking about water and "water" as we do and as Thales, Homer, and Virgil did. However, these philosophers are like Thales in one respect: they are driven by theory to conclusions that violate common sense.

Because water has been around for a long time, it is surprising that there should still be a question about what it is. The word "water" has also been around for a long time—not as long as water, of course, but long enough. It is thus surprising that there should still be a question about what it means. It is even surprising that such disparate questions should not be distinguished from one another, yet frequently they are not. In this essay I shall answer both questions, and in the course of doing so, explain why it is important to discriminate between them. The second is a linguistic question about the meaning of the word "water" in English (or its equivalents in such languages as Italian and Japanese, say), whereas the first is about a nonlinguistic constituent of the world, namely a particular liquid substance. Presumably, Thales was interested in the substantive question and not the linguistic question, so they should be distinguished. An English monoglot might not know what the Japanese word "mizu" means, while of course knowing what water is. My answers will take us deep into the central cores of the theories of meaning and reference, but they will also raise a more general question about the status of what is observable with the naked eye. This latter question I shall investigate in "Microscopic and Macroscopic," the essay to follow.

How is it possible that theories of meaning and reference can generate doubts about such seemingly obvious matters as what water is and what "water" means? Part of the answer is that one cannot know what "water" means unless one knows what water is. So that if there is a question about the nature of water, there will be a corresponding question about the meaning of "water." This principle—that there is a close relationship between what a given substance is and what a word referring to that substance means—is widely accepted by many of our best philosophers today. So formulated, the principle makes use of the concepts of meaning and reference, and thus takes us to the brink of the theories about these notions. But we shall have to go still deeper to understand why there should be a question about what water is.

Let us assume, for the moment, the principle asserting that there is a close connection between what a given substance is and what a word referring to that substance means. Then what additional reasons can be given for thinking that the nature of water is problematical? Odd though it may seem, a reason that Kripke and Putnam give is that anyone who lived before the nineteenth century did not know what water was. This seems like an incredibly paradoxical claim at first sight, yet they provide persuasive grounds for thinking that it is correct. They claim, as I have mentioned, that we shall find such grounds in recent developments in the theories of meaning and reference. So let us look for them there.

To the uninitiated, philosophy at times seems to consist of a set of receding questions that must be addressed before one can understand an answer in the foreground. And it is true that sometimes in trying to give these prior, background answers, a philosopher will never get around to dealing with the question at hand. I could easily find myself in this situation if I try to explain in detail what is meant by the "theories of meaning and reference." Yet unless I say something about these concepts, we cannot sensibly move forward at all. So I shall say a few words, no doubt excessively simplified.

TWO

From the time of the ancient Greeks to the present, philosophers have been attracted to puzzles. One of the earliest takes two forms: (1) How can we speak meaningfully/truly about what does not exist? (2) How can we deny the existence of something without first assuming that it exists, and thus contradicting ourselves? Contemporary theories of meaning and reference, building on the work of their early predecessors, are designed to answer these questions. Here I shall discuss only the first of these issues. The problem it generates concerns the nature of language and its relationship to the nonlinguistic world. The relationship between "water" and water is a special case of this general concern. The simplest theory about that relationship is that the words composing a language have the meanings they do because each of them refers to a particular object, process, event, or feature in or of the world. According to this account, the sentence "Plato was the author of the

Meno" is both meaningful and true, and the word "Plato," which occurs in it, is also meaningful because it refers to the person (entity, object) Plato.

But this theory implies that for words to be meaningful the objects they purport to refer to must exist, will exist, or have existed. And this principle engenders a difficulty. It seems obvious that the sentence "Hamlet did not really exist" is both meaningful and true when used about a character in a play by Shakespeare. It also seems that this sentence can be both meaningful and true only if "Hamlet" is meaningful. Yet the object it presumably refers to does not exist, will not exist, and never has existed. Therefore, if one is to maintain that "Hamlet" is meaningful, the simple theory correlating words and objects will have to be modified.

The most famous modern modification, due to the work of Frege and Russell, is that a distinction must be drawn between meaning and reference. Both hold that a term can be meaningful without referring to anything. This is true, according to Russell, of sentences containing the word "Hamlet." Russell called "Hamlet" an abbreviated description, a putative name that stood for a definite descriptive phrase such as "the central male character in the play *Hamlet,* by Shakespeare." In the context of a sentence, definite descriptive phrases (which contain the word "the" in the singular) enable one, according to Russell, to pick out, identify, or denote exactly one individual. In the context of a sentence, it is the meaning of these words composing the phrase that enables us to make such unique references. Russell's distinction between meaning and reference roughly corresponded to Frege's distinction between *Sinn* and *Bedeutung.* Every expression in a natural language such as English has a *Sinn* (meaning) but some expressions do not have a *Bedeutung* (reference), and "Hamlet" would be an example of such a term. According to Frege, it is the sense (meaning) of a term that allows us to pick out, or identify, its referent—if it has one. So here once again, there is a coincidence between Frege's views and Russell's. Both held that it is possible to speak meaningfully about the world without referring to existent entities. Both applied their theory to proper names such as "Plato" and to such general words as "gold" and "water."

In the past thirty years or so this theory has been attacked by a group of distinguished philosophers—Ruth Marcus, David Kaplan, Keith Donnellan, Howard Wettstein, Joseph Almog, Saul Kripke, and Hilary Putnam, among others—who advance a view they call a theory of "*direct* reference." According to this doctrine, proper names are not abbreviations for descriptions. Contrary to what Frege claimed, they do not have meaning (*Sinn*) but are used by speakers to tag or pick out certain objects or persons without the intermediation of meaning. In this sense, then, they are directly referential. According to some of these writers, mass nouns such as "gold" and "water" are also directly referential. They are also used to mention, pick out, or refer to certain sorts of substances without the interposition of meaning. Russell's and Frege's notion that we must appeal to the meaning of an expression in order to identify its referent is thus mistaken. With these preliminary remarks we are in a position to see how the thesis of direct reference can generate reasons in support of the notion that nobody living before the nineteenth century knew what water was or what "water" meant.

THREE

Putnam's famous Twin Earth scenario provides the explanation. It rests upon considerations deriving from the theory of direct reference. He asks us to imagine Twin Earth, a planet exactly like ours except in one respect, which I shall mention in a moment. It will be the same size, have the same appearance, have on it counterparts of each person who now exists on Earth. On Twin Earth there will thus be a Twin Hilary Putnam and a Twin Avrum Stroll and so on. Indeed, an observer, even a god, looking at the two planets from an external standpoint, would find them indistinguishable. So early in the history of Twin Earth there would have been a Twin Thales and a Twin Virgil, and the former would have claimed that everything is water, while the other would have written a book identical in name and content with the *Aeneid*. On Twin Earth there will also be a substance that Twin Earthlings call "water." In terms of its observable properties and its uses, it will be indistinguishable from water. But there will be one difference between these two worlds. When this substance on Twin Earth is subjected to chemical analysis, it will be found not to be composed of hydrogen and oxygen but of another combination of chemicals called XYZ that is distinct from H_2O.

According to Putnam, this is a possible scenario; we can easily imagine such a twin world. But if it is a possible scenario, then certain inferences about the theory of reference follow from it:

• Earthling and Twin Earthling can have the same concept of water in mind, namely that water is the liquid having the phenomenal properties mentioned above.

• The reference (extension) of that concept is a liquid that is H_2O on Earth and XYZ on Twin Earth (and where XYZ is different from H_2O).

• The liquids referred to by the same term "water" are different substances.

• Therefore, the views of Russell and Frege are mistaken. Since both Earthling and Twin Earthling grasp the same concept (i.e., have the same meaning in mind) and because that concept picks out two different references, H_2O and XYZ, it follows that meaning does not determine reference, as Frege and Russell had claimed.

• Even deeper, they were wrong in holding that "water" means the liquid having certain phenomenal properties. What "water" means has nothing to do with any such Fregean or Russellian sense or meaning but is wholly determined by what water is, and this in turn is determined by the chemical composition of water.

• The nineteenth-century scientific discovery that water is composed of H_2O resolved the issue of what "water" means.

• Finally, English speakers who lived before those nineteenth-century chemical findings and who therefore could not have known that water is H_2O were mistaken in thinking that water was *the* liquid defined by certain phenomenal properties. For the Twin Earth narrative indicates that *two different liquid substances* exhibited exactly those very same properties.

Putnam concludes that the observable properties of any natural kind do not determine its real nature. A natural kind is found in nature, as distinct from artifacts created by human beings. Chairs are not natural kinds, but gold, water, and tigers are. It is thus possible to imagine an albino tiger that is not striped and is not beige in color, yet its genetic make-up determines it to be a tiger and not its observable features. There are substances, such as iron pyrite, that look very much like gold and yet have a different chemical composition, so they are not gold. There is chrysoprase, an apple-green chalcedony that to the naked eye is virtually indistinguishable from jade but that is not jade. Once again the phenomenal characteristics of these natural kinds do not determine their true natures. In the case of water, its nature is determined by a chemical analysis, which finds it to be H_2O. Since that is not the composition of the liquid on Twin Earth, it follows that, despite its appearance, the latter is not water. Given the principle that the meaning of a word is determined by the nature of the substance to which it refers, it follows that "water" as used on Twin Earth does not mean what "water" as used on Earth means.

In effect, then, the scenario shows that "water" is a homonym (a word with the same sound but with different meanings). The word "bank" in English is a homonym: it can refer to one of the sharp slopes between which a river runs or to a commercial institution where money is deposited. The fact that a word has the same sound does not entail that it has the same meaning. So "water" means XYZ on Twin Earth and H_2O on earth and is therefore a homonym. This is a compelling analysis, almost universally accepted by philosophers of language and philosophers of science. But in my judgment it is wrong, and I will now try to show why.

FOUR

As I indicated earlier, Putnam and Kripke are each dealing with two different questions: what the word "water" means and what water is. They frequently tend to conflate these questions because they presuppose that the debate about what the word "water" means will be settled once it is determined what water is. At this time I do not wish to challenge the principle that the meaning of "water" is determined by what water is, only the special interpretation that Kripke and Putnam give to it, in which they assume that water is identical with H_2O. I will develop a "functional argument" below to demonstrate why this interpretation is mistaken. So, deferring that issue until later, I will now describe what Kripke and Putnam say about water and "water."

What, then, do they take water to be? Kripke proffers the following account:

I want to go on to the more general case . . . of some identities between terms for substances, and also the properties of substances and natural kinds. Philosophers have, as I've said, been very interested in statements expressing theoretical identifications; among them, that light is a stream of photons, that water is H_2O, that lightning is an electrical discharge, that gold is the element with the atomic number 79.[1]

Putnam's view is indistinguishable from Kripke's. He puts it thus:

Once we have discovered that water (in the actual world) is H_2O, *nothing counts as a possible world in which water isn't H_2O.*[2]

I think both Kripke and Putnam would agree that the expression "Water is H_2O" exactly captures what they intend. Moreover, both of them take this locution to be an identity sentence, so that the word "is" means "is identical with." Let me simplify what they intend by using the formula "Water = H_2O." I do not believe that anything substantive in the theory is affected by this notational simplification. Kripke states that he is speaking of "identities" between terms for substances and adds, "Philosophers have been very interested in statements expressing theoretical identifications." There is no doubt that both writers mean that water is identical with H_2O.

But if this is so, the theory is unacceptable, as the following counterexample will show:

- Water = H_2O
- Ice = H_2O
- Water = ice

48

The conclusion follows as an instance of the valid formula that if $A = B$ and $B = C$, $A = C$. But since the conclusion of the argument is false, at least one of its premises must be false (in fact both are). That the conclusion is false is obvious. Clearly, water is not identical with ice. If I ask you to put some ice in my glass, I am not asking you to put water in my glass. Water is a liquid and ice is not; water is transparent and ice is not. Indeed, water and ice stand in a virtually unique relationship to one another. Nearly all other liquid substances have solids that are more dense than they are. But water is more dense than ice, and therefore ice will float on water. Ice could not in truth, and perhaps not even meaningfully, be said to float on water if ice and water were identical. Nor could ice and steam be phases of water, i.e., subsets of water, because something cannot be ice (a cold solid) and water (a tepid liquid) at the same time.

Note that the argument could be extended by adding the premise "Steam = H_2O." If we add this premise, it follows that ice = steam, which is clearly false, even though the chemical composition of steam is H_2O. If Putnam believes that ice is identical with H_2O and steam is identical with H_2O, he would have to subscribe to the belief that ice is identical with steam, since both have the same chemical composition.

What is the import of such counterexamples for Putnam's and Kripke's theory? Since patently water is not identical with ice, nor ice with steam, and since water and steam and ice have the same chemical composition, it follows *that the differences among them cannot be accounted for in terms of their chemical composition*. Their differences will have to be explained in terms other than those referring to their common microcomposition—indeed, as I have indicated, in terms of their observable physical differences. And to do this, we shall have to employ the locutions

49 that ordinary, nonscientific human folk have used for this purpose since time immemorial. It is the phenomenal properties denoted by those words that allow us to make the distinction. These tell us that when water freezes it becomes ice, that ice is invariably cold but water is not, and that water is transparent whereas ice is not. None of these features is an underlying chemical component of water in the way that H_2O is. Yet they not only allow us to distinguish water from ice and steam from ice, *they are the only means we have for doing so.* It follows that water is not identical with H_2O, nor water with ice, nor ice with steam. All this is consistent with maintaining what is true, namely that the chemical composition of water is H_2O. For this statement, which speaks about the *composition* of water, *is not an identity sentence.*

Putnam's and Kripke's basic mistake is to think that it is. To put the point in the material mode of speech, we can say that their error is to have inferred from the fact that water is a substance composed of two parts of hydrogen and one of oxygen that it is identical with the union of those components. But as the previous argument shows, this is a sheer mistake, having such paradoxical consequences as that steam and ice, and that water and ice, are identical.

Their idea that one can state what a natural kind is in terms of a simple identity sentence is a common error. Indeed, it permeates the literature on direct reference, and we can find it in other authors as well. Here, for instance, is what J. J. C. Smart says:

When I say that a sensation is a brain process or that lightning is an electric discharge, I am using "is" in the sense of strict identity. (Just as in the—in this case necessary—proposition "7 is identical with the smallest prime number greater than 5.")
. . . Consider lightning. Modern physical science tells us that lightning is a certain kind of electrical discharge due to

ionization of clouds of water vapor in the atmosphere. This, it is now believed, is what the true nature of lightning is. Note that there are not two things: a flash of lightning and an electrical discharge. There is one thing, a flash of lightning, which is described scientifically as an electrical discharge to the earth from a cloud of ionized water molecules."[3]

This error arises, at least in part, from a failure to make certain distinctions that are crucial in understanding the science involved. Here is what Putnam, speaking as a philosopher of science, avers:

Suppose, now, that I have not yet discovered what the important physical properties of water are (in the actual world)—i.e., I don't yet know that water is H_2O. I may have ways of *recognizing* water that are successful (of course, I may make a small number of mistakes that I won't be able to detect until a later stage in our scientific development), but not know the microstructure of water. If I agree that a liquid with the superficial properties of "water" but a different microstructure *isn't really water*, then my ways of recognizing water cannot be regarded as an analytical specification of what *it is to be* water.[4]

We can contrast what Putnam says with what chemists tell us about water. But first note that in the preceding passage Putnam asserts that water is H_2O and that it is to be identified with its "microstructure," implying with this last remark that H_2O is the microstructure of water. Further, what I have been calling the "phenomenal" properties of water, Putnam calls the "superficial properties" of water. But scientists would deny both that the microstructure of water is H_2O and that the phenomenal properties, which they also call the "gross" or "physical" properties, of water are superficial. If these properties were superficial in Putnam's sense, any chemist would tell you that you could not distinguish steam from ice.

In contrast with Putnam, scientists distinguish between the gross or physical properties of a substance, such as iron (its rigidity, say), and its chemical properties, such as its disposition to rust when, in the presence of air, it comes in contact with water. Its properties, whether gross or chemical, are to be distinguished from its chemical *structure*. The term "structure" is used to speak both about the internal spatial arrangements of atoms within a molecule and about the internal spatial arrangements of the molecules within a substance. If one is speaking about a molecule of water, then the microstructure of that molecule would be the particular (and characteristic) arrangement of the hydrogen and oxygen atoms within it. If one is speaking about a natural kind such as pure water, the microstructure of the substance will be certain characteristic spatial relationships between its molecules.[5] In the case of steam, this is a virtually random set of relationships; in the case of water, the arrangement is complex, characterized by much molecular movement and tumbling; in the case of ice, the molecular arrangement is regular and crystalline.

Putnam's term "microstructure" blurs these distinctions and leads to serious confusions. The basic point is that there is not a one-to-one correspondence between the physical, chemical, or gross properties of water and its chemical components. Thus, water, ice, and steam all have the same chemical components. Each is composed of molecules containing two atoms of hydrogen and one of oxygen. Yet their gross properties are different, ice being rigid and water not. The example is directly relevant to the point I have been stressing above. Ice, water, and steam are all identical in chemical composition, but their physical properties are distinct. If each of them were identical with its chemical composition, each would be identical with the others, and then by Leibniz's Law, each would have identical gross properties. Since they obviously do not, it follows that none of them is identical with its chemical components (or with its "microstructure," as Putnam uses that term). Therefore, one cannot distinguish between them in terms of their chemical composition. It follows that Putnam is wrong in holding that water is *identical* with H_2O, and indeed that natural kinds in general are to be identified with their chemical composition. His mistake stems, as I have indicated, from not distinguishing the proposition that water is identical with H_2O and the proposition that water is composed of H_2O. The "is" in "Water is H_2O" is not the "is" of identity but the "is" of composition.

One can make the same point by adopting a technique made famous by Kripke. Kripke would ask, "Can you imagine a situation in which a liquid can have all the properties usually associated with water, such as being transparent, nonviscous, etc., and yet not be composed of H_2O?" Since the Twin Earth narrative gives one good grounds for saying "Yes," both Putnam and Kripke would argue that water cannot be identified with the liquid having those phenomenal properties. Both infer that water must therefore be the single liquid composed of H_2O. But this is a non sequitur, as my counterexample shows. Can one, I now ask, imagine something composed of H_2O that is not water? Of course, I answer: ice and steam (and these are real cases, unlike the Twin Earth examples). This shows by an argument parallel to that of Kripke's and Putnam's that water cannot be identified with its compositional constituents.

FIVE

How might Kripke and Putnam respond to these criticisms? I can think of two arguments they might offer. The first I will call "the melt-down argument." Take an ice cube, they might say, and just leave it on a counter. In a few minutes it will begin to melt, and the result will be water. Nothing in the ice cube has changed. It was water to begin with, and it is still water after melting. When they say that H_2O is the "essence" of water, they are referring to what all forms of water have in common. The conclusion to be reached is that all forms of water, such as ice and steam, are combinations of hydrogen and oxygen. This is the point of the identity thesis, and it is supported by what science has discovered about H_2O.

This argument has a strong initial plausibility, but it is unsound for several reasons. To begin with, it contains a false premise, i.e., that nothing in the ice cube has changed. In fact, the contrary is true. Ice is rigid, so a cube that began with a crystalline structure has altered its internal structure in becoming a liquid. In phenomenal terms, an object that is inert, hard, opaque, and cold to the touch has changed into a fluid that is transparent, tepid, and flows. What is true in the argument, as I have stressed above, is that ice and water are both composed of H_2O. But this truth does not entail that they are therefore internally (or for that matter, externally) the same.

The second argument I will call "the linguistic argument." According to it, there are two uses of "water." In the first use, it denotes a fluid that is transparent, tasteless, and odorless. But the second use is generic: one can speak of frozen water, water vapor, and liquid water. On this use, ice is frozen water, steam is water vapor, and the familiar fluid is liquid water. Each of these items is thus water, but in different states. Astronomers might describe Mars, for example, as possessing frozen water at one of its poles. The argument concludes that the common element that a solid, gas, and fluid contain is water in this generic sense.

This argument has something to be said in its behalf. It is true that persons sometimes do refer to ice as frozen water and to steam as water vapor. I have never heard the term "liquid water" used in ordinary speech, but in scientific contexts it is sometimes employed. I grant, then, that there are such uses as "frozen water" and "water vapor." The argument gets some of its authority by suggesting that a frozen Eskimo is an Eskimo, and pari passu that frozen water is water. But can we say that a vaporized Eskimo is still an Eskimo? It is dubious. More generally, my objection is that from such usages it does not follow that ice is identical with water or that steam is identical with water. The reason for this is that three new complex terms have been introduced. Each contains "water" but also a phenomenal term, such as "frozen," as a second constituent. We thus have not one term, such as "water," that is common to descriptions of ice and steam but three different terms that cannot in each case simply be reduced to "water." It is like the difference between olive oil and baby oil. The former is made from olives but the latter is not made from babies. What has happened here in the linguistic argument is, in effect, that "water" has been substituted for "H_2O." What proponents of this position really mean is that ice is frozen H_2O, and with that I agree. As I have stressed throughout this chapter, the common constituent of ice, steam, and water is H_2O. But that common constituent is not water, simpliciter.

There is a second objection to the linguistic argument. In referring to ice as "frozen water" and to steam as "water vapor," one is mentioning the phenomenal features of these things. One is no longer characterizing ice and steam simply as H_2O but as having such and such observable features. The existence of these features is determined by various states of the world, e.g., whether the temperature is below o degrees Celsius, and so forth. By introducing such terms as "frozen" and "liquid", Putnam's and Kripke's approach gives the game away. They are now agreeing with me that to discriminate ice from water, we must refer to their phenomenal properties. I conclude that this argument, like the first, carries no conviction.

SIX

But if water is not identical with a substance having those phenomenal properties, as Putnam and Kripke claim, or with a substance that is identical with H_2O, as I claim, then what can it be?

To this question I have an answer. To give that answer, I find it helpful to begin by considering two theses that Kripke advances in this connection. First, as an earlier quotation establishes, he states that "Water is H_2O," that "Light is a stream of photons," and, with J. J. C. Smart, that "Lightning is an electrical discharge," are identity statements.

Second, he holds that a natural kind is determined by (is to be identified with) its *internal* structure. He writes thus:

Even though we don't *know* the internal structure of tigers, we suppose—and let us suppose that we are right—that tigers form a certain species or natural kind. We then can imagine that there should be a creature which, though having all the external appearance of tigers, differs from them internally enough that we should say that it is not the same kind of thing. We can imagine it without knowing anything about this internal structure—what this internal structure is. We can say in advance that we use the term "tiger" to designate a species, and that anything not of this species, even though it looks like a tiger, is not in fact a tiger.[6]

These two passages raise some issues we have already examined but also some we have not. A consideration of these will help us with the question of what water is. First, by the examples he cites, Kripke suggests (though he does not explicitly assert) that there is a distinction to be drawn between the internal and external features of a natural kind. But is this true? If lightning is a natural kind, and is, as Smart claims, identical with an electrical discharge, then which of its features are internal and which external? Shall we consider the color of a bolt of lightning to be external? But external to what? Surely not to the electrical discharge, for presumably the color just is that discharge. Second, he claims that a natural kind is to be identified with its internal rather than external features. But I have already shown this thesis to be incorrect in the cases of ice and water. Later I shall show via a functional argument that there are other reasons for rejecting this claim. Once again we encounter what is endemic in philosophy: a theory whose plausibility diminishes as one expands the range of examples it should cover. Third, Kripke avers that the internal features of a natural kind are to be identified with its internal *structure*. Do we know that every natural kind has an internal structure? Kripke insists that this is so, even if we do not know what that structure is. Surely, this is a priori stipulation masking itself under the guise of scientific philosophy.

But as unconvincing as the claims above are, Kripke's and Putnam's insistence upon drawing an *exclusive* distinction between the external and internal features of a natural kind in order to lay the groundwork for their claim that it is the internal features that determine the kind in question is even less justifiable. That is, Putnam and Kripke assume (rather than argue) that if a natural kind like water has both internal and external features, one cannot identify the natural kind with features of both sorts. This is the whole thrust of Putnam's Twin Earth arguments and their Kripkean congeners. Their strategy is designed to force us to choose between competing alternatives: the phenomenal and the microstructural. But there is simply no reason to do so. A correct account of what water is will mention *not only its phenomenal features but also those that are not readily observable.*

There is thus a double mistake in Putnam's and Kripke's approach. First, they assume that one can give an accurate account of what water is in terms of a simple identity sentence, and second, they infer, via a factitious distinction between supposedly competing alternatives (phenomenal features versus microstructure), that water is to be identified with only one of these, namely its internal microstructure. In this latter case their theorizing is very traditional in generating pseudodichotomies—a point I emphasized in the previous chapter. In giving a correct account of what water is, I reject both their assumption and their inference. Instead, I submit, to understand what water is we need an extensive characterization (not a simple definition in terms of necessary and sufficient conditions or essences) that is open-textured. I will not attempt to give a full characterization here; it would require too much space. But I will now offer a shorter version of such a description—it expands what Thales might have given had he known modern science. I give it to illustrate the points that the characterization is complex, that it cannot be reduced to a simple identity sentence, and that it will refer both to features that are readily observable and to those that are not.

Water is a substance. That substance has various observable features: it is liquid, transparent, collects in pools, etc. (the "etc." informs the reader that in a fuller description other items would be added to the set of features). In its pure state, it is odorless, tasteless, colorless, and possesses a high degree of fluidity. In oceans, lakes, etc., it is generally found in an impure state, containing minerals, mud, and other substances. Pure water is composed of molecules each of which contains two parts of hydrogen and one part of oxygen. The microstructure of water is complex, because its molecules are in a highly active state that causes tumbling and other rapid movements. When water is cooled to the temperature of zero degrees Celsius, it freezes, forming ice, and when heated to 100 degrees Celsius, it boils, forming steam. It is more dense than ice, so ice will float on it. Its molecular *composition* does not change during these processes, but its *microstructure* does. (One can explain these scientific points at much greater length.) Water is and can be used for various purposes, such as . . . (and here a lengthy list would follow).

This complex statement describes accurately, though not completely, what water is. Note that it is not a simple identity statement of the kind that Putnam's and Kripke's approach requires, and in particular, that it does not *identify* water with any particular feature, whether gross or nongross. Further, unlike Kripke's and Putnam's approach, which gives a *static* description of water, the above is *dynamic*. It speaks about how changes in temperature, etc., affect the nature of the substance (I shall say more about this point in the next essay). Science is concerned not only with static features of the world (such as the microcomposition of water) but also with its dynamic features, and it is a serious deficiency in Putnam's and Kripke's approach to have overlooked this difference.

SEVEN

What has all this to do with the theory of direct reference? That theory, as I have mentioned, is a view about the nature of language, especially about the meaning and referential uses of certain categories of words, and not primarily a theory about the constituents of the world as in the writings of Thales. But because its proponents maintain that natural-kind terms directly refer to so-called micro-structures in the world, they believe that it is necessary to give an account of such structures in order to articulate and defend the theory. Hence the attempt to explain what water is via its putative microstructure. In particular, as I noted, Putnam and Kripke suppose that a good reason for believing that the word "water" means H_2O is that water is identical with H_2O. But since, as I have demonstrated, this identity claim is false, it is not a good reason for believing that "water" means H_2O.

But there is more to the theory than I have indicated so far. Taken as a linguistic thesis, the theory of direct reference makes another important claim. It holds that one can explain what "water" means by an ostensive definition. An ostensive definition is thought to be a paradigm of direct reference. It gives the meaning of a word by directly correlating the word with its referent. The technique rests upon the familiar principle that one can explain what "water" means by indicating what water is. One will point to a sample of H_2O while uttering the word "water." It is believed that an auditor will come to understand what "water" means via this ostensive procedure. I will now show that one cannot come to understand what "water" means in this way, and further, that it would not enable an auditor to distinguish between the supposedly diverse meanings of "water" on Earth and Twin Earth.

The direct-reference account implies that the process of ostension is similar to the following case. Suppose I take a small child to a zoo for the first time and point out various animals the infant has never seen before. I point and say "That is an aardvark," "That is a tiger," etc. In this way the child comes to understand what "aardvark" and "tiger" mean.

Here is Putnam's account of how one explains what "water" means:

Let W_1 and W_2 be two possible worlds in which I exist and in which this glass exists and in which I am giving a meaning explanation by pointing to this glass and saying "This is water." Let us suppose that in W_1 the glass is full of H_2O.[7]

To whom is Putnam giving this explanation? Presumably his auditor is not a foreigner, since Putnam uses English in communicating with that person. Is the individual a very young child, someone who does not know what "water" means? Let us assume so, since all normal adults and virtually all older children already know what "water" means. Yet as we shall see, the power of the example does not depend on the auditor's being a child, and I shall show that similar difficulties also arise for an adult. But by beginning in this way I can delineate the central issues more perspicuously. Let us therefore assume that Putnam is trying to explain what "water" means to a youngster. Then would his explanation be a good one? Could that person come to understand that "water" means H_2O via the process Putnam describes?

An immediate difficulty with it emerges from the identity thesis. Putnam says, "Let us suppose that in W_1 the glass is full of H_2O." But if the H_2O is ice, then Putnam will be pointing not at water, which is a fluid, but at a solid. One would thus need further explanation to get the child to understand that this solid will melt into a liquid and that the liquid is water. But this further explanation would require something other than an ostensive definition.

A second objection to the account is that if H_2O is the microstructure of water, as Putnam claims, how would the child know what Putnam is pointing at? Surely, with the naked eye the child cannot see the microstructure of water. So what will the child be looking at? Putnam states that he is pointing to a glass and saying, "This is water." Why shouldn't the child take Putnam to mean "This glass is water." After all, that is the most literal interpretation of what he said. So how does his auditor come to understand that Putnam intends to refer to the fluid rather than to the glass? Perhaps Putnam should have put a finger in the liquid, stirred it a bit, and then said, "This is water." But then, maybe, the child will have understood him to mean that his finger is water. How can he get the child to know that he means the liquid?

Let us suppose that somehow Putnam does succeed in getting the child to attend to the liquid in the glass. Then will the child be noticing the microstructure of water? Of course not. What the little one will be seeing is a liquid with certain phenomenal features. So how can Putnam's explanation teach the child that "water" means not the liquid having those phenomenal features but instead H_2O?

Clearly, it cannot. One would need a more elaborate set of instructions than Putnam provides in order to get the child to believe that "water" means a certain sort of microstructure. Those instructions, if they are to get off the ground at all, will have to include the locutions "H_2O" and "microstructure." I have just pointed out the difficulties in explaining ostensively what "H_2O" means. But the situation is as bad with "microstructure." On the assumption that the microstructure is not visible to the naked eye, how could Putnam get a young native speaker who does not know what "water" means to understand, especially by an ostensive process, what "microstructure" means? Indeed, where could one find a child who could understand Putnam's sentence "This is water" and yet not know what "water" means? Note also that nowhere in this process does Putnam talk explicitly about the meaning of "water." Instead, his effort is directed to getting the infant to recognize that the liquid in the glass *is* water. Even if the effort were successful, how would it help to explain what the word means? Surely, we need some additional explanatory procedures to progress from talk about a liquid in a glass to talk about the meaning of a word.

As I mentioned earlier, the difficulties I have described would exist if the person being given such an explanation of meaning were an adult. Such a person looking at a sample of what is called "water" on Earth could not distinguish it from a sample of what is called "water" on Twin Earth, since both specimens would have exactly the same phenomenal properties. For Putnam to explain that one sample consists of H_2O, whereas the other consists of XYZ, would amount to distinguishing them via definite descriptions. That is, Putnam would have to say something like "The stuff that is called 'water' on Earth is *the same stuff* as this sample here" (pointing to a liquid in a glass), "and by 'same stuff' I mean that it is composed of H_2O." That is just what he does say, as the following quotation makes clear:

Then the theory we have been presenting may be summarized by saying that an entity x, in an arbitrary possible world, is *water* if and only if it bears the relation *same* (construed as a cross-world relation) to the stuff *we* call 'water' in the actual world.[8]

Accordingly, his meaning explanation would no longer involve just directly referential terms but would identify water through the intermediation of a description: "the stuff that, like this sample, is composed of H_2O." So the direct-reference account would not work for an adult either, since that adult could not directly observe the underlying chemical components of the stuff that Putnam is pointing to.

The scenario becomes increasingly implausible as one explores it. It also fails, for example, to distinguish cases where one is being introduced to unfamiliar items, like aardvarks and tigers, from cases involving very familiar items, such as water and human beings. As with most philosophical theories, the theory of direct reference depends on too few examples. When the range of examples is expanded, it loses its credibility.

EIGHT

I will now propose an alternative to Putnam's account. Suppose that we wish to explain to a child what the word "water" means. How do we in fact go about it? We can exclude the direct-reference myths that we do this by showing a child a glass of water and saying "This is water" or by telling a child that what we now call "water" in the twentieth century is H_2O.

The notions of explaining, understanding, and meaning are connected elements in an ongoing instructional process designed to promote communication between human beings. Meanings play a crucial role in this process. They are the links that tie the chain of communication together. But the process is complicated. In teaching a tyke its native language, including what words mean, we do not begin with definitions, ostensive or otherwise. We train children as we train animals, i.e., to obey and to follow orders. We do not begin the training of animals with definitions. Moreover, early training is designed less to explain what words mean than to explain what things are. In training children, the emphasis is upon teaching them what water is, not what the word "water" means. We say "Don't spill the water," "Bring me a glass of water," "There is too much water in the glass. Pour some out," and so on. As Wittgenstein writes, "Children do not learn that books exist, that armchairs exist, etc. etc.—they learn to fetch books, sit in armchairs, etc."[9]

These kinds of training procedures initiate a child into a community united by common linguistic practices. Their effect is to explain in ways that are not totally explicit but that through a cumulative developmental process eventually endow a child with the understanding of what words mean and what persons mean by the words they use. This process can succeed only if the young can observe the things and their features that are being referred to. In the case of water, this means observing its phenomenal properties: its fluidity, transparency in small amounts, and so forth.

The outcome of the process is that the child, in an effort to communicate his or her thoughts to others and to understand theirs, learns to use the word "water" in a way that is consonant with community practice. He or she learns, that is, to apply the word to a liquid having certain overt properties and, beyond this, to use the word in a variety of other ways, as an active verb, for instance.

This learning process extends through time. At first a child may understand "water" only to mean a fluid that is tasteless and colorless and that is given to him or her to allay thirst. Later he or she may learn that this fluid, which is colorless in a glass, takes on a bluish hue in thick layers, that muds and salts dissolve in it, and yet that the word "water" is still applied to it. The child may also discover that when it is sufficiently cold, water is transformed into a different substance that his elders call "ice." How should one describe these supplemental pieces of information? Are they additions to the meaning of "water"? Let us not try to decide the matter here. What is clear is that such additional pieces of information allow for fuller communication between the child and others. The important point is that at this level of education all the components of the meaning of a word like "water" that a child grasps involve observable features, i.e., they consist of such concepts as being liquid, *being fluid, being transparent, being odorless, being potable.* Meaning thus arises as a function of what the child observes and experiences. And what the neophyte observes are the gross properties of water. As his or her education proceeds, the youngster may eventually come to learn (though not by seeing or experiencing) that water is composed of H_2O. Shall we say, as Putnam and Kripke insist, that children know what "water" means only at the end of this process, i.e., when they learn that water is composed of H_2O? Why should we? We do not, and we should not.

If Putnam and Kripke were right, no native speakers of English before 1800 could have known what "water" meant. This follows from their thesis that "water" means the same as "H_2O" and that nobody knew that the composition of water was H_2O before 1800. But if so, they could not have communicated with one another; they could not have sensibly given or obeyed such commands as "Don't spill the water" and "Bring me a glass of water." But since they did communicate with one another in saying these things and without knowing anything about the molecular structure of water, it follows that they did know what "water" meant and, accordingly, that the theory advanced by Putnam and Kripke is mistaken.

Putnam and Kripke have reversed the order of nature. Instead of beginning with the fact that early speakers of English communicated with one another and asking how this is possible, they have developed an a priori theory that makes the fact of such communication inexplicable. Here we have philosophical paradox in its strongest form.

For, contrary to what Putnam and Kripke say, these early training procedures do not make use of the techniques of direct reference, they do not rely on ostensive definitions, and they do not initially teach a child that water is composed of H_2O. Instead, they teach a child what "water" means by reference to what the child observes and manipulates.

The doctrine of direct reference cannot account for the developmental process I have described, or for the role that the phenomenal features of water play in determining the meaning of "water," or for the historical fact that early speakers of English obviously communicated with one another in using the word "water." These facts thus form decisive reasons for rejecting it.

NINE

But now someone might object as follows: "You have described how one *explains the meaning* of a particular word, but this is different from telling us what the word means. What does "water" mean in English? Indeed, how does one decide what any word means?" I begin my answer by noting that we are speaking about individual words rather than about phrases, sentences, or longer units of language like paragraphs and chapters. Unlike some of these longer units, words are the kinds of linguistic entities to which the question "What does x mean?" singularly applies. Indeed, they are paradigms of the linguistic units about which we can ask this question. *In general,* we cannot sensibly ask this question about a whole sentence (*pace* Frege), though we can *sometimes* ask it—say if one is trying to translate a sentence from a foreign language into English. One can then ask of the sentence itself, "What does it mean?" The answer will consist in translating it into a synonymous English sentence. But we do not normally ask what a sentence means, though, of course, we might be asking what somebody means in using the particular sentence he does. In contrast, even native speakers frequently ask what an English word means. In saying this, I nonetheless emphasize that the question is normally specific: it is about a given word and what it means. To ask in general what words mean, as many theorists from Russell to Putnam and Kripke have done, is to ask a question for which there is no decision procedure.

Fortunately, there exists such a procedure with respect to specific words, namely, to look up their meaning (or meanings) in a dictionary. This procedure does not apply to all words. In general, it does not apply to proper names. We cannot look up the name "John" in a dictionary, for example. Some writers have inferred from this fact that all proper names lack meaning. But this claim must be qualified when the range of examples is expanded. "Poland" for instance, is defined by my dictionary as a central European country. What is true is that for any word that is not a proper name, a good dictionary will give its meaning (in contrast, one cannot look up the meaning of a sentence or a paragraph in a dictionary).

When one looks up "aardvark," "tiger," and "water," the results are interesting. Here is what the *American College Dictionary* gives as the meaning of "aardvark":

A large, nocturnal, burrowing mammal of Africa, subsisting largely on termites, and having a long, extensile tongue, claws, and conspicuously long ears. There is only one genus, *Orycteropus*, constituting a separate order, Tubulidentata.

And here is what it gives for "tiger":

A large, carnivorous feline, of Asia, tawny-colored, striped with black, ranging in several races from India and the Malay Peninsula to Siberia.

Four other dictionaries I have consulted give similar characterizations. Webster's *Third New International Dictionary* gives this definition:

Tiger: A larger Asiatic carnivorous mammal having a tawny coat transversely striped with black, a long untufted tail that is ringed with black, underparts that are mostly white, and no mane, being typically larger than the lion with a total

68

length usu. of 9 to 10 feet but sometimes of more than 12 feet, living usu. on the ground, feeding mostly on larger mammals (as cattle), in some cases including man, and ranging from Persia across Asia to the Malay peninsula, Sumatra, and Java, and northward to southern Siberia and Manchuria. (P. 2392)

You will note that in none of these entries is anything said about the microstructure, DNA, or the internal structure of any of these natural kinds. Instead, the emphasis is on the phenomenal characteristics: in the case of a tiger, its having a tawny coat, black stripes, no mane, underparts that are mostly white, and so forth. What the word "tiger" means, then, is the animal having these particular features. Kripke is wrong in thinking that the meaning of "tiger" is determined by the "internal structure" of tigers.

Now Kripke might respond to this assertion by saying that there are animals we call "tigers" that do not fit the above description: albino tigers, three-legged tigers, two-headed tigers, and so forth. And he would argue that what determines all of them to be called "tigers" is their identical genetic makeup. But this is a sheer mistake. People do not call albino tigers "tigers" because of their genetic makeup, which in fact almost nobody knows anything about. Such aberrant animals are called "tigers" because experience, based upon observed properties, makes it plain that we can expect such deviations from the norm. That is, persons observing tigers over lengthy periods of time will note that some of them are of a slightly different color than others, are striped in different patterns, and indeed diverge in all sorts of ways from prototypical tigers. Experience teaches us that there is a spectrum of such features, an extreme example of which is an unstriped tiger, such as an albino. Thus it is still the observable features that decisively determine whether something is to be called "tiger" or not, and not the underlying structures of tigers. The case is thus parallel to that of "water."

The instance of tigers is interesting for another reason. Along with the fact that what is called "jade" has two different compositional elements, it gives us good grounds for holding that in general overt considerations, including the functions that certain kinds serve, are more decisive than microfeatures in determining what a word means. As I said earlier, it will provide good grounds for rejecting the claim that there is *always*—I stress "always"—a direct connection between what a word means and what the substance named by that word is composed of. In the argument that follows I shall show that the meaning of the word has little to do with the composition of the item but depends on the function it serves.

Take as an example the common noun "table." This is, of course, not a natural-kind word, but the point is applicable to natural-kind words, such as "water" and "jade." The term "table" refers to objects composed of glass, steel, wood, plastic, and other materials. The "microstructures" of tables will vary, depending on the material of which the table is made. Yet function determines whether we subsume objects having such diverse microstructures under the rubric "table." What counts as a table is the use to which the item is put, and not the material of which it is made. The meaning of "table" is thus determined by function or use, and not by material composition or microstructure.

Now it is easy to extend the point to natural-kind terms. Consider the following modification of the Twin Earth scenario by way of illustration. Suppose that for centuries now there has been considerable interaction between Earth and Twin Earth. Persons have been flying between these planets for eons, and for some time now planes leaving Earth have been stocking up on what Earthlings call "water," which they use for drinking, washing, cooking, and other purposes. Planes returning from Twin

Earth have been supplied with what Twin Earthlings call "water," and this liquid is used for the same set of purposes on the return trip. But let us suppose that before 1996 nobody had performed a chemical analysis on the fluids they all call "water" on the two planets, but in that year an analysis was done. It was then determined that the liquid on Earth was composed of H_2O and that the liquid on Twin Earth was composed of XYZ. Would the persons moving between the planets stop calling one of the fluids "water"? I doubt it. I think they would say that water is composed of different ingredients, depending on where it is found, or perhaps they would say it comes in two different forms, like jade. They would thus treat the word "water" in the way we now treat the word "table." Function would override microcomposition in such a case. The example shows that there are plausible alternatives to Kripke's contention that the microcomposition of a substance is *always* decisive in determining what we call that substance. With the sorts of modifications I have mentioned, similar comments apply to albino tigers.

I have said that the argument above functions as a counterexample to Kripke's and Putnam's assumption that the debate about the meaning of "water" will be settled once it is determined what water is. It does function as such a counterexample only on Kripke's and Putnam's further assumption that the nature of water is determined by its microstructure. I have indicated that "water" refers to a liquid having certain phenomenal properties. If these are the properties of water, as I have argued, then the debate about the meaning of "water" will be settled, but not as Kripke and Putnam think. The meaning of "water" will not be determined by the microcomposition of water. This is what I meant earlier when I said that I would not challenge the principle of a close relationship between being and meaning per se, only the interpretation that Kripke and Putnam give of it.

In concluding this chapter I should emphasize that there are nonetheless differences between the cases of "table," "water," and "tiger"/"aardvark." In good dictionaries, reference is made not to the microcomposition of tables but only to the function that such artifacts serve. In the cases of tigers and aardvarks, as we have seen, no reference is made to their DNA (or to any other genetic or "internal" or covert features). And as in the case of tables, definitions refer not to their "functions" but only to their phenomenal characteristics. Water differs from tables and from tigers/aardvarks in that all good modern dictionaries characterize it in terms of its phenomenal features, its various functions, and its chemical composition. *The American College Dictionary* says this:

Water. n. The liquid which in a more or less impure state constitutes rain, oceans, lakes, rivers, etc., and which in a pure state is a transparent, odorless, tasteless liquid, a compound of hydrogen and oxygen, H_2O, freezing at 32 F or 0 C, and boiling at 212 F or 100 C. It contains 11.188 percent hydrogen and 88.8812 percent oxygen, by weight.

The emphasis in this entry is upon the phenomenal features of water. But water is also said to be a compound of hydrogen and oxygen, H_2O. In mentioning that water is composed of hydrogen and oxygen, the dictionary, to be sure, does not state that water is identical with H_2O, as Putnam and Kripke contend. Yet its reference to the chemical components transcends the merely phenomenal, as in the case of tigers and aardvarks.

Since I am arguing that dictionaries give us the meaning of specific words, it would seem that I must be committed to the view that it is part of the meaning of "water" that the composition of water is H_2O. But am I committed to such a view? I do not think I am.

Dictionaries written before 1830 do not mention H_2O in defining "water"—see Thomas Sheridan's *A General Dictionary of the English Language* of 1780, and Samuel Johnson's *A Dictionary of the English Language*, 9th. ed., 1805, for example.

Given the difference between such early modern and contemporary lexical entries, we have at least five different options for describing what "water" now means.

1. We can say that the meaning of "water" changed after 1860.

2. We can hold that English speakers before 1860 did not know what the word "water" meant, since they did not know that water was composed of H_2O.

3. We might think that meaning is a matter of degree, the full meaning of "water" having been arrived at only after 1860.

4. We can abandon the notion that dictionaries give us the meaning of words.

5. We can assert that dictionaries give us the meaning of "water" in terms of the phenomenal characteristics of water and also give us certain supplementary pieces of information about water that are not parts of its meaning, the references to its chemical properties being such additional pieces of information. In the case of "tiger" we have a phenomenal account describing the appearance of tigers and certain additional pieces of information about tigers, for example, that they are found in Manchuria and Sumatra. We would not normally suppose that these latter pieces of information have much to do with determining what tigers are or what the word "tiger" means.

After reflecting on these five options, I reject (2) for reasons already stated and (4) on methodological grounds, i.e., it seems obvious that dictionaries do give us the meaning of words. I am unable to decide categorically between (1), (3), and (5), though I entertain (1) with considerable reluctance because I have the hard intuition that English speakers in the eighteenth century meant by "water" exactly what we mean today. I do not wish to deny that words do change their meanings, but I see no reason to believe that "water" is one of the words that has changed its meaning over time. Still, I am unable to mount a compelling defense of this intuition. For reasons explained earlier, I am attracted to (3) but with reservations about how to distinguish degrees of meaning and to what extent additional pieces of information play a role in determining the meaning. Thus I will defend (5). This proposition has the merit that it assimilates "water" to "tiger" and "aardvark," and thus gives us a uniform account of the meaning of natural-kind terms. That is, it asserts that the meaning of such terms is determined by the phenomenal features of the natural-kinds they refer to. Accordingly, that water is composed of H_2O and that tigers exist in Java are not strictly parts of the meaning of "water" and "tiger" but are supplementary pieces of information about those natural kinds.

What is really clear to me is that water is not identical with H_2O and that early speakers of English knew what the word "water" meant. Since Putnam's and Kripke's theory asserts or implies the negation of each of these propositions, it is to be rejected for misrepresenting some of the main features of the world.

Microscopic and Macroscopic

ONE

In the preceding essay, "Reflections on Water," I gave several arguments to show that water is not identical with H_2O and that the word "water" does not mean H_2O. One of these concluded that if the identity thesis of Putnam and Kripke were correct, it would follow that ice and steam are not only identical with water but also with one another. Since ice and steam are patently not the same, Putnam's and Kripke's identity thesis is mistaken. What is true, as I stated, is that ice, water, and steam are all *composed* of H_2O, but they are not identical with it. I shall call this the *compositional argument.*

I also developed a second argument, which I called the *functional argument,* to show that "water" does not mean H_2O, as Putnam had claimed in his essay "Meaning and Reference" of 1973. In 1989 in *Representation and Reality* Putnam revised his position, asserting then that "water" and "H_2O" are not *strictly* synonymous, but that the extension of "water," i.e., H_2O, is still the *dominant factor* in determining its meaning. This, in effect, was a reaffirmation of his earlier view that the meaning of "water" is not a function of its macroscopic features: its liquidity, potability, transparency, etc. Putnam also affirmed that this result applied to all natural-kind terms, such as "gold" and "tiger." The compositional argument and the functional argument are thus about two different things: the first concerns the nature of water, the second the meaning of the word "water."

As far as I know, Kripke's views about the nature of water and the meaning of "water" have not changed. Since Putnam's revisions seem more terminological than substantial, I shall focus here on the earlier position they both held.

According to the Twin Earth scenario in Putnam's paper, two observationally indistinguishable liquid substances on Earth and Twin Earth are both called "water." But they differ in composition, one of them being made of H_2O, the other of XYZ (where XYZ is not identical with H_2O). Accordingly, "water" refers to two different substances on the two planets, and therefore means different things. "Water" is thus a homonym, a term with the same sound but having different meanings. The argument thus presupposes that what "water" means is determined by its reference, and that in the case of the substance on Earth, its reference is H_2O.

My functional argument served as a counterinstance to the thesis that the microcomposition of a substance either determines, or is the dominant factor in determining, the meaning of the term denoting that substance. It demonstrated that other considerations may sometimes override microcomposition in determining what a term means. Tables made of different materials are still called "tables," despite their differing compositions. They are called "tables" because of the function they serve. "Table" is not a natural-kind word, to be sure, but the functional argument, with some modifications to incorporate the macroscopic features of things, was shown to apply to terms that are, such as "aardvark," "tiger," and "jade." In particular, both functional and macroscopic considerations apply in determining the meaning of "water."

Putnam's Twin Earth argument holds that water is necessarily H_2O, and accordingly that it is not possible for "water" in Earth English to mean something other than H_2O. The premise that water is necessarily H_2O is false, but even if it were true, the conclusion derived from it, that "water" must mean H_2O, is a non sequitur. I will show in Section 5 why the premise is false and why, even if it were true, the conclusion would not follow from it. These will be new arguments not mentioned in the previous chapter. I call these the isotope argument, the category-mistake argument, and the argument from isomers.

This chapter is still about water and "water" to some degree, but its thrust is quite different. It is centrally about the tendency of many recent philosophers to look for reality beneath the observable or phenomenal. This, as I shall show, is a serious error. My focus on water and "water" is designed to bring out the nature of this misconception.

TWO

Who are these philosophers, and what is their view? The main exponents of this position are, inter alia, the aforementioned Kripke and Putnam, but they are joined in advancing this doctrine by many other distinguished scholars, such as Stephen Stich and Paul and Patricia Churchland. The view has its provenance in Quine's naturalized epistemology and in the earlier forms of empiricism associated with Locke and Hume. It is not easy to give it a traditional name. One might describe it as a new form of empiricism or as a kind of scientific rationalism, but neither appellation fits exactly.

According to most textbook definitions, empiricism is the doctrine that all knowledge derives from experience. This statement is usually bolstered by the addition of the word "sense," so that "experience" in the formula becomes "sense experience," and sense experience is usually taken to be the product or result of causal sequences that have both external and internal physical or material origins. Thus the internal sources giving rise to feelings and other sorts of sensations, such as itches and pains, are said to have a neurological base, and this in turn is traced to microscopic elements that are ultimately material or physical in character. All of the external causes, of course, are said to be material or physical (these terms were usually not distinguished, and are frequently, though mistakenly, taken to be equivalent even today). The very formulation of "empiricism" in these terms thus implies the existence of an external world. But, of course, to imply that the external world exists is not to prove that it does, so the formulation does not, by itself, amount to a solution to that celebrated epistemological problem.

Admittedly, even with these additions, the definition of "empiricism" is vague and subject to other liabilities, but if in any sense it can be taken seriously, it is dubious that any philosopher has ever been an empiricist. Neither Locke nor Hume, generally regarded as exemplars of empiricism, would have conformed to that characterization. What Locke identified as "trifling ideas" seem to be specimens of what were later called "tautologies," and Hume in *An Inquiry Concerning Human Understanding* asserted that there is a kind of knowledge about the "relations of ideas" that does not depend on experience. Though their terminology was different, nearly all of the famous logical empiricists of the twentieth century—Carnap, Hempel, Ayer, and Schlick—drew a distinction between two different types of knowledge, a priori and a posteriori, and it was only the latter that was tied to experience.

These counterexamples suggest that a more refined definition of "empiricism" is needed. This might hold that all nonanalytic knowledge derives from sense experience.

Rationalism would then be the view that some nonanalytic propositions, such as "The mind/soul is immaterial" and "All properties must inhere in a substance," do not derive from sense experience. But this definition has the disadvantage that it depends on a sharp distinction between the analytic and the nonanalytic. Since Quine's "Two Dogmas of Empiricism" the distinction has been widely seen as problematical, and indeed, for Quine and for many others, it is not needed in order to characterize what is meant by "empiricism."

To use "empiricism," then, as a rubric for the doctrine I will be discussing below, I wish to suggest a better characterization that will include as empiricists many philosophers, such as those I have mentioned above. In virtually all earlier versions of the doctrine we find two notions usually thought to be complementary or mutually supportive:

1. Science and science alone is capable of providing a true account of reality.

2. Any such account must ultimately be grounded in observation or sense experience.

As Quine himself puts it, "Total science is like a field of force whose boundary conditions are experience."[1] And elsewhere he says, "Each man is given a scientific heritage plus a continuing barrage of sensory stimulation; and the considerations which guide him in warping his scientific heritage to fit his continuing sensory promptings are, where rational, pragmatic."[2] These various idioms are intended to capture what the older empiricists were referring to when they spoke of observation or sense experience.

This definition not only captures the intuitive content of the doctrine but it also provides a significant contrast with most classical versions of rationalism, which deny such a favored role to sense experience. It is also important to mention that earlier forms of empiricism took it as obvious that the concept of observation, when applied to the external world, refers to what one perceives with the naked eye as well as with instruments, and accordingly that the ordinary appearance of things is one—though not necessarily the only—grounding feature of science. But I shall not make this further feature a *defining* property of "empiricism" for reasons to be explained in a moment.

Quine would, I believe, support both of the preceding tenets, and therefore can also be classified as an empiricist, though, of course, he would deny that *single* observations are definitive in the construction of the "corporate body" that is scientific theory. As he says, "If this view is right, it is misleading to speak of the empirical content of an individual statement."[3] His holistic empiricism recognizes the importance of "sensory promptings," while rejecting the reductive dogma that individual observations play decisive roles in the construction of scientific theory.

Quine's rejection of the distinction in kind between analytic and synthetic statements is compatible with adherence to the dual principles I have mentioned. Quine is thus not rejecting empiricism but merely two conceptions that have traditionally been thought to be necessary to it but that under his construal are not. Identifying himself as an empiricist, he writes, "As an empiricist I continue to think of the conceptual scheme of science as a tool, ultimately, for predicting future experience in the light of past experience."[4]

My thesis in this essay is that proponents of these recent types of empiricism, if that is the right name for their views, have driven a wedge between the apparently complementary principles mentioned above. On the one hand, they hold secure the principle that science alone can discover the nature of reality, but on the other, their commitment to the observability principle is highly qualified. This qualification takes two different forms. First, they tend to minimize the importance for scientific theory of the observation of the macroscopic world, whether with the naked eye or with instruments. Their focus instead is on the microscopic or even submicroscopic world, and it is that world that they take to constitute reality.

The second qualification concerns the extent to which science does depend, even at the microscopic level, on observation. Since they acknowledge that some aspects of the submicroscopic world are not observable, at least with present levels of instrumentation, or perhaps even in principle, their account of reality goes beyond observation and is driven by theory. For them, then, science ultimately needs more than observation to determine the characteristics of the real world.

Such qualifications do not entail that these thinkers have abandoned the notion that observation plays some role in the development of scientific theory. To this extent they are faithful Quineans. But they do imply that they assign a lesser status to observation than the classical empiricists did. For Putnam and Kripke, the observable features of substances such as water or of animals such as tigers are invidiously described as "superficial" in contrast to their "internal, microscopic structures."

This deprecation of observation is reminiscent of certain ancient Greek attitudes in which a kind of tension is held to obtain between appearance and reality. In its most extreme forms, say in Plato's *Republic* and *Timaeus,* it gives rise to a fundamental opposition: what is observed is unreal, and what is real cannot be observed. That is because, for Plato, reality is hidden from any form of sense experience, lying behind the world of appearance as it were. Yet he was an avowed exponent of science. Georgios Anagnostopoulos has said this of Plato:

His views on the sciences clearly represent one of the earliest, if not the earliest, attempts to provide a philosophy of science.

And his is the attempt that has yielded that dominant conception of scientific thought which has often come to be identified with the name of Plato and has invariably been viewed as assigning to scientific thought those features that we associate with rationalism. That is, the conception that assigns to scientific thought the characteristics of being *a priori*, necessary, deductive, and thus denigrating the role of experience as well as the world of experience, or perhaps even eliminating these from the domain of scientific investigation and knowledge.[5]

As the quotation brings out, Plato believed that science and science alone can provide knowledge of reality, but given his attitude toward sense experience, he averred that science must transcend the observable to discover the real. In effect, he identified science with the careful and systematic employment of reason and with the denigration of observation. I should stress in this context that Plato's attitude toward observation went well beyond observation with the naked eye. Even the most sophisticated instruments could not, in principle, give us access to reality. Resonances of this view were to appear in Descartes two millenia later.

The early modern empiricists were also devotees of science (note that the subtitle of Hume's *Treatise* is *Being an Attempt to Introduce the Experimental Method of Reasoning into Moral Subjects*), but they diametrically reversed the Platonic emphasis, putting their stress on the sensible—on ideas, images, and impressions, i.e., on what were later to be called sense-data—as the sources of our knowledge of external reality. Concomitantly, they affirmed that the products of reason lack conceptual content. They anticipated Wittgenstein's remark that one who knows that it will either rain or not rain knows nothing at all about the weather.

This emphasis gave rise to another thesis often advanced by these earlier writers, and sometimes (erroneously) identified by commentators with empiricism, namely, that necessity is not to be found in nature (i.e., between matters of fact) but only in the mind. As Georgios Anagnostopoulos has indicated in the quotation above, this is in direct opposition to the approach of the classical rationalists. A corollary of this thesis is the contention that if propositions are certain they have no existential import, and if they have existential import they are probable only. (This is sometimes expressed as, though it is not synonymous with, the thesis that from tautologies only tautologies can be derived.) So for early empiricists, science, which is about matters of fact, is fundamentally tied to observation, and the Platonic thesis about the nexus between reason and science was accordingly rejected.

The new empiricism I am describing resembles both the older empiricism and Platonic rationalism, yet it differs from both. It is indeed an interesting question whether it has an earlier exact counterpart. Perhaps its closest prototype is to be found in Greek atomism. According to Sextus Empiricus, Democritus distinguished between different kinds of knowledge, a "bastard" knowledge that the senses provide and a "legitimate" knowledge that operates on the atoms, i.e., on objects too fine for the senses (here the naked eye) to perceive. Sense information is termed "bastard" knowledge because it is not trustworthy, a notion we also find to be central to the Platonic tradition, as I have mentioned above. The question then arises, What is the source of legitimate knowledge? Since the atomists had no instruments to perceive atoms, they could not claim it was observation in any *direct* sense of the term, and indeed, the textual evidence indicates that Democritus believed that it is reason, reflecting critically on the information or "bastard knowledge" generated by the senses, that gives rise to knowledge about atoms.

The relationship between sense experience and atoms, i.e., how the underlying reality of atoms is manifested in appearance and especially to the naked eye, is not very clear. What is clear is that atoms were not directly apprehensible by the senses. It could well be that Democritus was working toward a doctrine of dispositional powers of the sort Locke was later to develop. It was also possibly a primitive theory of representative realism, according to which the senses provided indirect information about reality. Of course, for Plato, atoms as particulars could not be real entities, so Democritus' atomism represented a radical departure from Plato's views.

The claims of the atomists about the existence and properties of atoms were thus mainly motivated by rationalistic, conjectural, or deductive considerations, rather than being based on direct observational findings. In this respect, and like Plato, they were driven by the need to find a compromise between the views of Parmenides and Heraclitus. It was a compromise that to some degree recognized the veridicality of the sensible world, even if only in the dispositional sense that by observing it, one could make sensible conjectures about the nature of atoms.

Hence in the atomists we encounter philosophers whose general doctrine, stated in a contemporary idiom, is a mixture of observation and theory—much of the latter taking the form of sheer speculation. Let us call their doctrine a type of "scientific rationalism." It was scientific as that notion was understood by the Greeks. But it was also rationalistic because it introduced reason where it believed observation could not play a role in the discovery of reality—rather than suspending judgment when observational evidence is not available, as Hume would later urge to be the only sensible decision—and because reason was taken to be decisive as to the nature of reality. In this last respect, the new empiricists hold views that are strikingly similar to those of the atomists, even though much of the microscopic world that constitutes reality for them is now observable with instruments.

What I wish to argue here is the following:

- These contemporary thinkers have wobbled between classical empiricism and a kind of scientific rationalism that, in complicated ways, disparages observation. As we shall see, science does not ignore observation at the macroscopic level.

- Because that is so, they fail in their avowed mission to be *the* philosophy that best explains and justifies the nature of scientific inquiry.

The contemporary picture is thus one of multiple crosscurrents stemming both from Quine's version of empiricism and the earlier varieties but now given a special rationalistic twist. The outcome of these confluences is a complex theory. It rejects the direct confrontation of macroscopic experience, which classical empiricism required, as well as the thesis that necessity is not to be found in nature. It agrees with the older empiricism that science alone will uncover reality, but like the atomists, it holds that reality is constituted by the microscopic (or submicroscopic) world and that at least some of the features of that world are apprehensible only by reason. To both of these traditions, it adds a touch of Aristotle in its search for the essence, and indeed the hidden essence, that lies behind the phenomenal world.

THREE

Of course, it may be wondered whether the preceding sketch does justice to these contemporary thinkers or whether it is a caricature. To avoid jousting with straw men, I shall now show that this new empiricism does espouse the views I have ascribed to it. I shall then go on to explain why its attempted reconstruction of scientific inquiry is abortive. That the writers mentioned above believe that science is the key that will open the door to reality is so well known that no extensive documentation is required, but the following brief quotations reveal how self-consciously explicit their commitment to this principle is.

In her book *Neurophilosophy*, Patricia Churchland agrees with Charles Sanders Peirce when she writes the following:

> In the idealized long run, the completed science is a true description of reality; there is no other Truth and no other Reality.[6]

In *Representation and Reality*, Putnam's scientism is manifest. According to him,

> Independence, Uniqueness, Bivalence, and Correspondence are regulative ideas that the final scientific image is expected to live up to, as well as metaphysical assumptions that guarantee that such a final scientific resolution of all philosophical problems *must* be possible.[7]

FOUR

In contrast to this unwavering commitment to scientism, and its firm rejection of the autonomy of philosophy, their view about the role of observation in scientific theory is highly qualified and, accordingly, is difficult to simply describe. Perhaps the best way of introducing it is to focus on what they say about natural kinds.

Let us turn to that task now. The essential point, as mentioned above, is that they denigrate the importance of the phenomenological characteristics of substances in their search for their hidden essences. That a *search* is required is another way of saying that the overt, observable characteristics of those kinds—the sort of features one can generally see with the naked eye—are taken not to be, or even to represent, the real nature of the kind under investigation.

In a widely discussed passage, Wittgenstein said this:

For they see in the essence, not something that already lies open to view and that becomes surveyable by a rearrangement, but something that lies *beneath* the surface. Something that lies within, which we see when we look *into* the thing, and which an analysis digs out.

"*The essence is hidden from us*": this is the form our problem now assumes.[8]

He also writes the following:

Philosophy simply puts everything before us, and neither explains nor deduces anything. Since everything lies open to view there is nothing to explain. For what is hidden, for example, is of no interest to us.[9]

Putnam and Kripke seem to have forgotten their Wittgenstein. In referring to Archimedes with approval, Putnam asseverates this:

When Archimedes asserted that something was gold, he was not just saying that it had the superficial characteristics of gold . . . ; he was saying that it had the same *hidden structure* (the same "essence" so to speak) as any local piece of gold.[10]

This passage expresses three of the main theses of the new empiricists: (1) that the phenomenological features of gold—its color, ductility, etc.—are superficial, which means, I take it, that in the quest for the real nature of gold, they don't carry much weight, (2) that the search for the nature of gold is a search for its essence, and (3) that this essence is something hidden, i.e., is not observable by the naked eye and perhaps is not observable at all.

In *Representation and Reality*, published some fourteen years later, Putnam expressed a completely contrary view. In this book he wrote thus:

MICROSCOPIC AND MACROSCOPIC

Part of my aim is to illustrate (by applying it to a particular problem) a philosophical attitude that gives up many traditional assumptions about Appearance and Reality; that gives up, for example, the assumption that what is real is what is "under" or "behind" or "more fundamental than" our everyday appearances."[11]

Yet there is more the appearance, rather than the reality, of change in his position. For later in the same work in speaking of water he reverts to his earlier view that the "essence" of water is H_2O. As he says,

In "The Meaning of 'Meaning'" I expressed this by saying that even in 1750 what the word "water" referred to in Earth English was H_2O (give or take impurities). The word "water" in Twin Earth English referred to XYZ (give or take impurities). To say that this is what the word "water" referred to in the two dialects is just to say that this is what the word *denoted* or was true of.[12]

At the end of *Representation and Reality* Putnam has changed his mind about Wittgenstein again. He admits that he "has not been quite persuaded by my Wittgensteinian colleagues that one should give up the effort to explain in philosophy."[13] Since Wittgenstein means by the "effort to explain in philosophy" the search for essences, and since the theory Putnam advances about natural kinds is the same in *Representation and Reality* as it was in his earlier books and essays, I think we should identify his real views with his practice rather than with the inconsistent meta-descriptions he gives of that practice.

Kripke also speaks about the quest to discover the real nature of species as a search for their essences. The following quotation is typical:

Note that on the present view, scientific discoveries of species essence do not constitute a "change of meaning"; the possibility of such discoveries was part of the original enterprise.[14]

As I mentioned at the outset, my thesis in this chapter is that the new empiricists deprecate the observation of the macroscopic in their efforts to depict reality. In the Twin Earth argument, they state, or at least strongly imply, that their views about natural kinds are based on an accurate scientific account of the relationship between the macroscopic and the microscopic. They also state, or again at least strongly imply, that this account, with some augmentation, can be used to support a linguistic theory of direct reference. (They do concede, of course, that part of the direct-reference theory, for instance its claim that proper names are rigid designators, is admittedly not based on science.) In the particular case of water, for example, their contention is that science has shown that water is identical with H_2O. On this basis they declare that the word "water" means H_2O. As promised, I shall now show that both claims are mistaken. The scientific account they give is not accurate, and their linguistic theory too is defective. Water is not identical with H_2O, and the word "water" does not mean H_2O. Though I shall be speaking about water and "water" here, my objections apply to the extrapolation of their views to all natural kinds and natural-kind words and, of course, still more generally to their denigration of the macroscopic. I have three arguments against their position: the isotope argument, the category-mistake argument, and the argument from isomers. Each of these has a scientific base.

I will begin with the isotope argument. In considering it, one should keep in mind that when Kripke and Putnam claim that water is identical with H_2O, they mean, as Putnam explicitly states, that each and every water molecule is H_2O. They take this thesis to be significant and not a mere tautology. It is nontautologous in the sense that whereas ordinary persons mean by "water" the liquid that falls from the sky as rain, collects in pools, etc., chemical theory shows that water is (ignoring impurities) necessarily H_2O. The isotope argument that now follows will show this claim to be false.

In 1931 Harold Urey discovered that the liquid ordinary persons call "water" is composed not only of H_2O molecules but of molecules composed of deuterium and oxygen. For this achievement Urey later received the Nobel Prize. Deuterium is an isotope of hydrogen, having an atomic weight double that of ordinary hydrogen. When it combines with oxygen it forms deuterium oxide, or D_2O. A collection of D_2O molecules is also called "heavy water," which is visually indistinguishable from normal water. Deuterium oxide has a molecular weight of about 20 (twice the atomic weight of ordinary hydrogen, which is 1, plus that of oxygen, which is 16), whereas ordinary water has a molecular weight of about 18. Heavy water is comparatively rare, since ordinary water contains only one atom of deuterium for every 6,760 atoms of hydrogen.

In 1934 E. Rutherford, M. L. Oliphant, and P. Hartreck bombarded deuterium with high-energy deuterons (the nuclei of deuterium atoms) and discovered another isotope of hydrogen that they called "tritium." This also bonds with oxygen, forming the molecule T_2O, which is heavier than deuterium oxide and is very rare in nature. To complicate matters still further, there are molecules whose chemical composition is symbolized as HDO, and there is an isotope of oxygen (oxygen 18) that bonds with various isotopes of hydrogen to form molecules that differ from any described above.

If one were to eliminate all sand, oils, salts, metals, etc., from the liquids found in the Pacific and Atlantic Oceans, one would obtain what Kripke and Putnam call "pure water." This they define as H_2O. But pure water would not be composed solely of H_2O. As the aforementioned history of chemistry indicates, it is a mixture of various kinds of molecules, such as H_2O, D_2O, HDO, and T_2O, all closely resembling one another but nonetheless different. These various molecules have different properties (e.g., boiling points, molecular masses, and so forth) and therefore are not identical. The statement that pure water is H_2O is neither a necessary nor empirical truth, since heavy water is not identical with H_2O. Pure water is thus like jade. It comes in various forms, not all of which are composed of H_2O molecules. Kripke's and Putnam's thesis that water = H_2O can be rejected because, like many philosophical conceits, it is based on too limited a gamut of samples. Moreover, since pure water is not identical with the total collection of H_2O molecules, it does not follow, even on their own semantic account, that "water" means H_2O. Their account, which I do not accept, would entail that "water" means the *aggregate* of H_2O, D_2O, and T_2O, through the whole range of molecular combinations of hydrogen and oxygen. But independently of the theory of direct reference, we shall find other reasons why "water" does not mean H_2O.

The isotope argument also gives scientific backing to my functional argument. I asseverated earlier that the function an object serves may be more important than its microcomposition in determining what it is called, and I cited tables as an example. It is their function and not the material from which they are made that determines whether they are called "tables." Let me apply the point to water. As I have just indicated, pure water is a melange of diverse molecules in a liquid state. The average person probably knows nothing about deuterium and tritium and their interactions with oxygen. For them, these microscopic features are irrelevant with respect to what they call that oh so familiar fluid. They call it "water" in part because of its phenomenal properties and in part because of its functions in allaying thirst, causing plants to grow, allowing persons to swim in it, and so forth. A well-known chemistry textbook begins a discussion of water by stressing its familiar properties and uses. As the context indicates, its authors assume that this is what ordinary persons mean by "water." As they explain,

Water plays a vital role in the various physical and chemical processes upon which life, as we know it, depends. It is the major constituent of both plants and animals and is found in tremendous quantities in rivers, lakes, oceans, and the huge polar icecaps. The absorptive processes by which nutrient materials are taken up by plants, the metabolic processes in plants and animals, and the elimination of waste products by animal organisms take place largely in aqueous solution or suspension. Evaporation of water from animal bodies keeps them cool, and the high specific heat of water causes large bodies of water to exert a strong moderating effect on the climate of neighboring land masses. In addition, water is an important industrial raw material.[15]

These remarks contain no references to H_2O or D_2O. Instead, they presuppose that function is essential in specifying the meaning of "water."

We can now move on to the category-mistake argument. Let me begin with the question, Why does ice float on water? I mentioned in the previous chapter that chemists, in speaking about *states* of water, use "water" in a generic sense. In such a case they allude to ice as "frozen water," to ordinary water as "liquid water," and steam as "water vapor." There are some objections to this generic use. I pointed out, for example, that "liquid water" sounds pleonastic to the ordinary ear. Accordingly, what chemists should be speaking of is not water but H_2O. Thus it would be more accurate to speak of ice as frozen H_2O or of water as liquid H_2O or of steam as vaporous H_2O. But if one employs this generic sense of "water," according to which steam, ice, and liquid water are all states or phases of water, then water in this generic sense is an unusual feature of nature.

The solid states of most substances are more dense than their liquid or gaseous phases, but this is not true of generic water. It has a solid state, ice, that is less dense than its liquid state. Moreover, in its liquid state it has the unexpected property of reaching its maximum density at about 4 degrees Celsius, and becomes less dense as it cools towards o degrees Celsius. When the liquid reaches o degrees Celsius. it turns into ice, which is still less dense. Another oddity of the liquid state is that it doesn't make any difference what its temperature is; it will *always* be more dense than ice.

The last point was graphically illustrated to me recently. I had lunch with Professor Eero Byckling, a well-known Finnish scientist, and in discussing the nature of water, he took the occasion to run a brief experiment at the table. Sitting before him was a cup of hot water into which he had planned to insert a tea bag. Instead, he dropped a cube of ice into the hot water and asked me to look at what I saw. What I saw was a piece of ice floating on water. As he then explained, ice is always less dense than water and will always float on water, no matter what the temperature of the water. Frozen water and liquid water thus differ in their physical properties, the former being less dense than the latter. It follows from Leibniz's Law that they cannot be identical.

The chemical explanation of why ice floats on water (i.e., why ice is less dense than water) is complicated. Here is a simplified account. Crystal studies show that in ice the oxygen atoms of the water molecules form a lattice in which each oxygen atom is connected to four other oxygen atoms by hydrogen bonds in a regular tetrahedral arrangement. This structure consists of columns of hexagonal, nonplanar rings. This is an open type of structure that accounts for the relatively low density of ice. When ice melts, some of these hydrogen bonds are broken, and the structure collapses to a more closely packed arrangement. Thus water occupies a smaller volume than the ice from which it is formed. In effect, then, there is more space between the molecules in a rigid lattice structure than in an arrangement where the molecules are tumbling, and this is why ice is less dense than water.

Furthermore, as the temperature of water rises, there is a further breaking of hydrogen bonds, and the volume continues to decrease until, at 3.98 degrees Celsius, the normal tendency toward expansion, which is due to the increased thermal vibration of the molecules, finally outweighs the contractive effect of the breaking of hydrogen bonds, and the liquid begins to expand. The existence of hydrogen bonds between water molecules is mainly responsible for the abnormally high melting point, boiling point, heat of fusion, heat of vaporization, and specific heat of water. The melting of ice necessarily involves the breaking of some hydrogen bonds. Since this requires the expenditure of energy, ice melts only at a much higher temperature and with the absorption of a considerably greater amount of heat than would otherwise be expected. Furthermore, when water is changed from liquid to vapor, all the remaining hydrogen bonds are broken.

I should add that under extremely high pressures the ordinary ice structure collapses to give other forms of ice (ice II, ice III, ice IV, etc.) and that all of these have a high density than ordinary ice (ice I). All of these forms of ice are less dense than water, and therefore all will float on water.[16]

This discussion brings us to the category-mistake argument. To simplify the discussion, I shall speak only about collections of H_2O molecules. The most important point to be made in this connection is that not all collections of such molecules are water. It depends on the nature of the collection, and this to a considerable degree is determined by such factors as air temperature and atmospheric pressure. Some collections are rigid, hard, and cold to the touch (ice I through ice VII). Some are liquid, tepid, and not solid. Ordinary persons call the latter aggregations "water" and the former "ice." It is a category mistake to infer from the fact that a particular collection of H_2O molecules is water that every such collection is water. This seems to be a mistake that Putnam and Kripke have made throughout their discussion of water.

It leads to another. "Water" does not mean H_2O, as they assert. For if it did and because water and ice are both composed of H_2O, it would then follow that the meaning of "water" would be ice. But this is clearly false. Since ice and water have different properties, the former being rigid and the latter nonrigid, the two are not identical. Therefore, if "water" meant ice, "water" could not mean water. Once again, we see that Kripke and Putnam are misled by their identity thesis into an incorrect linguistic theory.

It is important to stress that their doctrine, which appeals to science for its credentials, describes a science that almost no chemist or physicist would recognize. Virtually no scientist would agree that water is strictly identical with H_2O. Science begins with the observable world and does not disparage its gross properties, such as the liquidity of water and the rigidity of ice. Rather, in explaining what ice and water are, science in fact refers to the macroscopic properties of these items, to their chemical and physical constituents, *and* to the conditions that obtain in nature in terms of temperature, pressure, etc. The scientific picture is richer and more complex than Kripke and Putnam recognize.

We can now turn to isomers. As I have been asserting in this essay and as their own remarks abundantly confirm,

Putnam and Kripke aver that it is the microcomponents that determine the nature of any natural kind, as well as the meaning of the term denoting that kind. Let us move away from the case of water, since it raises special problems about the relationship between H_2O and the various forms it assumes under different conditions of temperature and pressure. But isomers involve a different set of relationships. Isomers are not phases or states of substances but independent substances. As such they provide a decisive counterinstance to the thesis that we can identify a natural kind, or indeed any substance, with its microcomposition.

Isomerism was first discovered at the beginning of the nineteenth century. The dominating chemical theory of the time held that all differences in the qualities of substances were due directly to differences in their chemical composition. But in 1824–1825, two chemists (Justus von Liebig and Fredrich Wöhler), analyzing two different substances (fulminic acid and cyanic acid, respectively), discovered that the composition of both compounds proved to be absolutely the same. Jöns Jacob Berzelius (1779–1848) shortly afterward introduced the term *isomerism* (from the Greek, meaning composed of equal parts) to denote the existence of substances having different qualities, both in chemical and physical behavior, and yet being identical in chemical composition. These phenomena were consistent with the atomic theory of matter, since a compound containing the same number of atoms of carbon, nitrogen, oxygen, and hydrogen as another might differ in internal structure by the different arrangements of those atoms and the molecules they form.

Water, ice, and steam are, of course, not isomers, but the mistake about identifying them with H_2O, and thus by the transitivity of identicals with one another, is analogous to the mistake one would make if one were to identify isomers with one another. Isomers are substances having exactly the same chemical components but with radically different arrangements of those ingredients. Thus ethyl alcohol, whose chemical formula is C_2H_5OH, and methyl ether, whose chemical formula is CH_3OCH_3, are each composed of two carbon atoms, six hydrogen atoms, and one oxygen atom. But the atoms bind to each other in different ways.

The substances in question are pure substances, i.e., they are not interconvertible, and are wholly different from one another, having different physical properties, such as their melting and boiling points, potability for humans, and so forth. There is no way of predicting these differences merely from knowing their chemical composition. Since they are pure substances, we can use Kripke's and Putnam's vocabulary and call them natural kinds. The example shows that Putnam and Kripke are wrong in holding that natural kinds are identical with their chemical components, since these are the same in all cases of isomers. The error of making such an identification was exposed nearly two centuries ago by the scientists I have mentioned above and by now, of course, is accepted scientific doctrine.

SIX

Let us return briefly to the theory of reference and to the meaning of "water." As I indicated in "Reflections on Water," Putnam and Kripke claim, in the simplest form of their theory, that "water" is a rigid designator, namely a term whose only "meaning" is its reference, and that in the case of "water" its reference is H_2O. I have produced a series of counterarguments to this theory both in "Reflections" and in this chapter. I would like to conclude my discussion of their scientific rationalism by contrasting what they say with what traditional empiricism would or might say about "water."

It is important to distinguish two differing sets of claims that Putnam and Kripke advance about the meaning of "water." The first is that meaning is not conceptual. As Putnam puts it, "Cut the pie any way you like, 'meanings' just ain't in the *head*!"[17] The second, is that the meaning of natural-kind words is determined by their reference.

Setting aside certain anachronisms, one might argue that such classical empiricists as Locke and Hume also espoused a referential theory of meaning. They, of course, invoked an "idea" terminology in their versions of empiricism. Today we speak about words and linguistic units in a way in which they did not. The two vocabularies are virtually equipollent. Their thesis was that all complex ideas could be reduced to simple ideas, and these in turn could be correlated with simple impressions that derive from sense experience. Thus the idea of a nonexistent entity, a dragon, could be shown to derive from experience, since its components—the head of a horse, body of a snake, etc.—were ideas that could be correlated with sense impressions. The mind had the power to combine such simple ideas into more complex ones, such as that of a dragon or unicorn.

Because these early empiricists did not know that the composition of water is H_2O (let alone D_2O, T_2O, etc.) they would have treated the idea of water in the same way. It is based on a set of observable properties.

Does it follow from such a "referential" view that meaning is not conceptual? I do not think it does. Clearly, the mind has the power to form complex ideas, so mental activity is relevant to what such ideas mean. But there is a more substantial point to be made here. Let us return to a modification of the Twin Earth scenario to see what it is.

Suppose that for centuries there has been air commerce between Twin Earth and Earth and that persons and vehicles engaged in these interactions have used the differing fluids they call "water" interchangeably, and also suppose that for eons now it has been known that the composition of these fluids differs, Earth water being H_2O and Twin Earth water being XYZ. Let us also suppose that water composed of H_2O is a unique substance that exists only on Earth. But tragically, this begins to disappear (perhaps as the earth warms up) and eventually vanishes completely.

Now if the meaning of "water" were H_2O and there were no H_2O anywhere in the universe, "water" would be meaningless on Kripke's and Putnam's view. Because "water" is a rigid designator, it will be meaningless if it lacks a referent. Would it then be meaningless on any referential theory? The answer is "No." A Twin Earth scientist writing about Earth could assert significantly and truly "Water no longer exists on Earth." That this sentence (a negative existential) is meaningful and indeed true shows that the meaning of "water" is not *wholly* determined by its referent, *if that referent is supposed to be* H_2O.

Two options remain for an empiricist committed to a referential view. The first is to maintain that the meaning of "water" is wholly determined by its referent but that its referent is not H_2O but rather an open set of the observable properties of water. As we have seen, this would be the option that a traditional empiricist would espouse. But as the preceding argument shows, one cannot simply identify the meaning of "water" with any set of existing properties, since true negative existentials are always possible with respect to any such set.

But there is a second possibility for the traditionalist, one that is not open to Putnam and Kripke. This would begin with the denial that "water" is a rigid designator.

Instead, it could be treated as a definite description à la Russell. On that analysis, even if water should vanish from the Earth and indeed from the universe, one could still meaningfully use the term "water" because one could construct a comparable concept based on the properties of existing substances that are liquid, transparent, potable, and so forth. One would thus treat water in the way that we now treat such natural-kind words as "dinosaur" or "dodo" or the way the classical empiricists treated "dragon." "Water" would thus designate a complex of observable characteristics, and thus would have a referential basis in experience. The sentence "Water no longer exists on Earth" would be analyzed as "There is no fluid on earth that exhibits the conjunction of such and such properties." Such an analysis would allow for meaningful and true negative existentials.

I suggest this interpretation of traditional empiricism because it approximates pretty well to how science uses language when it investigates nature. On this construal, the traditional-empiricist reconstruction of scientific inquiry depended on a referential theory of meaning, but it also insisted that the reference—a set of phenomenal properties—was something observable, either by the use of the naked eye or by instruments. Such a theory could reject the thesis that "water" is a rigid designator and in this way accommodate negative existentials. And for these various reasons it would provide a better account of scientific inquiry than that advanced by Putnam and Kripke.

SEVEN

I conclude that with its emphasis upon the macroscopic world the old empiricism of Locke and Hume did a better job of interpreting scientific practice than the new empiricism of Putnam and Kripke. Accordingly, if one is committed to empiricism as a philosophy, the argument of this essay would supply reasons for not abandoning that older tradition.

But how about empiricism per se? As I have indicated, both forms of empiricism adhere to the principle that science is the only key that will open the doors to reality. In a series of papers I have rejected that principle, and thus empiricism in any of its forms.[18] It would be impossible to rehearse the arguments of those papers here, but in effect they defend the autonomy of philosophy against the kind of scientism espoused by empiricists, new or old.

I thus agree with Wittgenstein, who, in *On Certainty,* says that there are aspects of reality not open to scientific investigation. These aspects, which, he avers, "stand fast for all of us," are presuppositions for science. They constitute the conditions that make science possible, rather than being part of its investigative subject matter. If science did not presuppose that the earth existed and that it is very old, its present research activities, as we now know them, would be incomprehensible. It is philosophy that has traditionally attempted to explore the nature of these presuppositions.[19] This is not philosophy's sole function, to be sure, but it seems to me beyond dispute that it is one of its central functions.

Examples

ONE

In *Philosophical Investigations,* Wittgenstein writes this:

It was true to say that our considerations could not be scientific ones. . . . And we may not advance any kind of theory. There must not be anything hypothetical in our considerations. We must do away with all *explanation,* and description alone must take its place. (Entry 109).

In using the word "we" Wittgenstein is, of course, speaking of philosophers, and his suggestion is that in doing philosophy, philosophers should replace explanation with description. What does he mean by "explanation" and "description" in this passage? Most exegetes have interpreted him as saying that to give an explanation is to advance a theory and that advancing a theory is tantamount to searching for the essence of things. On this account, descriptions are alternatives to theories. This elucidation is one that I too accept, as I indicated earlier in this work. In a recent article David Pears also construes Wittgenstein's descriptivism in this way, i.e., as a rejection of theorizing. As he says,

There are several kinds of philosophical naturalism and one of their leading ideas is that the right method in philosophy is not to theorize about things but to describe them as we find them in daily life. Wittgenstein's later philosophy is evidently a naturalism inspired by this idea.[1]

Whether Wittgenstein's descriptivism should be described as a form of naturalism and whether it should be assimilated to Hume's naturalism, as Pears intimates, or to F. J. E. Woodbridge's, as Howard Wettstein suggests,[2] are doubtful conjectures in my opinion. However, I shall not debate the issue here. There is a further reading of the passage that many commentators would accept, namely that Wittgenstein thinks of description as the proffering of examples (or cases, as he sometimes says, including intermediate cases). On this construal, an example-oriented approach to philosophical questions is also an alternative to theory building or the quest for essences. This is also a compelling reading of Wittgenstein, and it has obviously influenced my approach in this book.

There is, however, one thing about examples that Wittgenstein does not explicitly mention but that his meta-comments in the *Investigations* clearly presuppose: that examples have to be accurate. It would be disastrous to have examples misfire, to be found to be irrelevant, or not to be actual examples of whatever is being described. Such infelicities can and do occur in the philosophical literature. Hume, for all his ingenuity, often goes wrong in this respect. In formulating the argument from design, for instance, he offers as examples of machines such things as houses, ships, cities, and furniture.[3] In this list the only defensible example of a machine is a ship. Machines are human artifacts that do work and expend energy in performing certain functions: a sewing machine would be a prime example. Not every artifact that serves a function is a machine: tools (hammers, chisels, pliers) are not, nor are instruments (a scalpel, a thermometer). Some things with functional uses are neither machines nor tools nor instruments, such as a piece of furniture, a clothespin, or a house. None of these does work in the way in which machines do, and none expends energy in carrying out its function.

In the preceding paragraph I have given some examples of examples and some examples of things that fail to be examples in particular contextual situations. If one wishes to do philosophy by example, as I urge, it is important to get a solid purchase on what examples are, as well as how they function in human discourse. In this chapter I will address these topics. My approach is in the spirit of Wittgenstein: it begins with a description of the linguistic rules that govern the uses of examples. In effect, I shall be describing the rules for the correct use of "example" and its synonyms, such as "case" and "instance." But for us to understand how such principles work, I first need to describe a more general set of rules: those that govern whole groups of synonyms. I will begin with this latter task and will consider two assemblages of such synonyms. The chief or head word of the first is "copy" and that of the second is "example." I select these groups for two reasons: first and obviously, because of the emphasis I have put on examples in this study, and second and less obviously, because the results obtained will allow a new assessment of one of the most celebrated of all philosophical conceits, Plato's theory of forms.

TWO

I turn, then, to the "copy" and "example" groups. As groups, they differ in their logical properties. The words within each group are lexical synonyms. My procedure in characterizing the rules that govern such collections is purely descriptive. When I speak of "logic" or "logical conditions" or "rules," I am referring to existing rather than normative features of English. The procedure starts from the observation that natural languages contain complex networks of assemblages of synonyms. These range from somewhat diffuse collections that I shall call "clusters" to groups with tighter and more readily specifiable structures, and these I label "chains" and "rings." There are rules that govern word membership in particular groups and serve to distinguish them from other groups. Each word also satisfies specific rules that determine its particular meaning or use in English. I shall show that the relationships between what is general and what is particular in these cases bring us very close to the sort of relationships often described as obtaining between universals and particulars.

In Plato's middle dialogues there are two different accounts of this relationship. Plato sometimes uses the term "participation" (*methexis*) in referring to it, at other times the word "imitation" (*mimesis*). No doubt there are exegetical complications in explicating these terms, but it is nevertheless clear enough that Plato intends the relationships to hold between the forms and things like examples on the one hand and between forms and things like copies on the other. The two accounts differ, as Aristotle was well aware.[4] But they have something in common, which perhaps explains why Plato shifted between them—something that might be expressed in two sentences:

(1) If x is an example (copy, instance, etc.) of y, then x is not y.

(2) x is a particular (or individual thing), and y is of a higher order than x.

These formulas capture the two versions of the theory of forms. The first states that no example, copy, or instance of something is the same as that of which it is an example or copy or instance, and the second states that x is a particular or individual, whereas *y* is something other than a particular or individual. According to these formulas, universals (forms, ideas) cannot be identical with particulars, since they will always be of a higher order or type.

Later on I shall show that these formulas do not adequately explicate the relationships holding between examples and what they are examples of, between instances and what they are instances of, between copies and what they are copies of, and so forth. In particular, the relationships in these cases are more complex than Plato and other classical theorists depict them as being. The results of my analysis will amount to a new way of viewing the problem of universals.

THREE

As I have mentioned the main notions in my descriptive account are "cluster," "chain," and "ring," and to these I shall add "interdefinable" and "heartland." Let me briefly and very roughly indicate what I mean by each of these terms. I will then elaborate on and refine the account as the chapter develops.

A *cluster* is a set of words that fall into a natural grouping within a natural language. By a "natural grouping" I mean the outcome of a process that, put crudely, consists in developing a list of synonyms for a given word in that language. It starts with a given word, adds the synonyms of that word to the list, the synonyms of those words to the list, and so on. When no further synonyms can be found, the list is presumed to be complete. This process is most conveniently carried out by using a first-class dictionary, and therefore it would be somewhat more precise to say that a cluster is a set of words falling into a natural grouping as determined by a particular kind of lexical process. Though intuitively it might be thought that synonymity is transitive, i.e., that any set of lexical synonyms will have the same meaning, this is not true in general. Within a large group of words, such as one typically finds in a cluster, the beginning and end words may deviate considerably in meaning. "Copy," to illustrate the point, is the initial word of a cluster. One of its lexical synonyms is "counterfeit," whose meaning is not identical with "copy" but overlaps it. Through a series of lexical synonyms of "counterfeit," we eventually arrive at "bust." There is thus a strong deviation in meaning between the initial and terminal elements of the cluster.

Within clusters it is possible to find a sequence of words whose initial word and final word, and of course all intermediate words, have roughly the same meaning. Thus within the total set of words forming a cluster, narrower groups can usually be formed, depending on the size of the cluster, united by tighter meaning relationships. These I call *chains*.

A *ring* is a set of words whose members are *interdefinable*. "Interdefinable" is a term that refers to a particular kind of lexical process. The lexical process of moving from synonym to synonym will eventually close, i.e., will lead back to the original word. Generally speaking, rings will be subsets of clusters and chains. But, of course, it is possible for a given set of words to be a cluster, chain, and ring all at the same time. This is a rare phenomenon, but it can occur when the lexical process that generates a word cluster generates a small number of words, these are then found to be united by a meaning bond, and it turns out that the lexical process exhibits closure. The internal relationships within clusters, chains, and rings usually differ, as I have indicated, but each of these word/word relationships can be thought of as types of family resemblances. So synonym clusters can also be roughly characterized as family resemblances, a notion that Wittgenstein develops in the *Investigations*.

By "heartland" I mean that rule (or normally set of rules) that every word must satisfy to be a member of a particular group. It may not be possible to find a heartland for every cluster that the lexical process generates, but as we shall see, some clusters do have heartlands. As I have been urging throughout this study, one must look at cases individually. Chains will always have heartlands, since these will be the set of rules that determine word membership in the chain. One may also find special conditions that apply to rings, so that there are "ring heartlands" that differ from "chain heartlands" even when the rings are subsets of chains. Heartlands are thus the linguistic analogues to what Plato might have called "essences." They are the set or sets of rules for determining membership in a group, and thus for determining the nature of the group in question.

In summary, then, what I am asserting in the account above is that certain kinds of lexical processes will generate sets of words, some of which are united by specific rules or sets of rules. A description of these may thus be called the "logic" of the particular group.

All of the preceding ideas are elaborations on a basic observation, which is that words do not occur randomly in natural languages but tend to collect into groups united by complex sorts of synonymity relationships. This observation can be confirmed by following the lexical processes I shall describe below and then examining the semantic properties of the resulting groups of words. But it also has an intuitive basis, which I shall now proceed to illustrate.

Suppose that one gives a native speaker of English the task of continuing to assign words to collections already containing some words. The condition that one begin with already formed collections is not necessary, as I shall show later, but it makes it easier to explain the point at this stage. Here are two such collections and a pool of words from which the native speaker is to select:

Collection A   *Collection B*

asserption   example

declaration   illustration

affirmation   specimen

Pool

proposition

trunk

sample

case

box

statement

instance

    It is predictable that any native speaker would put "proposition" and "statement" in collection A, and "sample" and "instance" in collection B. That person would probably not know what to do with "trunk" and "box," and might hesitate over "case," especially if one thinks of it as denoting a receptacle and thus as belonging in the same group as "trunk" and "box." But after some reflection, the informant would probably see that it too should go into collection B.

    Why are these responses predictable? A plausible answer is that the native speaker intuits some meaning relationship that unites "assertion," "declaration," and "affirmation" and distinguishes them as an assemblage from "example," "illustration," and "specimen" and, moreover, from "trunk" and "box." My task here is to make this kind of intuition more precise and to show in detail what sorts of meaning relationships these are.

The observation, then, is that there are many such collections of words—words united by some kind of meaning relationship. I now produce some other examples of such mélanges in order to support this claim:

Collection C	Collection D	Collection E
copy	sameness	multitude
duplicate	identity	number
replica	equality	host
facsimile	coincidence	crowd
effigy	identification	throng

Any native speaker can see immediately that these groups involve different meaning relationships, and therefore that in sorting words it would be a mistake to assign, say, "crowd" to collection C or "duplicate" to collection E. These are, of course, collections separated by gross differences in meaning. It does not follow, therefore, that even a native speaker could always clearly see to which collection a word belongs, or even whether it belongs to more than one collection. Would one put "model" into collection B or collection C or both? So it is important to reinforce one's intuitions by a process that is reasonably mechanical for forming such groups of words, and this is where the dictionary becomes helpful.

Since in some vague sense all the words in each of the above groups are synonyms, the problem in effect is to find the total number of synonyms each group (or any group) will contain. Palpably, all the examples of collections I have produced are incomplete. Many words not cited or mentioned in my "pool" could be quickly added to each of the above collections by a native speaker. But how would one know that one had not missed any?

Obviously, the answer is that if one wishes to know how many words each collection would ultimately have, the pool of words one would have to begin with would have to include all and only those words that belong to the English language. Unless the pool is of this order of magnitude, one cannot be sure that one has not overlooked some word in making assignments to the various collections. A first rate, up-to-date dictionary may be thought of as such a pool, or reservoir, of words. I admit that dictionaries differ in quality, that they have special biases, and that no dictionary contains all the words that belong to, or have belonged to, English, but we have no more convenient source from which to select words for forming such collections.

Furthermore, a dictionary is more than just a collection of words. It is a thesaurus of their uses and, as we saw in "Reflections on Water," a repository of all sorts of supplementary information. It is thus possible to use a dictionary as if it were a native informant, only one with a much better memory bank than most of us have and with a much keener ear for the distinctions that the language embodies. Unlike most native speakers, it thus "knows" all or nearly all the words in the language and all of their main uses, and it sorts them so as to make them virtually instantly available. It is thus a kind of "ideal" native speaker, that is, a person whose word capacity is indefinitely large and whose recall ability is almost instantaneous. Such an ideal speaker would be optimal for playing our game—for assigning words to groupings united by some kind of meaning relationship. Though in principle the informant might have some difficulty in apportioning words to categories (and it is not clear that every word belongs to some such category), he or she would be able to do so for most words. In practice, the native informant would thus come close to completing all the possible group collections the language contains.

We may think of one who uses the dictionary in this way as approximating an ideal native speaker. Such a person will be drawing upon the dictionary's expansive "knowledge" of the language in a way in which one cannot possibly draw upon one's own more limited resources, even as a native speaker. For no native speaker is familiar with all the words and their uses in the language. The native speaker's powers of recall are limited, as are his or her powers to discriminate quickly between closely resembling uses of words. To say these things is, of course, not to imply that a native speaker can only reproduce fragments of good dictionaries. Linguists often point to the ability of native speakers to produce new and grammatically correct sentences.

In the light of these general comments I shall apply all this machinery to a given group of words. Using the dictionary, I will now form a cluster.

FOUR

We can pick any entry, for example, "copy." To make sure that the resulting collection is united by some kind of however vague meaning relationship, I will invoke specific rules in forming a cluster. To begin with, all the words in a cluster must be of the same grammatical category. Suppose that we regard "copy" as a noun. We cannot include, in the list of words we then generate, the various synonyms of this word when it is used as a verb, for instance. For the verbal form of "copy" we find as synonyms such words as (to) "mimic," "ape," "mock," "burlesque," and "imitate." The noun expansion of "copy" clearly would not include "ape" (i.e., an ape) among its synonyms.

A first rule in forming a cluster, then, is that the same grammatical category be preserved in spinning out the synonyms of the word. In addition, for reasons I shall not bother to expatiate on here, the rules mandate that one ignore obsolete and archaic words when they are so marked, and the various types of specialized uses (when so marked or indicated), such as those occurring in music, law, business, etc. These stipulations rule out "copiousness" as an archaic form of "copy," and "copy" in the sense in which it is used in newspaper offices, i.e., as written material to be set up for printing.

So let us begin with "copy" as a noun. The fact that we can start from scratch shows that the ability to form clusters does not depend on starting with prearranged groupings of words. We first check the entry expansion of "copy." By "entry expansion" I mean a single definition. Generally speaking, each entry will have a number of entry expansions. An entry expansion is thus the sort of thing that is usually called a "dictionary definition."

In *Webster's Third New International Dictionary* we find six entry expansions for "copy" as a noun. Because five of these are archaic, obsolete, specialized, or technical uses, we can eliminate them in constructing our cluster. Entry expansion 2 reads, "An imitation, transcript, or reproduction of an original work (as of a letter, an engraving, a painting, a statue, a piece of furniture, a dress)." At this point, some (but a minimal amount) of intuition is needed. We must select those words in the entry expansion of "copy" that more or less match its sense. These are, in the case above, "imitation," "transcript," and "reproduction." We add these to the list that originally included only "copy," arriving at a total of four words.

We now check the entry expansions of the three new words added to the list. For "imitation," as a noun, only one of its entry expansions is relevant. It reads, "Something that is made or produced as a copy: an artificial likeness: COUNTERFEIT." "Likeness" and "counterfeit" match the sense of "copy," so we add them to the list, which now consists of six words. A check of the entry expansion of "transcript" includes "copy" and "reproduction," which are already on the list, and a new word "rendering." We now go to the entry expansions of "reproduction" and find "copy," "likeness," "counterpart," "reconstruction," and "replica." The new words are "counterpart," "reconstruction," and "replica." The list has now expanded to nine words. By checking the entry expansions of "likeness," "counterfeit," "counterpart," "reconstruction," and "replica," more words are added. The list generated by following this technique to a point where no new words appear is the following:

Collection C, expanded

copy	likeness
duplicate	picture
facsimile	bust
replica	portrait
transcript	effigy
reconstruction	figure
model	statue
counterpart	icon
rendering	image
reproduction	similitude
representation	painting
counterfeit	drawing
imitation	semblance

I shall henceforth refer to this group of words as the "copy cluster," since I generated it by the lexical process described above, beginning with the word "copy."

Having generated this cluster, I am now in a position to describe its rules and ascertain whether it contains chains and rings. It has four rules, and it contains both chains and rings. I cannot show in detail, for reasons of space, how the rules apply to each of the 26 words in the cluster, but they do. In what follows, I shall select words more or less at random from the list as illustrations.

Rule 1   If *A* is a copy of *B*, then *A* is not *B*.

The second "is" in the formula needs clarification, but even at a preanalytical level it is clear that it has something to do with sameness. Since the principle denies that *x* is *y*, it affirms that in some important respect, copies and what they copy are not the same. This seems true even though copies may resemble or even be indistinguishable from what they copy. Plato saw the point clearly in holding that individual men, tables, and beds were never identical with the forms they copied, but he thought that the principle implied that copies were always of a different order from what are copied. Whether this inference is justified is a matter that I shall consider below. But even now one can say that the principle would hold in the following sense: if *y* is an original object and *x* is a copy or duplicate or replica of it, then *x* will never be the same object as *y*. A bust of Socrates will not be the same object as Socrates; a replica of the Taj Mahal will never be the same object as the Taj Mahal.

Not only will *x* not be the same object as *y*, but the converse also holds. The relationship, "being a copy of" is asymmetrical. It is also intransitive, since it is not always the case that if *x* is a copy of *y*, and *y* is a copy of *z*, that *x* is a copy of *z*. And it is irreflexive, since *x* cannot be a copy of itself. All the words belonging to the copy cluster denote relationships having these properties and lacking those of being symmetrical, transitive, and reflexive. The substantive philosophical point is that all the words, when given the above interpretation, do satisfy the first principle of Platonism, namely that if x is a copy, replica, duplicate, etc., of y, then x is not y.

Rule 2 If A is a copy, etc., of B, A resembles B.

Once again, it is difficult to state with precision what "resembles" means in this context, but I shall not worry the point at this time. It should merely be noted that there are degrees of resemblance. At one end, the resemblance may be that A and B look exactly alike. A good photocopy of a document may be visually indistinguishable from the original, and a duplicate key may look exactly like the original key. At the other end of the spectrum, there are cases in which A just barely resembles B. In fact, the words in our list can pretty well be ordered in this respect. If A is a facsimile of B, it will stand higher in the list than if A is a semblance of B. If A is an effigy of B, the resemblance may be remote.

Yet even where an effigy is the crudest sort of figure, it will have to resemble the hated person, or the spell won't work. The dictionary confirms this judgment in two ways: it traces the etymology of "effigy" back to Latin, where "effigies" meant a copy of an object, and it explains in such locutions as "to burn or hang in effigy" that it is "an image" of the person that is so treated. But as it goes on to say, the effigy does not have to be realistic: it may be either a "full or partial representation, esp. of a person." It is thus part of the logic of "copy"-cluster talk that A may be a poor, distorted, inept, amateurish copy or effigy or likeness of B while still remaining a copy or effigy or likeness of B.

EXAMPLES

The principle also captures something of what Plato meant in discussing the forms. It is plain that he thought that individual men, particular tables, this or that bed resemble their corresponding archetypes, and no doubt this is why he uses the term "mimesis" to describe the relationship.

Rule 3   If *A* is a copy, etc., of *B*, *A* is typically the product of human contrivance.

The rule distinguishes things that nature creates, such as natural kinds, from things that human beings create. The word "typically" occurs in the rule, since we occasionally use some of these words to speak about natural objects. Thus one may find a rock formation in the desert that is a "duplicate" of a famous statue. Or again, one may find two natural objects, say two rocks, and describe them as "duplicates" of one another. *The Oxford English Dictionary* explains that this use is derivative and entered the language some two centuries after what I am describing as the standard use of these words. The point is particularly important in attempting to understand Plato's theory of ideas, since he thinks not only of artifacts, like tables and beds, as "copies" or "imitations" or "replicas" of the forms, but also of natural objects, such as men, trees, and clumps of mud in the same way. But they cannot be: the logic of the language rules out this possibility unless these words are being used in derivative or extended senses.

Rule 4   All the words in the cluster satisfy the matrix "*x* is a ____ of *y*."

This formula will always produce well-formed sentences if we replace the variables by certain English words and fill the blank with one of the terms belonging to the cluster ("This is a reproduction of El Greco's *Toledo*"). The formula emphasizes that replicas are always replicas of something, copies are always copies of something, busts are always busts of something, and so forth. If Plato thought of particulars as always being copies or replicas, then the logic of the language would have made it easy for him to draw the inference that what they are copies or replicas of are not particulars. I am not suggesting that it was only for this reason that he was led to hold that prototypes are of a different logical order from their copies or imitations, but it is possible that this factor played a role in his thinking.

The conjunction of these four rules I call "the 'copy'-cluster heartland." It constitutes the common thread of meaning that unites these words, and thus forms a particular assemblage.

SIX

Let me now turn to a discussion of the chains and rings we find in the cluster. If we look again at the words in collection C, (the "copy" cluster), it is obvious that they can be divided into smaller groups, united by autonomous meaning relationships. For instance, "statue," "bust," "portrait," "effigy," "figure," and "picture" seem closer in meaning to one another than they do to "transcript," "facsimile," and "duplicate." We can therefore select from the "copy" cluster a subgroup of words connected by relationships over and above the four rules that all the words in the cluster satisfy. Such a subgroup is what I mean by a "chain." Notice that chains are not formed by lexical processes as clusters (and, as we shall see, rings) are. Here a considerable degree of intuition and sensitivity to the language is necessary. It is, of course, possible that the "copy" cluster contains many chains, but I want to concentrate on one, which I shall call "the 'replica' chain." It contains the following words:

The "replica" chain

replica

reproduction

reconstruction

transcript

facsimile

duplicate

model

copy

imitation

counterfeit

Though chains are not entirely formed by lexical processes, they play a role in helping us form a chain. As I have mentioned, the words in the "replica" chain form a nearly autonomous group. They appear in the entry expansions of one another, and are virtually absent from the entry expansions of the remaining words in the "copy" cluster (e.g., "semblance," "similitude," etc.). This tends to confirm our intuition that words like "replica," "transcript," "duplicate" have a different logic (are governed by different rules) than "figure," "bust," "portrait," etc.

However, the matter is somewhat more complicated than this simple description indicates. There are four words that connect the members of the "replica" chain with the remaining words in the "copy" cluster. Two of these are "imitation" and "counterfeit." As the dictionary tells us, though "imitation" refers back to "likeness" and has "counterfeit" in its entry expansion, "counterfeit" does not connect up with the remaining words in the "copy" cluster. Its entry expansion includes "replica." On the other hand, none of the words in the "replica" chain refer back to "counterfeit" or "imitation," with the exception of "copy," which has "imitation" in its entry expansion. There is thus some question about whether these words belong to the chain, and this is a matter we shall have to decide by other than lexical criteria (see below).

The other two words that have relations with the remaining words in the "copy" cluster are "reproduction" and "copy" itself. Indeed, they have extensive connections with the words in the "replica" chain and with the words in the "copy" cluster. For this reason, one might call them "bridge words." There is some reason to put them with the "replica"-chain words because, as we shall later see, they satisfy the same logical principles as the other words in the chain. In terms of their logical properties, therefore, they belong in the "replica" chain, though in terms of their lexical functions, they play a special, intermediate role, connecting the words in the "replica" chain with the remaining words in the "copy" cluster. In a sense hard to define, they may well be more "basic" than the other words in the cluster. I call it "'copy' cluster" in part for this reason. I should also mention that two of the remaining words in the "copy" cluster also seem to have similar bridging functions, namely "counterpart" and "representation." They are clearly governed by principles different from those that govern the words in the "replica" chain, so I do not include them there.

Let us now turn to the rules that govern word membership in the "replica" chain. There are three such rules.

"Replica" rule 1 If x is a replica, duplicate, copy, etc., of y, then there must be or have been an "original" that x replicates, duplicates, or copies.

This precept is somewhat complicated. In what might be called prototypical cases, replicas, copies, duplicates, etc., are made from an original object, such as an original manuscript, key, tape, and so forth. It is, of course, possible that at some later time the original object has ceased to exist. Thus it is possible to replicate a replica, to copy a copy, to make a transcript from a transcript, and so on. In such cases the object used is an "original" to the copy or replica made from it. Let us call the original item the "absolute original" and the copy a "relative original." In general, it is thus not true that if x is a replica or copy of y, y is an absolute original. What is true is that if x is a replica or copy of y, then y is either an absolute or relative original. The preceding principle must be understood in this sense.

This condition eliminates some of the words in the "copy" cluster from potential membership in the "replica" chain. It is possible to make paintings of "human beings" like Sherlock Holmes who never existed and who are therefore not copied by the artist. It is possible to make busts, representations, drawings, and statues of things where there is not now and never has been an original (e.g., a statue of Medusa). The point, as I say, is complicated, since one might make a drawing of, say, Cyclops from a verbal description in a text. Shall we say that such a description functions as an absolute original? I would be inclined to say "No." Though the drawing may be based on a verbal description, it is hardly a copy or facsimile of it in any familiar sense. But in accordance with the example-oriented anti-synoptic approach adopted in this book, one should be flexible about how to describe such cases. Rule 2 of the "copy" cluster requires that there be a resemblance between pictures, effigies, representations, etc., and what they are pictures, effigies, and representations of. In some cases one may determine the resemblance from a verbal description. Any bust of Socrates will have to be snub-nosed, for example, and any bust of Medusa will have to have snakes as her hair. Yet even in these cases we cannot say that such busts are exact, good, or bad copies, replicas, of their supposed originals.

"Replica" rule 2 If x is a replica, duplicate, etc., of y, then y exists or has existed.

This rule is closely related to the previous one and is relevant to some of the issues I have just discussed. There are transcripts of the Sacco versus Vanzetti trial, but not of the impeachment proceedings of Franklin Delano Roosevelt. There are reproductions of Picasso's *Guernica,* but not of his portrait of Generalissimo Francisco Franco. It is possible to find a copy of the first page of the Massoretic text of *Isaiah,* but not of the canonical *Book of Manasseh.* I can make a counterfeit of an American silver dollar, but not of an American silver three-dollar piece. I can make a duplicate of the key to my office, but not of the key to the Kingdom of Heaven. Again I should emphasize that the difficulty in making copies, reproductions, counterfeits, etc., of these latter things is not a practical difficulty but a logical one: the rules for the uses of these terms eliminate such possibilities when the object never existed. All the words in the "replica" chain except "model" satisfy this requirement. It is possible to make models of things that don't yet exist, as a pollution-free internal-combustion engine. In contrast, the remaining words in the "copy" cluster do not obey this principle. Thus, as mentioned above, there are statues of Bacchus, icons of the Angel Gabriel, pictures of Satan, busts of centaurs, and paintings of just about anything: fictional, imaginary, real, or even impossible, such as some of the Escher sketches.

"Replica" rule 3 If x is a replica, etc., of y, x may be indistinguishable from y.

This rule, which members of the "replica" chain satisfy, is a stricter variation of the condition of resemblance, which all words in the "copy" cluster satisfy. As we have seen, replicas, duplicates, effigies, and busts must to some degree resemble the objects they are replicas, duplicates, effigies, and busts of. But "replica" rule 3 allows something further: that absolute originals and their replicas, duplicates, and copies may be indistinguishable from one another.

Once again, it is difficult to give a simple characterization of the notion of "indistinguishable" as used in the maxim. Manifestly, it does not mean that under no circumstances or conditions can replicas be distinguished from what they are replicas of. Most of the time this can be done, and it is one of the implications of the general principle applying to all the words in the "copy" cluster that if x is a replica of y, x is not y. So something weaker and more flexible is required.

Roughly speaking, the formula means that in certain not unnatural circumstances x can pass for y, or be taken for y. A duplicate key, for instance, might be of a different color or even of a different metal from the original and still be called a "duplicate" because it opens the car door (though if its appearance and constitution vary too much, one might call it an "extra key"). But to the naked eye, an *exact* duplicate might be indistinguishable from the original key, even in good light. Talk about duplicates is a good illustration of how broad a range of examples can be subsumed under this rubric.

Let us consider some cases. A replica of Henry VIII's crown may be smaller, made of different material, and have red cut glass rather than rubies in it. It might be of the same size, weight, and shape, have the same detailed engraving on the base, and be made of a metal visually indistinguishable from the original gold. Even a professional thief, seeing it under optimal conditions of illumination, might be taken in. These same remarks apply to full-scale models, perfect counterfeits, excellent copies, and so on.

But they do not apply, in the same way, to the remaining words in the "copy" cluster. In good light, or in not unusual circumstances, a picture, portrait, bust, effigy, statue, icon, or drawing of y (where y is a person) will not pass for y. The notion of "passing for" is also open textured and must be interpreted with flexibility. A statue in Madame Tussaud's (if moved to a different locus and in indifferent light) might pass for a living individual, but closer inspection will show it to be a replica. But no amount of inspection might indicate whether a given item is the original or a duplicate key. In general, then, though paintings, portraits, drawings, statues, etc., must resemble the things they are paintings, portraits, etc., of, they do not satisfy the stronger condition of passing for the items they are paintings, portraits, etc., of.

These three rules give us the heartland for the "replica" chain. To be a member of the chain, a word must satisfy the initial set of conditions that apply to the "copy" cluster and the stronger conditions that apply to the "replica" chain.

SEVEN

Let us now turn to a still smaller group within the "copy" cluster, a ring. As the metaphors suggest, rings are closed, while chains may not be. The "replica" chain in fact does not close, while two rings it contains do. When a set of words forms a ring, its members are said to be "interdefinable." As I will employ the term "ring," a defining condition of a ring is that its members are interdefinable. "Interdefinability" describes a lexical process that begins with an entry and will lead through a set of entry expansions back to the original entry.

It is perhaps worth mentioning that in this situation "interdefinable" is not used in any traditional philosophical sense, i.e., in the sense in which philosophers sometimes speak of "real definitions," "analytical definitions," and so forth. In that use, "brother" and "male sibling" are interdefinable. Neither is the term to be identified with what are called "dictionary definitions," i.e., with the sorts of things that I have been calling "entry expansions."

Rather, "interdefinability" refers to a certain kind of lexical process that uses expressions found *in* entry expansions. Entry expansions, or dictionary definitions, have the characteristic that they can be read right off, but whether a set of words is interdefinable (closes) is something one must discover. I have suggested that interdefinability involves *synonyms*, but even this word can be misleading if it is given a traditional construal. Interdefinability is part of a complex process of moving from entry expansion to entry expansion, using some degree of intuition and judgment, until the agent finds himself back at the original entry. The words that are the stepping stones in this process are *never exactly identical in meaning* with the original word, and therefore are not synonyms in that sense, if this is what philosophers mean by "synonym."

Following the sort of procedure just described, one can generate within the "replica" chain two rings. We cannot complete the closure process by starting with "imitation," "counterfeit," or "model." We have already seen that "model" occurs marginally in the "replica" chain, but the stronger conditions rings must satisfy will give us additional grounds for excluding it. "Counterfeit" and "imitation" are both absent from either ring and are therefore excluded by the lexical process. The resulting rings are the following:

Ring 1	*Ring 2*
reproduction	reproduction
reconstruction	reconstruction
replica	replica
facsimile	duplicate
copy	copy
transcript	transcript
reproduction	reproduction

To obtain these rings at all, we must start with "reproduction"; otherwise we find that we are blocked (as in the case of "model," whose only entry expansion is "representation," which is not a term in the "replica" chain) or, in trivial cases, that the rings close too early. The only difference between the two rings is that one contains "facsimile," the other "duplicate," but neither contains both of these words. Since intuitively "duplicate" and "facsimile" would seem to belong to either set, one possible explanation for this puzzling phenomenon is that the dictionary I have used (*Webster's Third New International*) is somehow aberrant with regard to its pattern of entry expansions. So as not to complicate matters at this point, let us treat the two rings as one, i.e., as a group of seven words containing both "facsimile" and "duplicate."

I do so to raise the question of whether there is some further set of rules that the members of this ring satisfy but that not all the members of the "replica" chain satisfy. It seems to me that there are. Here is one:

Ring rule 1   If x is a replica, reconstruction, facsimile, copy, etc., of y, then both x and y are particular things.

It is this rule that excludes "model." Models are normally particular things, but they represent things that are not necessarily individual or particular. This is the case with the theoretical models made by economists and psychologists, which are simplified representations of complex forms of human behavior. Such forms or patterns of behavior are not normally thought of as individual or particular things. Indeed, models are often resorted to just when a phenomenon must be represented that cannot readily be visualized or directly observed, such as the pattern of electrical charges called an "atom" or the complex configuration of buying patterns in an economy that is called "inflation."

The words that belong to the rings, however, describe relations between individual things or particulars. One cannot have a replica of infinity or Newton's First Law, though one can have a replica of the particular page on which that law is printed. One cannot make reproductions of Hadrian's instructions to his architects, but one can of the villa they built for him at Tivoli. One cannot make a facsimile of the gross national product or of human frustration, though one can of documents that mention the GNP or that describe various forms of human frustration. And similar comments apply to the remaining words in the rings. This condition—that when x is a copy, replica, duplicate, facsimile, etc., of y, x and y are *both* particulars or individuals—is clearly of the greatest importance with regard to the problem of universals. But I shall defer comment on this matter until later.

There is finally one other logical principle that the words in the ring must satisfy:

Ring rule 2 If x is a replica, copy, etc., of y, y must be a human artifact.

The rule states that y is something that comes into being through human contrivance. The principle thus excludes cases where y is a natural object, such as a river, stream, hill, tree, plant, or rock. We can make drawings of trees, portraits of human beings, and statues of horses, but we cannot make replicas, copies, facsimiles, transcripts of these things. But why, one might ask, can't we make a replica of, say, an existing horse. The answer is that "replica" has the sense of repeating or duplicating something. A replica or reproduction would not duplicate that animal. It can't run or sire other horses. One of the common uses of "replica" is where a replica indicates a reproduction of an art object, such as picture or statue, created by the maker or performed under his direction. A horse is not a man-made object and therefore cannot be duplicated by any artifact.

The issue about the nature of clones might be raised at this point. Here we enter the world of biology, and complications arise. There are technical and popular uses of this term. In the strict technical sense, clones are made from the same genetic material. They are thus similar to identical twins. How shall we think of such twins? We would not characterize one twin as a replica or copy of the other. The relationship between them is tighter. Twins should be distinguished from visually indistinguishable cigars of the same brand. None of the cigars are clones (i.e., identical twins), since they are not made of the same genetic material. And "identical" ball bearings are not like identical twins, "identical cigars," or true clones. All these cases should be distinguished from one another. We typically do so by special idioms. We can say of visually indistinguishable cigars that they are "qualitatively but not numerically identical," for example. But we would not say that they are replicas and copies of one another. Each of these cases must be assessed on its own merits.

Let us return, then, to the straightforward cases covered by ring rule 2: replicas of Michelangelo's *David*, reproductions one can buy of Botticelli's *Birth of Venus*, reconstructions of the fortress at Masada, and transcripts of the Scopes trial. But all of these are human artifacts in the sense in which I am employing the term. And, of course, it doesn't just happen that there are no reproductions of George Washington or transcripts of trees: the rules governing the uses of these words excludes that there can be.

The implications of these findings for Platonism are great. We have already seen that if Plato thinks of particulars as copies of the forms or universals, the logic of the language requires that as copies they be man-made things and not things like human beings or clumps of mud. But these latter findings show that the other terminus of the relation, the form, cannot be as depicted by him. If individual tables and beds are copies of forms, forms must also be individual things. And further, they must be the sorts of things brought into existence by human endeavor. Neither of these conditions seems compatible with the usual interpretation of the theory. But as I mentioned earlier, I will defer a more intensive discussion of Platonism until later.

In the light of the foregoing comments, I will conclude this section of the chapter by suggesting an alternative characterization of a ring. This way of describing rings does not mention closure or interdefinability. No doubt the alternative descriptions are mutually implicative, but I shall not attempt to prove that here.

A ring, then, is a set of words such that (1) every word in the set is to be found in the entry expansion of at least one other word in the set, and (2) for any word w in the set, every word in the entry expansion of w that matches the sense of the ring is to be found in the set. This is not to be taken as a formal definition, because the term "ring" appears in the definiens and also because the somewhat vague sense of the term "the sense of the ring." But in these specifications are to be found the ingredients that a more precise characterization would incorporate.

In this part of the essay I have not described the differences among the uses of the individual words within the "copy" cluster but merely certain general rules that all the words satisfy. Nor have I contrasted the "logic" of the "copy" cluster with that of the "example" cluster. In the next section I shall briefly compare and contrast these clusters and then investigate the uses of some of the key words in each. I will then be in a position to discuss Plato's theory of ideas.

EIGHT

Starting with the word "example" and following the lexical procedures described above, we can generate the following collection, which I shall call "the 'example' cluster."

The "example" cluster

example	exemplar
instance	ideal
model	beau ideal
case	standard
illustration	prototype
sample	indication
specimen	form
pattern	

This is a highly complex group of words, and accordingly it is difficult to find a rule or set of rules to which they all conform. One rule they satisfy is that they are susceptible to the formula "x is a ___ of y." With appropriate substitutions for the variables x and y, the results of filling the blank with words from the list will always result in well-formed English sentences, such as "This is a specimen of blood," "Smith is the very prototype of evil," "This is a standard of achievement unparalleled in this century," and so forth. Insofar, as this is so, these words have something in common with those in the "copy" cluster. Note that only one word, "model," appears in both the "copy" cluster and in the "example" cluster. Since the logical conditions it must satisfy in being a member of the two clusters are different, we can predict that its role as a member of the "copy" cluster will not be the same as its role as a member of the "example" cluster. This is another way of saying that it will mean different things in the two cases.

The chains and rings in the "example" cluster are particularly interesting. "Example" is its head word, with the remaining words tied to it directly or at most one entry expansion away. "Example" thus has several functions. It is the core word of the cluster. It also functions as a bridge word, connecting the various chains and forming the nucleus of the cluster. It is also a member of one of the chains, the "instance" chain, and a member of the "sample" ring within it. The "sample" ring consists of six words: "example," "sample," "instance," "specimen," "case," and "illustration." These words are interdefinable and exhibit closure.

There are three chains within the cluster, each radiating away from "example" and tending to collect around a core word. Two of these chains begin from the two words that are the only synonyms given for "example" in *Webster's Third New International Dictionary,* namely, "instance" and "model." "Model," in turn, directly gives rise to "pattern," which then forms a grouping of its own.

We thus have three main subdivisions to the cluster, each chain being relatively, though not entirely, autonomous. The core words for the chains are "instance," "model," and "pattern," each with more or less its own set of words. The words within the chains tend to play the same kinds of logical roles, i.e., have roughly the same uses and meanings within the language. We thus have within the cluster three broadly different kinds of logical roles represented, i.e., words that tend to function like "instance," like "model," or like "pattern."

In pointing out that the words within each chain tend to play the same sorts of logical roles, I should also stress the converse of this observation, namely that each word in the cluster has its own logic (use, meaning). I can say "This is a sample of his urine," or "This is a specimen of his urine" but I cannot say, without a change of sense, "This is an illustration of his urine" or "This is a case of his urine." The words may have overlapping functions in some contexts, and thus may be interchangeable in those contexts, but the fact that they are not everywhere interchangeable shows that each has its own specific meaning or use. In asserting here that the words in chains have resembling or sometimes overlapping uses, I do not wish to be understood as saying that they do not have their own special uses. At the same time, I wish to emphasize that the words in each chain tend to have uses that resemble one another more closely than they do the uses of the words in contiguous chains. The three chains are composed of the following words:

The "instance" chain	*The "pattern" chain*
instance	pattern
example	example
specimen	model
indication	exemplar
illustration	archetype
case	prototype
sample	paradigm
pattern	form

EXAMPLES

The "model" chain

model

example

prototype

archetype

form

ideal

beau ideal

standard

criterion

test

gauge

touchstone

yardstick

Though the words in the "example" cluster fall into these three chains, they don't do so neatly. The lines of division are not clear-cut, since many of the words have extracatenate connections, which the lists do not perspicuously bring out. Nevertheless, even from the lists one can see that the groupings follow a pattern, and in particular that the "instance" chain is relatively more autonomous than the "model" and "pattern" chains. Since "instance" is not in the entry expansion of "model" while "pattern" is, one should not be surprised. This finding suggests, correctly, that we can expect words in the "instance" chain to have a more homogeneous use than those in the "model" and "pattern" chains.

For our purposes, the most important factor that emerges from a perusal of the lists is that "model" and "example" are ambiguous. It can be seen that "model" appears in two of the chains, the "model" chain itself and the "pattern" chain, but not in the "instance" chain. From this finding we can predict that it will not have uses resembling "instance" words but will have uses resembling the words in the "pattern" and, of course, "model" chains. "Example" appears in all three lists, and this suggests that it will have a complex logic, resembling the uses of the words in the three chains. To see whether these expectations can be confirmed, let us look into the matter more closely.

As I have already observed, "model" is a member of an entirely different cluster of words, the "copy" cluster. As such, it has a use that resembles that of words like "copy," "replica," "reproduction," and "duplicate." This use is captured by sentences like "He built a model of the Taj Mahal out of white cardboard paper for his son" or "That is a full-scale model of a Fokker D-7." A model is this sense is a reproduction or replica, usually (but not always) smaller than what it replicates. Typically, a model is an individual thing that occupies a specific place in the space-time order. But it is seldom, if ever, *typical* of what it copies. Models simply replicate or reproduce the original object. I have said that copies resemble their prototypes, but it would be misleading to say that they are typical of them. In this sense, models play different roles from examples, instances, samples, and specimens, which are not only individual things but are also usually typical or representative in character. It is this difference, I submit, that explains why "model" does not occur in the "instance" chain.

"Model" does, to be sure, have close lexical ties to a group of words some of whose uses parallel the uses of the words in the "instance" chain. These are some of the words in the "pattern" chain, such as "prototype," "archetype," "paradigm," and "exemplar." "Model" is also a member of the "pattern" chain, but as I shall note below, its uses do not resemble those of "prototype" and "archetype" when these function like "instance" words. That they do so function is surprising but is confirmed by the dictionary. Archetypes, prototypes, paradigms, and exemplars are often individual items (as are samples, examples, etc.), and when they are, they are typical of something (as are samples, examples, instances). "He is the archetype (prototype) of the stuffy reactionary" refers to a single individual and says of him that he is typical of a certain class.

But "model" doesn't seem quite at home here: it would be somewhat odd to say "He is the model of the stuffy reactionary" if the sentence is intended to be equivalent to the former. Nor does it go at all well as a replacement for these words in "He was the prototype or archetype middle linebacker: stocky, thick-chested, bull-necked." This result tends to reinforce our finding that when "model" is used as a member of the "pattern" chain, its use differs from those of the words in the "instance" chain. My first point, then, is that in its first use "model" belongs to the "copy" chain and not to the "instance" chain.

"Model" has a second, somewhat subtle use, one that connects it with the "pattern" chain, and in particular with "pattern" itself. "He built his home on the model (pattern) of an old farmhouse," where the old farmhouse is intended to be the model. Or "He followed the French model (pattern) of instruction in his lectures to the end of his life," where the French pattern is what he followed. In this use, models are prototypes or archetypes when these are neither instances (i.e., not typical of anything) nor copies (not reproductions or replicas of anything). "He made many models of the coin before he was satisfied with one," "The ancient pattern (model) of life no longer appealed to him," "His father was the model for one of the most famous characters in contemporary fiction," and "This was the original die (model, prototype) from which the coin was struck" are all sentences conveying this sense. It is often prepositions, like "for" and "from" rather than "of," that convey the idea that a model in this sense is an original item, as in the previous two sentences. The point is that when thus used as prototypes upon which other things are based, models stand at the opposite end of the relationship depicted in Plato's metaphor. They belong to the upper terminus and not its lower. And they are neither typical of nor copies of anything. An original die is not typical of the coins struck from it, nor does it copy them. Models as originals and models as copies both play roles, but different roles, in the relationship Plato describes in his metaphor.

There is a third use of "model" to be distinguished, one that brings it into close relationships with such words as "ideal" and "standard," words found in the "model" chain itself. A model in this use is something worthy, and in particular, worthy of emulation. "He was the very model of a modern major general," "His paper is a model of scientific argument," "His written addresses are models of clarity, order, and style" convey the sense intended. Words like "ideal" and "standard" virtually incorporate this commendatory sense, in a way in which "model" does not. The fact that someone's father was the model for a character in a novel does not mean that his father was a person worthy of emulation. Models as prototypes, i.e., as progenitors of objects, can thus be evaluatively neutral in a way in which models as ideals are not. There are some interesting intermediate cases, for example, references to model prisoners. It should be noted that models in this "prototype" use do not have to be individual things, nor are they generally typical or representative of anything. And, of course, seen from the standpoint of Platonism, they would be objects of the upper terminus.

"Example" is subject to much the same pattern of ambiguity as "model." It also tends to have three distinct uses, one perhaps less perspicuous than the others but, I think, still different from them.

When "example" is employed as a member of the "instance" chain, its use is sharp and clear. There it functions like "sample," "specimen," "case," "illustration," and, of course, "instance." These words denote *individual* items, episodes, facts, or aspects of situations that are typical or representative in character. The logic these words share as members of the "instance" chain shows that Plato's intuitions were not wholly misplaced. He thought of them as relational words, i.e., as typifying or representing something and also as denoting particulars. His picture of the relationship put particulars at the lower terminus, whereas the things typified stood at the higher terminus. He, of course, thought of these "higher" items as forms or universals, i.e., as entities that are not particulars. Samples, examples, etc., are individual items, facts, etc., and they are typical of something. But whether in every case that something is an entity of a different order or type, as Plato believed, is another matter entirely.

The second use of "example" is less sharp. It is a use that "example" shares with "model," though the affinities should not be pushed too far. In this "prototype" use of "example," it resembles certain uses of "archetype," "paradigm," "exemplar," and, of course, "prototype." To say that Smith made many prototypes of a die before arriving at his final model is to say that he made many examples (but not copies) of the die. One might even say that what he arrived at was the final example. In this use, examples are not typical or representative of anything. The earlier examples do not typify the final example, since it has not yet been made, and the final example (the die) doesn't typify what can be struck from it. All these objects are progenitors or potential progenitors of something else. They thus stand in certain kinds of relationships to these other objects, so that they seem to find a home in the Platonic model. But if examples in the "instance" sense belong to the lower terminus of the relationship, then examples in this "prototype" sense belong at the other end of it. In saying this, I do not mean to imply, of course, that examples are always examples of examples.

The third main sense of "example" resembles the use of "model" that carries connotations of value, except that in the case of examples they can be either positive or negative. One can compare "He is an example we can all be proud of" with "He is the very model of a modern Major General." We often use the verbs "provide" and "sets" instead of "is" in speaking about examples in this sense. "He provides an example for us all" or "He set an example for us all" illustrate the point. Examples in this sense are not always things to be emulated; they in fact are often cited as things to be avoided. "Learn from me," Mary Shelley writes, "if not by my precepts, at least by my example, how dangerous is the acquirement of knowledge."[5]

I may summarize the preceding discussion as follows. I have distinguished three roughly parallel uses for "model" and "example." We sometimes speak of models as if they were copies, replicas, or duplicates. As such they are almost always individual things. But they are not typical of what they copy: they simply reproduce it. We sometimes speak of examples as if they were instances, specimens, and samples. These are sometimes thought to be things like copies, replicas, and duplicates, since they are individual items. But we have seen that they are not, since they are typical or representative in character. From this description, it is plausible to infer that they are "particulars" in Plato's sense and also that they stand in a relationship of some kind to what they typify or represent. Plato thought that the relationship should be described as holding between entities of two different types or orders, with particulars being items of the lower order. Whether this inference is justifiable is something I shall discuss below.

We sometimes speak of models and examples as if they were prototypes. In this sense, they are originals or progenitors. Once again the Platonic metaphor seems to apply, since it seems plausible that they stand in some kind of relationship to whatever they generate, or to whatever is based on them. When "example" and "model" are used in this "prototype" sense, they differ in an important respect. Examples are almost always individuals, while models (which are sometimes patterns) need not be. But in neither case do models or examples typify the objects that have these relationships to them.

Finally, "example" and "model" have evaluative uses that they do not typically possess as members of the "instance" chain or the "pattern" chain. But they differ in one respect. Models are always things worthwhile (a "model" student) and in particular are the sorts of things worthy of imitation or emulation. Examples may be worthy, but they can also be things having a negative value. Generally speaking, examples, in either the commendatory or pejorative senses, are individuals (like Smith, who should or should not be emulated), while models (which resemble ideals and standards) may not be. In neither case are they usually typical of anything; indeed, the reverse is true. It is because models or examples are outstanding or egregious, and thus differ from the typical individual who wishes to emulate or avoid them, that they can function as examples or models in these ways.

In the light of the preceding comments, I am now in a position to make the first of three hopefully major points about Platonism.

First, I mentioned at the beginning of the chapter that the relationships between examples and copies, on the one hand, and what they are examples and copies of, on the other, are more complex than Plato depicts them as being. I am now in a position to substantiate this claim.

To begin with, Plato tends to conflate the uses I have distinguished. He fails to articulate the distinction between examples and copies, though his two versions of the theory of forms strongly suggest that he must have intuited the difference. He sometimes speaks as if forms are prototypes that generate items (an idea that influenced Plotinus) and of which particular beds, tables, and men are instances, copies, examples, replicas, etc. When speaking in this vein about particulars as copies, he fails to appreciate that such talk makes sense only if the forms themselves are individuals or particulars. He also sometimes speaks as if the forms are ideals or standards that ought to be emulated and as if "lower-order beings" should strive to come up to these ideals or standards (an idea that influenced Aristotle). As such forms may occasionally initiate behavior, but sometimes they do not. What, for example, does the standard meter bar in Paris generate? And though Plato is correct that ideals and standards are not necessarily individual things, he fails to see that sometimes they are.

Above all, Plato fails to see that the conceptual model he is working with is simplistic and too rigid. For him, the world contains only two kinds of things: particulars and universals. Each has its own special role, and their roles cannot be interchanged. Particulars always stand at one end of the relationship (the lower end), while forms always occupy the other (higher) end. But as I have indicated, when examples are prototypes or ideals, they too can serve at the "higher" terminus. In such cases, there thus may be no need to invoke new entities, forms, at all, or if there is, then it does not follow that they are the only things that can function at the higher terminus of the relationship depicted in Plato's schema.

"Lower" for Plato is not a neutral term: his use of it carries invidious overtones. It typically has the sense of "inferior." An individual man is less perfect than the ideal man, an individual triangle cannot come up to the level of the perfect triangle, and physical objects are less real than the forms, and therefore they are all less desirable. Plato has indeed captured some of the resonances we associate with copies. A copy of a painting is generally less valuable than the original, a copy of a birth certificate may not be accepted by the Immigration and Naturalization Service, and so forth. But there are exceptions. And Plato's schema does not allow for these. It is a serious defect that it cannot accommodate counterexamples to its synoptic worldview.

Finally, I wish to stress that the relationships within the model are more complex than Plato makes them out to be. Here one must be sympathetic to Plato. There is no doubt that he was sensitive to some of the differences between copies and examples, and his talk of participation, on the one hand, and of imitation, on the other, reflects a struggle to clarify the relationships involved. But what is missing from his efforts is a sense that the relationships may be pluralistic. As we have seen, it will not do to characterize in simple terms the relationships holding between these various items. Thus the relationship between a sample and what it is a sample of will be determined in part by the fact that it is a sample, and not an example or illustration or specimen or case, and in part by the kind of thing it is a sample of. A sample of cloth may be less than the whole bolt, but is an example of a grammatical mistake less than the whole mistake?

My second point deals with an inference that is basic to Plato's entire enterprise.

Copies, replicas, examples, samples, instances, and specimens have something in common. Each of them is, in some sense, different from the items they are copies, replicas, examples, etc., of. The theory of forms is based on this insight. I have expressed this idea in terms of the formula "If x is a ____ of y, x is *not* y." Plato would have said, I believe, that this formula is true when any of the words belonging to either the "copy" cluster or the "example" cluster replace the blank in it. Plato inferred from this principle not only that x and y must not be identical but also that they must be items or entities of a different order, and specifically, that y must be of a higher order than x.

There is some support for this further inference in language. We speak of "samples of y," "examples of y," "copies of y," and so on. The "of" locution strongly suggests that two different things stand in a certain typal relationship to one another, and that x is the lower member. My point is that Plato was mistaken in holding that if x and y are different, they must be different in kind, i.e., that they must be of a different type or order.

It is true that if x is a word belonging to the "copy" cluster, the principle "If x is a ____ of y, then x is not y" holds. But it holds only in the sense that x is not the same object as y. A copy of a will is not the same object as the original will, nor is the duplicate key I have in my pocket the original key. But it does not follow that because they are copies or duplicates, they are therefore objects of a different order from their originals. Indeed, the converse is true. It is generally true that copies, duplicates, replicas, etc., are things of the same kind, type, or order as the things they copy, duplicate, or replicate. If they were not, it would make no sense to speak of exact copies, exact duplicates, and exact replicas. With regard to "copy" talk, therefore, it clearly does not follow that x and y are of a different order, even if we grant that the principle "If x is a ___ of y, then x is not y" is true for the words in this cluster.

The matter is more complicated with regard to the words in the "example" cluster, but again it is evident that Plato's inference does not go through. The complications concern the interpretation of the words "is not" in the above formula. It seems true to say that examples, samples, instances, illustrations, cases, and specimens, are in some sense all different from what they are examples, samples, etc., of. A sample of wine taken from a cask may be physically located at a distance from the cask, and it will have a different size and weight from the wine that remains in the cask. Accordingly, one might be tempted to speak of it as a "different object" from what it is a sample of, especially if one thinks of identity in terms of Leibniz's Law. If x is a sample of y and x is physically separated from y, then x is not identical with y, according to Leibniz's Law. But there is something peculiar about describing a sample as a different *object* from what it is a sample of. Is a particular illustration of the grammatical mistake a different object from the grammatical mistake? This is hardly the most felicitous way of characterizing the respects in which x and y differ.

It is even misleading to describe samples of wine and the lot of wine being sampled as "different objects but objects of the *same* kind." The words "same kind" are not used in this way. One might say that though a diamond necklace and an imitation necklace (i.e., an exact copy made of glass) are not the same object, they are objects of the same kind or type (both are designed to be worn by someone). It is thus a feature of "copy" talk that if x is a copy of y, x will not only differ from y but also may be said to be the same kind of object as y. But it would be strange to say this of two batches of wine, one of which is a sample of the other. For we want to say something stronger about this relationship. It is not that the batches are of the same *kind* but rather that both batches are exactly the same wine. Chateau Brane-Cantenac and Chateau Cantenac-Brown, whose provenance is the parish of Margaux, are the same *kind* of wine, though not the same wine, in contradistinction to Chateau Mt. Redon, which comes from the Rhone Valley and is not the same *kind* of wine as either.

The principle that thus holds of the words in the "sample" ring of the "example" cluster ("example," "sample," "case," etc.) is this:

(1) If x is a _____ of y, then x is y.

This principle applies in the sense that when words belonging to the ring are substituted for the blank in the formula, the following inferences go through: If x is a sample of wine, x is wine. If this is a specimen of urine, it is urine. If what Jones has is a case of measles, then what Jones has is measles. It is also true that if x is sample of *a* y, then x is *a* y. Thus if Los Angeles is an example of an American city, then Los Angeles is an American city. (I think the difference between the two formulations is important, but will not speak to it here, since it does not affect the point at issue, namely that samples, examples, etc., do not differ in kind or order from what they are samples or examples of.)

To say this is not to deny that samples are in some sense different from what they are samples of. But what I am now stressing, and what the formula illustrates clearly, is the converse point. In some important sense, samples are the same as what they are samples of. If I give you a sample of the wine of Chateau Cos d'Estournel, what you sip *is* the wine of Cos d'Estournel. In taking a sip, you do not drink all of the wine of Cos d'Estournel, to be sure, but what you are drinking does not differ in order, type, or kind from the wine of Cos d'Estournel. If what I have in the test tube is a specimen of Smith's urine, I may not have all of his urine in the test tube, but what I do have there is Smith's urine, and not something of a higher type or different order. Examples, samples, instances, cases, illustrations, and specimens are typical of what they are samples, examples, and specimens of precisely because they do not differ in kind from those things.

Etymology supports this contention. The lexical investigation above established that "example" is the key word in the cluster and that the other words in the "sample" ring are intimately tied to it. Etymologically speaking, we find "example," "sample," and the archaic forms "essample" and "essaumple" to be variations of the same word. All of them derive from the Sanscrit "sam," and this is also our word "same." Examples and samples are what they are because they are the same as what they are samples and examples of. There is thus justification on linguistic grounds for asserting that samples of wine *are* wine. To say either that samples are not identical with what they are samples of or that at most they are the same *kind* of thing is to miss the power embodied in this etymological point.

This brings me, then, to my second major criticism. We saw that Platonism could be formulated in terms of the following two principles:

(2) If x is an example (instance, copy, etc.) of y, then x is not y.

(3) If x is an example (etc.) of y, then x is a particular (or individual) and y is of a higher order than x.

My point is that neither the "participation" nor the "mimesis" version of the theory of forms satisfies the conjunction of these principles. Ignoring some of the differences between "copy" talk and "example" talk that I just mentioned, let us suppose that (2) holds. Let us suppose that samples of wine differ (perhaps in quantity) from what they are samples of and that copies differ (are different objects) from what they are copies of. But if (2) holds, then (3) does not. It is false that copies are always of a different kind or order from their originals. What is true is merely that copies are not the same objects as their prototypes, but it is manifestly false that they are *always* objects of a different kind, order, or type from them. "Copy" talk provides Plato with the difference he needs between x and y, but it does not provide him with a difference in order, type, or kind. Even if copies are sometimes "inferior" to their originals, they are not always so.

A similar point may be made with regard to the words in the "example" cluster. For as we have just seen, if x is an example, sample, instance, etc., of y, then, contrary to what (3) requires, x is the same as y and not of a different order, type, or kind from y. If it were, then x could not be typical of y. In neither case, then, does Plato get the sort of "gap" he needs between examples and copies, on the one hand, and what they are examples and copies of, on the other. Neither the "participation" nor the "mimesis" account of the relationship between particulars and universals will do.

After all this, one may begin to wonder what differences there are between samples, examples, illustrations, cases, and instances. My third major point depends on answering this question, that is, on moving "inside" the ring and working out the specific rules governing the use of each of its words. Since I have already done this, I can categorically say that the information cannot be reproduced except at some length, and therefore not here. My point is likely to be less compelling without the backing such a detailed statement would provide: I am therefore asking the reader to take my word for one finding, namely that the same object or thing may be either a sample or an example.

The difference between examples and samples is not always a matter of what sort of object one is dealing with, but in many cases, and pretty characteristically, it is a matter of the use to which a certain object is being put. We use examples in situations where we do not know what something is, have never seen it, and want to find out what it is. If an Eskimo has never seen cloth and wants to know what cloth is, we show him an example, a swatch cut from a bolt of Harris Tweed, say. If, however, the Eskimo already knows what cloth is but wants to know what Harris Tweed is, we show him a sample. Not any old piece of cloth will do in the latter situation: it has to be Harris Tweed. But it can be the same piece of cloth we showed him before. Samples are thus used in circumstances where more detailed information is required, and the use of samples presupposes a certain amount of background information that the use of examples does not. But this does not imply that in every case the objects that are samples or examples (or instances, specimens, cases, illustrations) are therefore different objects. Most of these words have overlapping uses; in some cases one can be substituted for another. If I am asked to bring in a specimen of urine, what I bring in may be regarded as a sample of urine. But if I am asked to bring in a specimen of an African bee, it would be peculiar to describe this as a case or a sample of an African bee.

More can be said about this, but that is enough for my purposes. This finding is relevant to Platonism in two different ways. First, it casts doubt upon the merit of the model Plato employs in his statement of the theory of forms. That model suggests that where there are different words, there must be correspondingly different objects. It suggests that examples are different kinds of particulars from copies, for instance. And it thus makes it plausible to hold that the relationships depicted in the model hold between objects of different kinds. Plato's quest is thus conceived of as one that turns on finding the right sorts of objects in order to form a perspicuous view of the relationships involved—hence the two versions of the theory of forms, each of which utilizes different sorts of objects.

I suggest, on the contrary, that the different relationships involved are not to be accounted for in terms of kinds of objects but in terms of the uses to which even the same objects may be put. When Plato's principle—one word, one object—is pushed further, it gives rise to a search for special objects that occupy the upper terminus of such relationships, objects of a different kind or order: universals. But as we have seen, samples of wine and lots of wine are at best dubiously described as different objects and are certainly not to be described as objects of a different order or kind. The search for such special objects is thus unnecessary and is a good example of how theory tends to ignore or misrepresent the pluralistic world in which we live.

The second respect in which this finding is relevant to Platonism may be put as follows. In the course of his extensive writings on the theory of forms, Plato uses an argument whose conclusion is that certain concepts or notions or ideas—certain sorts of abstract entities—must be distinguished from (and indeed exist separately from) their exemplifications or instances. I have elsewhere called this the "detachment argument." Put abstractly, it states that if x is an example of y and if z is an example of y and if x and z are different, then neither x nor z is y. Plato interprets the "is" in the conclusion to mean that x is not identical with y, in a sense of "identical" that might be expressed in Leibniz's Law, and this implies that x and z are not things of the same order as y. The point of the argument is to establish that exemplifications differing from one another cannot be identical with what they exemplify, and if not, that one cannot discover the essence or form of y by using examples.[6]

Something like this argument (it obviously could be more carefully formulated) has been part of the received opinion in philosophy since the time of Plato. It has given rise to a tradition that has deprecated the use of examples, and indeed has identified "reason" with the kind of knowing that does not involve the use of examples. The scientific rationalism or new empiricism I described in the previous chapter is a contemporary version of the tradition.

I now propose that we stand the Platonic tradition on its head. The preceding investigation indicates that when someone does not know what something is, one can find out what it is by means of examples. This is true even though examples may differ from one another. If Smith and Jones don't know what snow is, have never seen snow before, and don't understand your description of it, they can find out what snow is by seeing examples of it, even though what you show each of them may be different in some respects from what you show the other. It is possible for them to find out what snow is because *all* examples of snow *are* snow and because all examples of snow do not differ in kind from snow. The search for the essence of snow, for a form hidden from possible observation, is unnecessary and misguided. To shift into Platonic language, I am saying that examples of snow capture the "essence" of snow because they are snow. This is, then, why we can replace explanation by description.

Reference Theories and Fiction

ONE

In "Identity and Necessity" and in *Naming and Necessity*, Saul Kripke advances two theses that are now widely regarded as central to the theory of direct reference: (1) proper names are rigid designators, and (2) rigid designators are terms that pick out the same object in all possible worlds.[1] With respect to the first thesis, Kripke explains that by a proper name he means only those things that in ordinary language would be called "proper names": the name of a person, a city, a country, etc. Frege had used "name" in a wide sense to include declarative sentences and definite descriptions, but this is a usage that ordinary speech would not sanction. So the class of what Kripke is calling "proper names" excludes definite descriptions and declarative sentences. Hence, (1) should be understood as expressing a thesis about proper names as these are understood in ordinary discourse.

We have seen in chapters 2 and 3 that Kripke also states that natural-kind terms are rigid designators. But natural-kind terms are not proper names, so not all rigid designators are proper names. Some are mass nouns, such as "gold" and "water." I shall therefore ignore his discussion of natural-kind terms in this chapter and focus only on proper names. I argued in those previous chapters that Kripke's account of natural kinds and of natural-kind terms suffers from severe difficulties. The idea that proper names are rigid designators seems initially exempt from many of those difficulties, but we shall find that it has its own share of troubles.

With respect to (2) Kripke states that by "rigid designator" he means a term that designates the same object in all possible worlds. He emphasizes that this formulation does not mean that the object exists or must exist in all possible worlds, i.e., that it necessarily exists. As he says,

All I mean is that in any possible world where the object in question *does* exist, in any situation where the object *would* exist, we use the designator in question to designate that object. In a situation where the object does not exist, then we should say that the designator has no referent and that the object in question so designated does not exist.[2]

Kripke expands (2) to distinguish rigid from nonrigid designators. Most definite descriptions, though not all (such as "the square root of 25"), are nonrigid. To say they are "nonrigid" means that on different occasions or in different circumstances they may pick out different individuals. "The owner of the house next door" is an example of a nonrigid description. A proper name, in contradistinction, designates just one individual, including references to that individual in counterfactual circumstances (e.g., "Clinton might have lost to Bush"). In speaking about Clinton in such a case, one is speaking not about a Clinton counterpart but about Clinton himself.

On this theory of direct reference, proper names function like tags. A name is applied to an individual and sticks to that individual in all circumstances, actual and possible. The terminology of "tagging" was first used by Ruth Marcus in "Modalities and Intensional Languages," published in *Synthese* in 1961. The paper was also presented in a lecture in February 1962 at the Boston Colloquium for the Philosophy of Science in conjunction with a commentary by W. V. Quine. Saul Kripke was present and participated in the discussion.[3]

Marcus introduced this locution in arguing that a true identity sentence whose flanking expressions are proper names (tags) is necessary and not contingent. Thus a statement like "Plato is Plato" is necessarily true. Her account of proper names is close to Mill's. She says, "A proper name (of a thing) has no meaning." She also pointed out that descriptions are not tags. Kripke accepted both her interpretation of proper names as tags and her analysis of true identity sentences that contain tags as necessary. Thus for Kripke to say that a proper name is rigid is tantamount to saying it is a tag. But Marcus states, "Proper names are not assimilated to what later came to be called 'rigid designators' by Saul Kripke, although they share some features with rigid designators."[4]

Kripke also agreed with Marcus and against Quine that even if one tags the same object twice with different names, say the planet Venus tagged with "Phosphorus" and "Hesperus," the identity sentence containing those names is necessary and not contingent. According to Kripke, Quine was confusing the concept of contingency with that of aposteriority. It was an a posteriori discovery that one had tagged Venus twice, but "Phosphorus is Hesperus" is nonetheless necessary and not contingent.

A controversy has recently developed over the question of whether Kripke's main ideas were taken, with insufficient attribution, from Marcus. The issue has been carefully and fairly described in "Whose Idea Is It, Anyway," by Jim Holt.[5] I do not wish to enter into the dispute. But since this essay concerns the relationship between the theory of reference and the analysis of fictive talk, I should point out that the antecedents of both Marcus's views and

Kripke's are to be found in Russell. In *Modalities,* Marcus meticulously describes Russell's influences on her views, and how her views resemble and differ from his. I shall say more about Russell's views in "Holism: The Chicken or the Egg" below, but a few words are apposite now.

Russell drew a distinction between proper names and descriptions. He later modified his position so that what ordinary persons regard as proper names are really abbreviations for descriptions. Proper names, on his modified view, are demonstratives and indexicals, such as "this," "that," "here," and "now."[6] But before arriving at such a counterintuitive result, he argued that an identity sentence such as "Scott is Scott," where both occurrences of "Scott" are names, is trivial. In effect, though he did not use the terminology, he was saying that the sentence was a necessary truth. He also distinguished "Scott is Scott" from "Scott is the author of *Waverley.*" Both are true, but the latter contains a descriptive phrase and is therefore not trivial. Accordingly, one might have expected him to say that "Scott is the author of *Waverley*" is an identity sentence but contingent. However, Russell gave an entirely different and unexpected analysis of it. He denied that it was an identity sentence at all. His contention was that it was a complex general sentence. This is the famous analysis given in his theory of descriptions. Marcus and Kripke disagreed. They both interpreted such sentences as identity sentences but denied they are necessary. What Russell, Marcus, and Kripke all accepted was that proper names differ from descriptions in the logical roles they play, and therefore that one cannot substitute descriptions for names in every context in which the latter occur.

In effect, all three philosophers were arguing that a description has (or expresses) a sense and it is via the intermediation of its sense that it denotes or picks out an object. Proper names differ. Their relationship to what they name is direct and without intermediation. Russell, of course, did not use the terminology of "tagging," and Marcus did not use Kripke's terminology of "rigid designation," but the ideas they had about proper names are remarkably similar. What Marcus and Kripke also saw and emphasized as against Russell is that in employing definite descriptions misidentification can occur. But a proper name requires ostension at some juncture, and this means that the "referent of a proper name remains fixed, even where attributions claimed by narrative are in error," as Marcus puts it. She adds,

On this account "proper name" is a semantical, not a merely syntactical, notion. Reference is supposed. We may mistakenly believe of some syntactically proper name, say "Homer," that it has an actual singular referent and is a genuine proper name, but if its use does not finally link it to a singular object, it is not a genuine name at all.[7]

Or again:

Proper naming as opposed to describing defines a special basic relation between a word and a thing in a linguistic institution. Naming relates a word introduced into an actual language in the actual world to a thing that is there to be encountered in the world when the event of naming occurs. Acts of naming are acts of actual language users. A possible object is not there to be assigned a name.[8]

Therefore, a designator cannot be a proper name unless there exists a particular individual that it tags. As we shall see in a moment, the idea that there is a direct relationship between such a name and its referent has important ramifications for such theories in speaking about fictive objects. As Marcus says,

It is not, I will propose, the general absence of "identification *conditions*" that makes possibilia problematic. It is that possibilia cannot be objects of reference at all.[9]

Kripke's version of the theory of direct reference had another merit. In emphasizing that he was speaking about proper names as they occur in ordinary speech, he was able to give an account of names as rigid designators that avoids the implication that a possible world is "a foreign country, or a distant planet way out there," as he puts it.[10] Talk about possible worlds, on his analysis, is thus translatable into ordinary discourse and becomes talk about counterfactual situations involving a tagged individual. Thus his theory does not require a special interpretation of the role of proper names in such contexts.

Yet despite their merits, all of these views have difficulties in analyzing the role played by proper names in reference to fictional objects. Kripke was very much aware of the problem. In *Naming and Necessity* he says,

Concerning rigidity: In many places, both in this preface and in the text of this monograph, I deliberately ignore delicate questions arising from the possible nonexistence of an object.[11]

Keith Donnellan's interesting variant of the direct-reference account, which he calls "the historical-explanation theory," distinguishes the nonexistent from the fictive nonexistent. His approach deals only with the former. As he informs the reader,

What is to be excluded from consideration here is an account of discourse about fiction. (This is not, of course, to say that such an account is not in the end needed.)[12]

The problem is straightforward. If fictive objects do not exist and have what ordinary persons would call "proper names" (e.g., "Sherlock Holmes," "Hamlet," "Santa Claus"), there is no way of tagging them. You cannot attach labels to the nonexistent, as the previous quotations from Marcus make plain. So clearly their "names" cannot be rigid designators. The direct-reference theorist thus faces a conundrum. Here are some possible options for such a theorist:

1. Abandon the notion that proper names are rigid designators (tags).

2. Adopt a Russellian analysis that says that in fiction so-called "proper names" are abbreviations for descriptions, while maintaining that in ordinary, nonfictive discourse they are tags.

3. Argue that in central cases (nonfictive contexts) proper names are rigid but that in fictive language they have a symbiotic, derivative, or secondary use. To say that they have such a derivative use does not necessarily mean that they have to be analyzed as definite descriptions.

4. Hold that fictive language presupposes a "fictive existence operator," so that fictive objects do exist in fiction and therefore can be tagged by fictive proper names. Tagging would thus be relativized to a particular body of discourse.

There are other possibilities as well, but the preceding list brings out the nature of the dilemma. None of these options is attractive for direct-reference theorists. To abandon the notion that names are rigid is simply to abandon the theory. To accept the Russellian account that fictive names are descriptions is to abandon the Kripkean notion that proper names are what ordinary persons describe them as being. To adopt the notion that fictive names are derivative or symbiotic and are about fictive objects, in some unspecified sense of "about," seems simply to beg the question. This seems to be the difficulty in Vendler's subtle account.[13] To accept the fourth option that one can "tag" fictive objects obviously involves an extended or stretched use of "tag." What seems to be undeniable is that one cannot tag the nonexistent.

　　　The conundrum arises because the following principles seem to be in conflict.

- Proper names are rigid designators.

- A rigid designator is a tag, and therefore requires the existence of something to be tagged.

- Fictive objects do not exist, and therefore cannot be tagged.

- Fictive objects have proper names.

- A proper name is what is ordinarily meant by a proper name.

TWO

It should be noted that another presupposition lies submerged beneath the options just described. It is that there is something special about the language of fiction. When one uses proper names in fiction, the assumption is that they cannot be used as they are in referring to existent persons, places, or things. Now ordinary persons do not think very deeply about the kinds of problems that beset philosophers. But let us attribute a kind of latent view to them. This is the view that words like "Sherlock Holmes" and "Hamlet" are proper names, no different from names like "Saul Kripke" and "Ruth Marcus." But if so, what are they the names of? The answer might be, They are the names of fictitious characters, Sherlock Holmes and Hamlet. Why shouldn't fictive objects have names, the answer might continue, just as nonfictive objects do?

　　　The "plain man" might even offer two simple arguments in support of this position. Here is the first. Suppose one were to ask an ordinary person to pick out the proper names in the following list: "John," "the first person to step on the moon," "a horse," "Medusa," "Smith," "the chancellor," "Santa Claus," "Einstein." There is almost no doubt that the ordinary person would select "John," "Medusa," "Smith," "Santa Claus," and "Einstein" as proper names and would reject "the first person to step on the moon," "a horse," and "the chancellor" as proper names. Two of the selections are the names of fictive entities. Therefore, such entities have proper names.

The second argument might run as follows: Suppose someone is looking through a book of names in order to select one for a newly born male child. That list might include "Hamlet," "Sherlock," and "Lancelot." These are names made famous in Western fiction, yet they can be used as the names of existing persons. So why think they are not names when used in fiction? A name is a name is a name in any context, Gertrude Stein might have said. So ordinary persons find no obstacle in identifying these words as proper names. Let us call this latent outlook "the commonsense view of names."

Now nearly every philosopher from Russell to the present who has thought about fictive language would disagree with that view. They might argue that it rests on a confusion. They might say that a list or book of names contains not *proper* names in a strict sense of the term, that is, names of actually existing individuals, but rather only potential names. Potential names become proper names only when they are applied to persons, and then they function as tags. It is therefore misleading to think of potential names as proper names per se. This response is interesting, but I think it begs the question. It assumes exactly what is in dispute: that N is a proper name only if it is applied to an existing person, place, or thing. It is therefore not a compelling objection.

I will argue in the rest of this essay that the commonsense view (whether it is actually held by any nonphilosopher or not) is right, and I will offer additional arguments in its support. These will claim that it is a mistake to think of proper names as tags and that it is also a mistake to conflate mentioning or referring to an object with identifying or picking out the object.

My approach, as the reader might guess, deflates theory. I submit that complex theories about the nature of language have driven philosophers to views that are replete with difficulties. One of these is to deny the obvious, namely that "Santa Claus," "Medusa," and "Pegasus" are proper names. A second difficulty is to presuppose that the language of fiction is special and differs fundamentally from nonfictive discourse. Almost all the famous twentieth-century theories of meaning and reference, including recent direct-reference theories, give rise to these misconceptions, and I shall now investigate the question of why this is so. At the end of this inquiry I will defend a conception of "proper name" that differs from those of both Russell and the direct-reference theorists.

THREE

To obtain a perspicuous view of these developments, one should consider them from a historical perspective. From the time of the Greeks to the present, the relationship between language and the world has been of fundamental concern to philosophers. As I pointed out in chapter 2, the problem of explaining how one can speak meaningfully about the nonexistent has been a central issue. Up to World War II, this continued to be the case. Philosophers such as Meinong, Frege, and Russell concentrated on meaning and less on reference.

At some point around the middle of the century there was a shift in emphasis from meaning to reference. It is a complicated exegetical question why and how this happened and who was responsible for it. One might at first glance suggest that Quine was responsible. In one of his early papers, Quine drew a distinction between meaning and naming.[14] It thus seemed that he was on the verge of propounding a direct-reference theory. But he wasn't, and didn't. Instead, under the influence of Russell, he argued that proper names, including fictive names, are analyzable as descriptions, and accordingly that "whatever we say with the help of names can be said in a language which shuns names altogether. To be is purely and simply to be the value of a variable."[15] So names have no special referential power, on his theory. Instead, the quantificational apparatus of language, of which descriptions are a part, bears the burden of reference. In the end, his philosophy of language more closely resembled the views of Frege and the later Russell than it did those of Marcus and Kripke.

Who, then, can be identified as the main source of the new outlook? I suggest it was Strawson. His celebrated paper "On Referring" (1950) was a turning point. It began by rehearsing the debate between Meinong and Russell over nonexistence and argued that both had confused questions about meaning with questions about reference. The classical issue about the connection between language and the world was henceforth to be viewed from this perspective. Therefore, I propose to take Strawson as a starting point and to show, via his essay, how the theory of reference produced the kinds of difficulties mentioned in the previous section.

Strawson's paper turns on a fundamental idea, namely that one must distinguish the formal grammatical characteristics of linguistic units (e.g., whether they are nouns or declarative sentences, etc.) from the use to which they are put. The failure to make this distinction is the basic mistake that Strawson finds in Russell's theory. It gives rise to all sorts of conceptual errors, including those about how fictive language is to be described. Strawson thus begins by speaking about the uniquely referring *uses* to which certain linguistic expressions can be put. These are locutions that one uses in mentioning or referring to an individual or thing in the course of making a statement about that individual or thing. As examples of expressions that can be put to such a use, Strawson lists singular demonstrative pronouns ("this," "that"), proper names ("Venice," "Napoleon"), singular personal and impersonal pronouns ("she," "it," "he"), and definite descriptive phrases ("the so-and-so"). His point is that these expressions *per se* do not refer to or mention anyone or anything, and that declarative sentences containing them do not make statements that are either true or false. It is only when such linguistic entities are put to some use that one can speak about their referring or statement making functions. On this account, statement making and referring are complementary activities that typically go hand in hand. To borrow a phrase from Wittgenstein, one might interpret Strawson as claiming that it is the *use* that gives such linguistic units their life.

The preceding account of Strawson's views is, of course, well known, since his paper has achieved the status of a classic in recent philosophy. One might have thought, therefore, that its essential bones would have been picked clean. But strangely enough, the theory he advances about the nature of fiction has escaped extensive critical examination. This is particularly surprising, since it is plausible and represents an advance over any proposed by his immediate predecessors. In what follows, I will show why it is plausible, why it represents an advance over older accounts, and why I believe it ultimately fails as an account of fictive discourse. In Strawson's work one can also find the ingredients of a solution to the problems generated by *direct*-reference theories, as I shall argue later.

The theory is expounded by Strawson as an alternative to three theories that he believes various philosophers have held about the nature of fiction—views that seem to him radically mistaken. Although I shall not explore these views at length, I would like to discuss them briefly in order to indicate how Strawson's own account differs from them and why he thinks (as I also do) that it represents an improvement on them. But before doing so, I propose to set the stage by asking why his predecessors thought there should be a problem about the nature of fiction at all? As we have seen, they were not particularly concerned with reference per se. Yet reference was involved in some way or other. So where did they locate the nub of the problem?

The answer lies in their adherence to the correspondence theory of truth. The theory has historically been stated in various ways, but on any typical formulation of it, including such semantic versions as Tarski's, truth is considered to be a relation obtaining between items belonging to two different categories. How these categories are constituted and what sorts of items can properly be said to belong to them are much debated matters in contemporary philosophy. Accordingly, there is a vast literature on the question of whether it is sentences (as Tarski thought) or propositions (as Russell thought) or judgments (as Moore thought) or beliefs (as Chisholm thought) or what is said (as Aristotle thought) or statements (as Strawson was to argue) that are the "bearers" of truth, and thus that properly belong to the first category. And there is an equally vast literature on the question of whether it is facts or states of affairs or what is the case that constitute the items to which they correspond. Finally, the literature on what is meant by "correspond" is no less extensive. Recently, for

164

example, it has been argued that because convention T
describes not a language-world relationship but a lan-
guage-language relationship, Tarski's formal definition of
truth in terms of satisfaction is empty of substantial philosophical content. But leaving aside concerns of this sort, I
only wish to emphasize that in all formulations of the
theory two different categories of items are involved and
truth is seen as a relationship holding between some items
of the one sort and some of the other. Accordingly, characteristic formulations of the theory state that a proposition is true if and only if it corresponds to what is the case
or that a sentence is true if and only if it corresponds to
the facts. Thus, whether Tarski's is really a correspondence
theory or not is too complicated a matter to be pursued
here.

It is also part of this doctrine to think of states of
affairs, facts, etc.—that is, items of the second sort—as
themselves composed of various kinds of constituents or
objects, such as persons, places, or things. It is this part of
the theory that traditionally imported, though generally in
an inexplicit form, the concept of reference. We shall see
how this works later. Thus, the fact that the cat is on the
mat, to which the true sentence "The cat is on the mat" is
said to correspond, is made up of such objects as a cat and
a mat, and standing in a certain spatial relationship to one
another. These constituents in turn are viewed as possessing
various features, qualities, characteristics, or properties
and/or (as in the above example) standing in certain kinds
of relationships to one another.

Those who espouse the correspondence theory are
thus disposed to think about truth in two different, but
closely connected, ways: they think, first, that a sentence
(proposition, statement, etc.) is *about* its corresponding
states of affairs, facts, etc., and, second, that in such a case

its predicate term is true *of* the object referred to by the subject term. The operative notions of the theory are thus two: A sentence (statement, proposition, etc.) is said to be *true simpliciter* when, in being about some state of affairs or fact, it corresponds to such a state of affairs or fact. Its predicate is also said to be *true of* some object or constituent of such a state of affairs or fact under such conditions. Many writers fail to distinguish these two uses of "true" and shift unreflectively between them.

Strawson is a case in point. In his work, "true" and "true of" are conflated and give way to talk "about" objects. According to Strawson, when a statement is true, it is "about" the objects being referred to by the speaker. The problem of fiction arises for him in terms of the question "How can a statement be about a fictitious object, since such an object does not exist?" His answer, which is a sophisticated version of option 3 mentioned in section 1, is that they are about such objects in a "secondary" or derivative sense of "about." Other writers, Quine for instance, explicitly make the distinction between "true" and "true of." For him, it is the predicate term or the verb phrase that is "true of" the object and the sentence per se that is "true" simpliciter. In Marcus and Kripke a proper name allows one to speak *about* the object. In this respect, their views have some affinities with Strawson's, but there are substantial differences as well.

The point to be emphasized in this connection is that the correspondence theory typically requires not only the *existence* of such items as states of affairs and their analogues but also the *existence* of the items comprising them before a statement or a sentence can be said to be either true simpliciter or to be true of those items. These two notions are beautifully conflated in Aristotle's famous formulation of the concept of truth: "To say of what is that it is not, or of what is not that it is, is false; while to say of what is that it is, or of what is not that it is not, is true" (*Metaphysics*, bk. 4, chap. 7).

By itself, of course, the correspondence theory raises no special difficulties about fiction. But when coupled with two further conditions, it directly gives rise to the problem. The first of these is that some of the sentences or statements about the characters or events in fiction seem to be true *simpliciter*. Thus it seems flatly true to say that Ethan Frome limped, that he was taciturn, and that he lived in a New England city called "Starkfield." But, second, if it is true to say these things *about* Ethan Frome, then according to the correspondence theory, it follows that there must exist, or have existed, someone *of* whom these statements are true.

When the second condition is added to the above, we have the problem in a full-blown form. For although it seems persuasive to say that such sentences are true simpliciter, and hence true of such entities, we also know that fictitious entities do not exist and have never existed. We know, that is, that Ethan Frome was never born, that he never died in New England, and that there is not and never was any such place as Starkfield—in short, that there does not exist, and never has existed, anyone or any place of whom these statements can be true. Put succinctly, the problem of fiction arises when, for this class of sentences, the ascription "true" seems to entail the ascription "true of" and yet there is nothing to which the latter ascription can apply.

FIVE

What, then, does one do when faced with such plausible but conflicting ways of speaking about fictitious characters or objects, such as Ethan Frome? The attempt to answer this kind of question gives rise to three theories that Strawson rejects. As we shall see, each of the theories concerned (and this is also true of Strawson) refuses to abandon the traditional correspondence account of truth; each in short, casts about for ways of dealing with fictitious entities, objects, and events that are compatible with the correspondence account.

The first group of such theorists is usually depicted as grasping the nettle and its seemingly paradoxical consequences, that is, as agreeing or perhaps reluctantly conceding that such objects and characters do exist. According to Barry Smith in his brilliant book *Austrian Philosophy*, Meinong espoused such a view, holding that the Fountain of Youth, the Round Square, the Golden Mountain, and Hamlet really do exist, since true judgments can be formed about them. Meinong's view, Smith states, originated in Twardowski's *On the Content and Object of Presentations of 1894* and embraced an ontology that contends that transcendent objects are divided into the two classes of existing and nonexisting. Meinong's theory provides an account of how mental acts are directed toward the objects mentioned in fiction and even toward impossible entities of every sort. As Smith puts it, "Meinong sought to free himself from that 'prejudice in favour of the actual' which had in his eyes been characteristic of all previous metaphysics."[16]

Meinong's view is more complicated than I can pursue in detail here. It turns on a distinction between subsistent and existent objects. On one reading of his theory, he seems to be committed at most to the position that fictitious objects exist "in some sense or other," and thus not to be a straightforward representative of this position. Russell, of course, thought he was, and interpreted him as a philosopher who is willing to accept the paradoxical consequences of the correspondence theory. Let us assume for our purposes, as Strawson also seems to have done, that Russell was right. Insofar as this is so, Strawson is in opposition to Meinong, or indeed to anyone, if there be such, who has ever held that such objects literally *exist*, call it what one may. If we label this the first of the three theories under consideration, we can say that Strawson categorically rejects it: there is no doubt in his mind that such objects as Sherlock Holmes and the Fountain of Youth do not exist in any literal sense of the term.

A second view rejected by Strawson but clearly held by a number of philosophers is to be found in Russell's early work. This view exhibits a "more robust sense of reality" vis-à-vis fiction, as Russell puts it in describing himself.[17] Russell starts from the position that characters in fiction or mythology do not exist and have never existed, that is, "were not composed of flesh and blood." Russell, like Meinong, was also unwilling to abandon the correspondence theory. Russell's solution to the dilemma was to state that no person named "Ethan Frome" exists or ever did exist—that no demographic chart of the period or place in which Ethan Frome supposedly lived would have included his name—but that what did exist were certain words printed in various books or documents, words purporting to describe someone.

His way of stating this point was to say that the apparent proper name "Ethan Frome" is an abbreviation for such describing phrases, and that all sentences containing this apparent name as a primary occurrence are literally false, since they in fact described nothing. This result amounts to the application of his theory of descriptions to fiction, and it contains three parts importantly different from one another: (1) that no persons, under a certain description, ever lived in Starkfield, (2) that talk about Ethan Frome must be translated into, or be understood as, talk about words and sentences appearing in the novel *Ethan Frome* by Edith Wharton, and (3) that the sentences purporting to be about a certain person named "Ethan Frome," when taken literally, are all of them false.

This set of conditions, when conjoined, provides an overall account that is inconsistent with the position that Ethan Frome literally exists or did exist. It is important to note that not all the elements comprising this account are incompatible with the view that Ethan Frome exists *in some sense or other*. In particular, premise 2, that talk about Ethan Frome is to be understood as talk about words and sentences in a certain novel, is consistent with the thesis that Ethan Frome exists as a character in a novel, but more of this later. We can summarize this second view as maintaining that such fictitious objects or characters do not literally exist and that sentences purporting to be about them are all of them literally false. Strawson demurs from the second part of this assessment; as we shall see, he denies that such sentences are always literally false.

There is, finally, a third view that Strawson rejects. This is a view attributed to some of the logical positivists. According to proponents of this view, the characteristic sentences of fiction or mythology—being about "objects," "places," and "events" whose existence can neither be confirmed nor disconfirmed by any empirical procedures— are not cognitively meaningful at all. Given that every meaningful sentence is either a tautology or verifiable in principle, and accordingly is either true or false, and given that the characteristic sentences of fiction are neither tautologous nor verifiable, it follows that they are neither true nor false. This strategy provides another way of saving the correspondence theory by arguing, in effect, that it does not apply to the language of fiction. In saying this, however, I should emphasize that some of these philosophers held that sentences of fiction are or might be meaningful in derivative or secondary senses of meaning—perhaps being "pictorially" or "emotively" meaningful, as Herbert Feigl once suggested.[18] The notion that they are meaningful in a derivative sense suggests that these writers might have been attracted to option 3 of section 1.

SIX

We have here, then, three views—all of which Strawson rejects:

• The view that some of the characteristic sentences of fiction are literally true, and hence that the items to which they refer must exist or have existed. On this view, the ordinary conception of proper names is retained. "Hamlet" is a proper name and refers to an object that exists (in some sense).

• The view that such sentences are always false when the names of fictitious objects have a primary occurrence in them. On Russell's view, sentences containing empty proper names are to be analyzed in accordance with the theory of descriptions, and in that account, proper names are abbreviations for descriptions. They thus differ from what ordinary persons would call "proper names."

• The view that such sentences are literally, or factually, meaningless. The sentences are meaningless because their descriptive components are meaningless. And these are meaningless because they do not denote anything.

Of course, it is important to stress that theorists who espoused the latter two views did not regard *all* the sentences that occur in fiction as being false or nonsensical, nor did they regard all the proper names that occur in them as lacking reference. Such a sentence as "George Washington was the first president of the United States of America" might well appear in a work of fiction and, depending on the context, would not only be meaningful but also true in a straightforward sense of the term. In that sentence, as so used, "George Washington" would be a proper name and would have a referent.

Rather, such theorists denied that what I have called "the characteristic sentences" of fiction are true in a straightforward sense of the term. As an example of such a sentence, I might cite the following, taken from Henry James's novel *The American:* "Christopher Newman stood gravely silent while his native penetration admonished him." Some of these theorists, to be sure, held even stronger views about such sentences, extending the class of characteristic sentences of fiction to include those uttered *about* the characters in fiction by readers and critics. An example of such a sentence might be "Christopher Newman was an American who traveled to Europe in the nineteenth century," or to hearken back to an earlier example, "Ethan Frome was born in Starkfield and was a taciturn man who limped." According to these philosophers, because the names of the characters mentioned in these sentences have a primary occurrence in them, they cannot be regarded as literally true. Moreover, the so-called "proper names" cannot be proper names, because they lack referents.

The reason why some philosophers have supposed that such sentences as these cannot be true and must either be false or nonsensical is thus simple to explain. In the cases mentioned, their argument might run as follows: Since the characters Christopher Newman and Ethan Frome do not exist and have never existed, are not and have never been creatures of flesh and blood, these sentences (and their names) cannot literally be about anyone or anything. Insofar as they purport to be about two human beings who lived in the nineteenth century, they are literally false or without cognitive sense, depending on how one analyzes them.

Strawson, as I have indicated, rejects each of these accounts. It seems clear to him that it is wrong to say that such objects really exist and also wrong to say that sentences like those I have quoted are either false or nonsensical. Against those philosophers who say that such sentences are nonsensical, Strawson invokes the technical distinction between a *sentence* and the *statement* that someone on a particular occasion uses the sentence to make. The point of the distinction is to establish that such sentences are perfectly meaningful, even though in fiction they may not be employed by those who utter them to make statements that are either true or false. For example, if someone were now to say "The King of France is wise," that person would be uttering a sentence (of English) that is perfectly meaningful. But even if that person were genuinely serious in saying what he does, he would not be employing it to make a statement—that is, something that is true or false—since there is no King of France. Before a sentence containing a referring expression in the subject place, such as a proper name, can be used to make a statement, the item mentioned by the subject term must exist. Strawson's views here prefigure those that Marcus and Kripke were to adopt later.

The point that Strawson wishes to emphasize is that the sentence, being a standard sentence of English, is meaningful. Therefore, on particular occasions it can be used to say things that are true or false; that is, it can be used to make a statement. If the history of France should suddenly alter, the sentence "The King of France is wise" might be employed to make a true statement about a future or present monarch of France. And possibly in the past, say in the reign of Louis XIV, this same sentence might have been used to make a true statement about that monarch. Accordingly, Strawson would argue, such a sentence as "Christopher Newman stood gravely silent, while his native penetration admonished him" is not nonsense. It is a meaningful sentence, since it could be used on some occasion to speak about some actually existing person, Christopher Newman and, in being so used, perhaps to make a true assertion about him. The view that such sentences are in general nonsensical is thus to be rejected. In this respect, Strawson's argument effectively illustrates how misleading general theories can be.

Against those philosophers, like Russell, who claim that such sentences are *always* false, Strawson adopts an analogous procedure. He again appeals to the distinction between a sentence and the use to which it can be put for making true or false statements. His contention is that, taken by itself, a *sentence,* as distinct from a statement, is *never* true or false, even if it is meaningful. Unlike the positivists, who held that every meaningful sentence is either true or false, Strawson drew a distinction between the meaningfulness of a sentence and its capacity, under various conditions of use, to be either true or false. On particular occasions it may be used by someone to make a (true or false) statement about someone or something. But this is possible only if that someone or something exists or has existed. It is at this point that reference enters his account. Unless there is something to be referred to— named or described—the sentence is neither true nor false. Since Christopher Newman, the character mentioned in James's novel, does not exist and has never existed, sentences in that work containing the expression "Christopher Newman" are not being used to make either true or false statements about anyone. It is thus incorrect to say, as Russell did, that sentences like these must always be false.

What, then, is Strawson's own view about the nature of fiction? In the light of what I have already said, the answer is readily at hand. For him, works of fiction deal with make-believe. Since this is so, the characters mentioned in fiction do not really exist, and accordingly, talk about them does not raise considerations of truth or falsity. But they are not nonsensical either. The proper way to assess the language of fiction, in his view, is to see that the sorts of sentences he describes as "overtly fictional" are not being used to make statements at all. For the statement-making use of language *presupposes* that the items being referred to by the speaker do in fact exist. And for Strawson, this is true not only of the characteristic sentences that occur in works of fiction but also of those characteristic sentences that are uttered about such works. He writes in this connection,

And this is where the distinction I drew earlier can help us. The sentence, "The king of France is wise," is certainly significant: but this does not mean that any particular use of it is true or false. We use it truly or falsely when we use it to talk about someone; when, in using the expression, "The king of France," we are in fact mentioning someone. The fact that the sentence and the expression, respectively, are significant just is the fact that the sentence *could* be used, in certain circumstances, to say something true or false, that the expression *could* be used in certain circumstances to mention a particular person; and to know their meaning is to know what sort of circumstances these are. So when we utter the sentence without in fact mentioning anybody by the use of the phrase "The king of France," the sentence does not cease to be significant; we simply fail to say anything true or false because we simply *fail* to mention anybody by this particular use of that perfectly significant phrase. It is, if you like, a spurious use of the sentence, and a spurious use of the expression;

though we may (or may not) mistakenly think it a genuine use.

And such spurious uses are very familiar. Sophisticated romancing, sophisticated fiction depend on them. If I began "The king of France is wise," and went on, "and he lives in a golden castle and has a hundred wives," and so on, a hearer would understand me perfectly well, without supposing *either* that I was talking about a particular person, or that I was making a false statement to the effect that there existed such a person as my words described. It is worth adding that where the use of sentences and expressions is overtly fictional, the sense of the word "about" may change. As Moore said, it is perfectly natural and correct to say that some of the statements in *Pickwick Papers* are *about* Mr. Pickwick. But where the use of sentences and expressions is not overtly fictional, this use of "about" seems less correct, i.e., it would not *in general* be correct to say that a statement was about Mr. X, or the so-and-so, unless there were such a person or thing. So it is where the romancing is in danger of being taken seriously that we might answer the question, "Who is he talking about?" with "He's not talking about anybody," but in saying this, we are not saying that what he is saying is either false or nonsense.[19]

As this quotation indicates, Strawson's approach to the problem of fiction rests upon the assumption that any solution to it must leave the correspondence theory intact. Thus, like the other writers I have mentioned, he wishes to give an analysis of what he calls "overtly fictional" sentences that will be compatible with adherence to the correspondence theory of truth. He does this by denying, in effect, that the correspondence theory is directly applicable to such overtly fictional sentences. For him, as we have seen, considerations of truth or falsity arise only when, for a given class of sentences, certain existential presuppositions are satisfied. The items being referred to must in fact exist. Since this condition is not satisfied by overtly fictional sentences, the correspondence theory does not apply to them.

I said earlier that Strawson's approach to the problem of fiction has marked advantages over those of his predecessors. I also stated that it has serious defects. I now wish to speak to each of these points.

The advantages are twofold. In arguing that the characteristic sentences of fiction are never employed for statement-making purposes, Strawson provides a conceptual wedge for distinguishing fiction as a *genre* so that the paradigms invoked by Meinong, Russell, and some logical positivists do not apply. Whether Kripke was in fact influenced by Strawson on this point is not clear, yet his view that proper names as tags cannot apply to fictive entities suggests such an influence. Like Strawson, he draws a sharp line between the fictive and nonfictive for semantic purposes.

As a result of Strawson's analysis one is now able to look at works of fiction with a freer eye and without assimilating its language to that provided by models derived from science and earlier versions of logical theory. He thus clears the ground for an appraisal of fiction in its own terms. But it is also true that he fails to exploit the full range of possibilities embodied in this move. In arguing that "overtly fictional" sentences can *never* be true or false, he falls heir to a mistake that parallels what he exposes in Russell, who simplistically analyzes all such sentences according to one pattern—being literally false. Strawson's simplistic mistake is to argue that all such sentences, when used in fiction, are neither true nor false in any straightforward sense of these terms. As we shall see, this is a serious mistake, but one need not be committed to this inference in accepting the important distinctions upon which it rests. When these distinctions are developed in a different direction, it becomes possible to characterize fiction in new and perspicuous terms.

A second commendatory feature of his account lies in his refusal to assume that the issue about fictive discourse concerns ontology, to be resolved by an appeal to the facts. While conceding that some persons, perhaps young children, might take fictional accounts to be descriptions of real persons and of real happenings, he thinks that most people do not, indeed, that this is not where the issue lies. He does not suppose, that is, that most people believe that Sherlock Holmes and Ethan Frome were real persons, that their names might be found in demographic lists of nineteenth century Englishmen and Americans. Russell speaks about Meinong as if the latter were suffering from just this sort of confusion, and he presents the theory of descriptions as if it were a conceptual device for exorcising the haunting belief that fictitious objects really exist.

But for Strawson, it is a serious defect in Russell's account that he should have posed the issue in these terms. Strawson sees clearly that it is not an ontological question but rather an issue about how fiction is to be characterized or described. The issue of whether fictitious objects exist is thus at no time an open question for him. Of course, such objects, places, etc., do not exist, and given this fact, what remains open for profitable discussion is how to analyze the overtly fictional sentences that purport to be "about" such objects, places, and events.

This perspective transforms the issue in three ways: first, by shifting the question of the status of objects of fiction from the center of consideration; second, by locating its crux in the question of how fiction is best to be described or characterized; and third, by identifying this last question with the question of how *the language of fiction* is to be analyzed. The first two transformations are wholly admirable. They not only free us from the bondage of past conceptual confusion, but they also point the way to new and fruitful solutions. In these respects, then, Strawson's work represents an advance over that of his predecessors. But at the same time it involves serious confusions of its own, insofar as it identifies questions about how fiction is to be characterized with questions about the language of fiction. In the next two sections I shall illustrate why and how this is so.

NINE

___

The matter is complex; unpacking it, I find that the conflation of the issue of how to understand fiction with the issue of how to analyze fictional discourse rests upon five mistaken principles, or theses. These are (1) that there is a special language of fiction; (2) that, accordingly, there are "overtly fictional" sentences that belong to, or even make up, this language; (3) that such sentences are never true or false, since certain existential presuppositions fail to be satisfied; (4) that, accordingly, making statements within or about fiction is not possible through the use of such sentences and the putative proper names they contain. All of these mistakes depend on a fifth error; they rest on what I shall call an "axiom of referring." Strawson's formulation of the axiom is this: "It would not in general be correct to say that a statement was about Mr. X, or the so-and-so, unless there were such a person or thing" ("On Referring," p. 35 in the Flew anthology). Other philosophers have advanced variations on this theme. For example, in *Speech Acts,* John Searle states, "Whatever is referred to must exist" (p. 77), and he calls it "the axiom of existence."

As the quotation from which Strawson's remark is taken indicates, he is making a claim about everyday discourse. His contention is that in ordinary English it is not, strictly speaking, correct to claim to be speaking about someone or something unless that someone or something exists. The word "about" plays a key role in this contention; by altering Strawson's formulation slightly, we can see that the principle on which he relies states the following:

Axiom of referring   One cannot use a term to refer to (speak "about") a thing unless that thing exists.

It is this principle that I call the axiom of referring, and it is from this principle that the foregoing mistakes derive.

How they derive from this so-called "axiom" is too complicated to be explored here in detail, and in any case, such an exploration would represent a divagation from my main line of argument. But broadly speaking, a summary version of the diagnosis would show that if one begins from Strawson's "commonsense outlook," i.e., if one starts from the premise or assumption that fictitious objects do not exist, then it is natural, following the axiom, to assume that one cannot speak about such objects in any straightforward sense of "about." The direct-reference theorists have pushed this intuition even further in arguing that proper names are tags and that one cannot tag, and hence cannot name, anything that does not exist. This inference in turn gives rise to the notion that it is impossible to make statements about, or refer to, fictive objects, since for the class of sentences involved, the requisite existential conditions have not been satisfied. But this ploy depends crucially on the idea that there is a class of "overtly fictional" sentences whose members can be identified. This step, finally, presupposes that there is a special "language of fiction" composed in part of such sentences. All these moves culminate in the view that the question of how fiction is to be characterized is seen as identical with the question of how such characteristic sentences are to be analyzed. This is, in essence, the package that Strawson presents us with.

This diagnosis, to be sure, does not show that the principles appealed to by Strawson are mistaken. On what grounds, then, do I advance this further claim that they are? And what bearing would such a claim have, if true, upon efforts to give a characterization of fiction? In the next section of this chapter I attempt to answer these questions.

TEN

I have indicated above why I think the "axiom of referring" lies at the source of four serious mistakes Strawson commits in his consideration of fiction. To establish individually and sequentially that each is a mistake would involve dealing with them in the kind of detail that is impossible here. My strategy instead will be to show why the axiom of referring is not acceptable. Remarks about the other four principles will be made *en passant* in the course of dealing with the axiom of referring. This analysis will lead us to a solution to the problem of the relationship between proper names and their fictive referents.

What I will attempt to show is that the axiom of referring is either vacuous, a kind of tautology if true (hence my reference to it as an "axiom"), or if not vacuous, false. It is doubtful, in fact, that Strawson would wish to defend it on the ground that it is a tautology, since he thinks that it involves a significant claim about everyday speech. This claim is to the effect that it is not in general correct to say that one can speak about an object, in a straightforward sense of "about," unless that object exists. This claim thus parallels the direct-reference notion that one cannot tag an object unless the object exists. Thus the more important challenge here will be to show that Strawson's claim is simply false.

First, then, I wish to show that an argument that Strawson adduces in support of the axiom is not sound. This move, even if correct, of course does not show that the axiom is false, but it will neutralize a main ground for holding it to be true. My argument is as follows. According to Strawson, in an ordinary sense of the word "use," we may say that *the same use* is being made of a referring expression if that expression is being used (say by two different people) to refer to the same object or thing. Thus, A, who says "The Queen of England is wise," and B, who says "The Queen of England is married," are both making the same use of the expression "The Queen of England" if they both use it to refer to the same person, for example, Elizabeth II.

On the other hand, if the same expression is used to refer to different individuals (Elizabeth I and Elizabeth II), then a *different* use is being made of it in those circumstances. From the conjunction of these principles, Strawson infers that an expression *has a use* only if there is an object to which it refers or can refer to. When this condition is not satisfied, "no use" is being made of the expression. Or, as he puts it in the long quotation I gave above, "it is a spurious use of the expression." This is why a sentence containing the expression cannot be "about" anything in a straightforward sense of "about."

The notion that an expression has a use if and only if a particular individual exists to whom it can refer is simply, in a different guise, the axiom of referring. The direct-reference thesis that one cannot tag a nonexistent object is a variant of this same "axiom." We thus find Strawson appealing to an axiom that is analogous to what he attacks Russell for espousing. In Russell, the axiom states that "N" can be a genuine proper name if and only if there exists an

N that "N" names. Strawson's axiom is thus a variant of the "Fido"-Fido theory of naming that he himself goes to such pains to discredit in "On Referring."

But interpreted as a claim about ordinary English, this principle is clearly false. No dictionary I have consulted, for example, gives an entry expansion for the term "use" that corresponds to anything like this axiom. In brief, my contention is that Strawson's argument in favor of the axiom of referring stems from a misuse of "use," and accordingly that the argument does not go through. There is thus no reason, if his argument supposedly supplies such a reason, for accepting the claim that we cannot refer to objects that do not exist. There is thus no reason to believe that because they do not exist, we cannot refer to such fictitious objects as Ethan Frome or the Golden Mountain.

One might wish to defend the axiom by arguing that Ethan Frome "exists in fiction" and because he exists in fiction, we can refer to him. This is to select option 4 of section 1. To push this point, a proponent of option 4 might say that if Ethan Frome did not exist at all, in fiction or otherwise, we cannot refer to him at all, and the axiom would hold. But in effect, this is to imply that in those cases where we cannot form names or descriptions, nothing exists to be named or described. But this is to beg the question and to render the principle vacuous. A variant of this move is to hold that it is a mistake to think that everything that exists must occupy spatiotemporal coordinates or be composed of corporeal matter. On this view, everything—in a broad sense of "thing"—exists, and the axiom holds. But as I have indicated, such a doctrine renders the axiom tautologous, and therefore this is not an interpretation of it that Strawson would support.

Independent of this negative result, there are positive grounds for believing that we do in fact use language to refer to nonexistent objects. These grounds stem from the fact that we do say things that are true or false about such objects. It is true to say that Ethan Frome limped and that he was born in Starkfield, and false to say otherwise. In saying these things, we are speaking about Ethan Frome, not in any secondary sense of "about," if there be such, but in the same sense of "about" in which I have been speaking about Saul Kripke in the course of saying that he had advanced such and such a doctrine about natural-kind terms and proper names. More generally, whatever can be said about nonfictional objects can be said about fictional objects, and whatever can be said in our daily talk outside of fiction, can be said within or about fiction. The "language of fiction" includes jokes, lies, true and false statements, direct and indirect references, asides, and every possible *use* of language.

Strawson's approach to the language of fiction goes wrong through his adherence to the axiom of referring. His reliance upon it disposes him to say that since "overtly fictional" uses of language do not refer to anyone or anything, considerations of truth and falsity do not arise when sentences containing certain referring expressions are employed to speak *about* fictitious objects. He thus concludes that such sentences form a special class differing from nonfictive sentences in involving spurious or empty uses of language, and that this difference marks the difference between fiction and nonfiction. In the end, the difference between fiction and nonfiction thus coincides, in his view, with the difference between the statement-making and non-statement-making uses of language. But, as I have indicated, this is far too narrow, far too inaccurate, a base for characterizing fiction.

In this chapter I do not propose a general characterization of fiction, even assuming (what is dubious) that this is possible. Instead, I wish to rule out some characterizations that purport to be characterizations of fiction and, in the course of doing so, to make two general points about fiction.

In the revised version of "On Referring" that appeared in the Flew volume, Strawson drew a distinction between what he calls sophisticated and unsophisticated fiction. According to him, the unsophisticated kind begins, "Once upon a time there was . . . ," while the sophisticated kind might begin, "The king of France is wise, and he lives in a golden castle and has a hundred wives." Since these are his examples of fiction, it appears that Strawson thinks of fiction as characteristically dealing with make-believe and therefore tends to look for language that can be clearly recognized as dealing with make-believe. No doubt such opening phrases as he cites do often mark the opening of fairy tales, and no doubt fairy tales deal with make-believe, but it is highly dubious that children's stories of this kind are to be taken as paradigms of fiction. Like many theorists, Strawson is working with too limited a set of examples, as we have seen in previous chapters. Compare and contrast the examples he gives with the opening sentences of a work of fiction, *A Rebours,* by J. K. Huysmans:

To judge by such family portraits as were preserved in the Chateau de Lourps, the race of the Floressas des Esseintes had been composed in olden days of stalwart veterans of wars, grim knights with scowling visages. Imprisoned in the old-fashioned picture frames that seemed all too narrow to contain their broad shoulders, they glared out alarmingly at the spectator, who was equally impressed by the fixed stare in the eyes, the martial curl of the moustaches and the noble development of the chests encased in enormous steel cuirasses.

Though this passage mentions "olden days of stalwart veterans of the wars," it is not overtly connected with make-believe. Indeed, there is no way of telling from the language per se who or what the author is describing; therefore, from a *sample* of the words the author uses, one cannot determine that he is writing fiction. His words could equally well apply to an historically accurate account of his or some other family.

A serious mistake of Strawson's, and of many writers who have dealt with the problem of fiction, is to assume that there are tell-tale hints in the language per se that indicate whether the work is a work of fiction or not. It may be characteristic of works of fiction that they deal with events that never happened or with events that happened differently from those described or with "persons" whose names never appeared in any demographic list, but in general this cannot be determined by fixing even on sentences or paragraphs that are in Strawson's sense "overtly fictional." In fact, many works of fiction use real people and real events as integral parts of their story. When an author sets a detective story in San Francisco, it is typically the real San Francisco that he is referring to, not a fictive San Francisco, even if some of what he says about the real San Francisco is not true. He does this to evoke certain sentiments and other reactions the reader already has about the real city. This is part of how the novel works. The point is perhaps easier to see with respect to historical fiction. If a novelist writes about George Washington, it is the real George Washington that is being referred to. The novelist relies upon the reader's knowledge of Washington to supply all sorts of information that would otherwise be tedious or even impossible to supply.

My first point, then, is that it is typically whole works, whole stories, that are to be described as fiction, and that such an ascription to a story or narration is an assessment or judgment that the reader makes about such a work on the basis of considerations extraneous to the language in which it is couched. To be sure, we do speak of particular descriptions of events, happenings, and characters in a given work as "fictitious," but from this it does not follow that the works containing such descriptions are themselves fiction. Consider the conversations between the members of the Persian court in Herodotus's *History*. They might well be (in fact, they are usually described as) fictitious, since Herotodus never witnessed them, but neither his account of what happened nor the overall work itself is to be characterized as fiction. Moreover, from the fact that such conversations are fictitious, it does not follow that the persons to whom they are attributed are fictitious. Real persons might well have been the speakers of words that are wholly made up by an author. The appellation "fiction" properly belongs to a whole work and only derivately to individual descriptions within it.

My second point is this: fiction accordingly contains no characteristic set of words or uses of language on the basis of which per se they can be determined to be fiction. As I have stated above, fiction, not untypically, involves all possible uses of language and in principle can contain every conceivable well-formed sentence of the language in which it is written. The idea that there is a special category of fictive sentences and that the members of this category can be identified, at least partly, with those whose existential conditions fail to be satisfied is thus a philosophical fiction about fiction.

ELEVEN

What significance do the preceding remarks have for direct-reference theories? I submit that we should abandon the "axiom of referring" in any of its forms. This has the following consequences: (1) It entails that the proper names used to refer to fictive entities, such as "Sherlock Holmes" and "Odysseus," really are proper names and are not to be distinguished from the names of nonfictive entities, such as "Saul Kripke" and "Ruth Marcus." (2) It entails that we should abandon the notion that proper names are tags. I agree that if a tag is a label that one can apply to an object, one cannot tag things that do not exist or that are mere possibilia, as Marcus argues. Thus abandoning the notion that proper names are tags, we can then use proper names to refer to fictive entities just as ordinary speakers do. We would thus need no special theory about proper names as used in fiction. (3) It entails that we do not have to construe proper names as abbreviated descriptions in fictive contexts. They are just proper names in the ordinary sense of that term. So Russell's theory of definite descriptions and the theory of direct reference are both excluded. (4) It entails that there is no difference in referential power between names and descriptions. I can refer to a neighbor as "the bald man next door" or as "James Wilson." Which I do will depend on various contextual factors, but naming has no special referential sanctity in such cases. Depending on circumstances, either expression can do the job equally well. (5) It entails that in doing philosophy by example, as I have been urging throughout this study, we must distinguish between such notions as mentioning x, and referring to x, and also between such notions as picking out x and identifying x. Tagging, on direct-reference accounts, presumably *always* involves picking out or identifying something. These two feats are not only different actions (e.g., I can pick out items from a group without being able to identify them); they are also completely different from either mentioning or referring to something. Both of the latter are actions I can perform without picking out or identifying anything. I can mention by name and say that Jack the Ripper was the person who murdered x, without being able to identify Jack the Ripper by sight or in any other way, and certainly without being able, let us say, to pick him out of a group of suspects in a police lineup.

So my conclusion is that Strawson was right in at least one fundamental respect about how various linguistic expressions can be used for referential purposes. Proper names, descriptions, demonstrative pronouns, etc., can be used to refer to or mention a particular individual, place, or thing. But Strawson was wrong in thinking that if the "individual" or "place" is fictional, the reference has to be indirect, or to be "about" the individual in a secondary sense. If we distinguish referring, whether in fictive or nonfictive contexts, from tagging, then there is no special problem about how to describe the use of proper names in fiction. As referring expressions, their functions are identical in all contexts.

ONE

In the previous chapter we saw wide divergencies in how direct-reference theorists answer the question "Do proper names have meaning?" Kripke, for example, is very cagey in this respect, and it is difficult to decide whether he does or does not hold that proper names have meaning. Some theorists, following the early Russell of "On Denoting" and the very late Russell of the *Inquiry into Meaning and Truth* and *Human Knowledge,* assert that proper names mean the objects they denote. As Ruth Marcus says, "Speaking slightly paradoxically, the 'meaning' of a name *is* its referent."[1] Others, belonging to the tradition initiated by Mill, claim that proper names are, strictly speaking, "meaningless." This is a position that at other times Marcus has also espoused. On that view, proper names simply function as tags or labels. All direct-reference theorists agree, of course, that proper names differ from definite descriptions in their semantic functions, and that proper names lack connotation or *sinn.*

All Russellian and Millian views give rise to difficult puzzles. For example, Mill states that some sentences containing proper names are meaningful, and indeed that some are true. But how can they be meaningful? Intuitively, one tends to think that the meaning of any complex expression is a function of its simpler constituents and if any of them lacks meaning, the complex expression will as well. Therefore, if a proper name occurring in a sentence is meaningless, the sentence will be meaningless too. There are analogous difficulties for the position that proper names mean their bearers but have no meaning in an intensional sense. Again, if propositions are the intensional meanings expressed by sentences, one must explain how a proposition can have meaning if one of its key constituents lacks intensional meaning.

In this chapter I wish to look at Russell's own views about these matters, since they are the source of most contemporary theories of direct reference. Russell's theory is unusual in one respect. He asserts, as mentioned, that proper names have meaning but only in a denotational sense. Most contemporary direct-reference theorists claim that descriptions possess meaning in an intensional sense, so they have no trouble explaining how sentences containing descriptions can be meaningful. Their trouble stems from proper names. But Russell denies that descriptions have any meaning at all outside of the sentential contexts in which they occur. This is what he means by saying that descriptions are incomplete symbols. His problem is thus the reverse of theirs. It is to explain how a sentence containing a description can be meaningful. Semantic holism, in certain forms, is one answer to all of these problems. That kind of holist will argue against any compositional thesis that holds that the meaning of a complex expression is a direct function of the meaning of its constituents. Instead, he or she will give an account of meaning that gives primacy to whole units rather than to their parts. Russell's theory of descriptions is an ingenious form of holism. But there are many kinds of semantic holism. To distinguish his from others, I shall begin with some general comments about holism.

In the philosophy of language it is generally agreed that holism is the doctrine that meaning is to be located in units of language that are larger than subparts of those units. This has become, especially since the work of Quine, the preferred view of many contemporary philosophers. In the twentieth century there have been, and still are, two main versions of this doctrine. The first states that the basic unit of meaning is the sentence (proposition, statement, assertion) in contrast to sentential constituents, such as individual words or phrases. The second contends that the basic unit of meaning is the whole language in contrast to any of its subconstituents, including sentences as well as individual words and phrases.

Frege and the early Wittgenstein are philosophers who subscribe to the first version. In the *Tractatus,* for example, Wittgenstein writes, "Only propositions have sense; only in the nexus of a proposition does a name have meaning" (prop. 3.3). As the quotation indicates, Wittgenstein is explicitly asserting that *only* propositions have sense or meaning and by this implying that no larger or smaller units do; in particular in asserting that only in the context of a proposition does a name have meaning, he is implying that names do not have independent meaning. So it is the proposition (an entity expressed by a sentence) that is the basic unit of meaning. There is a slight use/mention confusion in his remark, since names and sentences are linguistic entities, whereas propositions are not; so na es do not occur in propositions. But we can set aside this terminological point and (using his parlance) say that for him, names have meaning in a nonbasic way. It is clear from the quotation that he is denying the famous Russellian view that names have independent meaning—independent, that is, of any context.

The later Wittgenstein, Quine, and Putnam have espoused the second version of holism. As Wittgenstein tells us in the *Investigations,* "To understand a sentence means to understand a language" (sec. 199).

In a later essay Quine describes his position as follows: "The primary reference for my holism is 'Two Dogmas'."[2] If we look at that early text (1950) we find him saying,

The dogma of reductionism survives in the supposition that each statement, taken in isolation from its fellows, can admit of confirmation or infirmation at all. My countersuggestion, issuing essentially from Carnap's doctrine of the physical world in the *Aufbau,* is that our statements about the external world face the tribunal of sense experience not individually but only as a corporate body.[3]

A similar view is found in Saussure, who writes this in his *Course in General Linguistics* (p. 120):

Whether we take the signified or the signifier, language has neither ideas nor sounds that existed before the linguistic system, but only conceptual and phonic differences that have issued from the system. The idea or phonic substance that a sound contains is of less importance than the other signs that surround it.

These quotations reveal a different point of view from the first one mentioned. Their authors are now taking "a language," "the corporate body," or "the linguistic system" to be the basic repository of meaning. Sentences, ideas, phonemes—i.e., subunits of "the corporate body" or the system—have meaning only in a parasitic or perhaps symbiotic sense. They obtain whatever meaning they have as parts of synoptic wholes.

Both of these contrasting versions of holism rest upon a plausible assumption, namely that what is true of a whole is not necessarily true of any of its parts. So a nation can be said to be populous, though this predicate cannot sensibly be applied to any of its citizens. A good reason for distinguishing between the meaning of the whole unit and that of its parts is that some (or perhaps even all) of its parts may not have independent meaning. In such a case one can ascribe the predicate "meaningful" to the larger but not to the smaller unit. The early Wittgenstein, as we have seen, adopts just this stance. Ferry and Renaut interpret Saussure as espousing a similar view. According to them, he is saying that apart from a "chain of signifiers" no signifier "can be grasped in itself" (*French Philosophy of the Sixties: An Essay on Antihumanism* [1990], p. 137).

As mentioned, there are many variants of holism. It has been argued, for example, that constituents of semantic wholes may have independent meanings and yet in aggregate their meaning does not always equal that of the whole. A different thesis is that sentences have a certain kind of independent meaning but that one cannot understand what they mean until they are embedded in a broader context, such as the whole language. And sometimes it is suggested that individual sentences can be understood not on their own but only when used in particular contexts, some of which may not be linguistic. The essential point that distinguishes holism as a semantic theory is the priority (however construed) it gives to larger rather than to smaller units of language.

TWO

In this chapter I will focus only on the first of these views, i.e., that the sentence rather than the system or the language is the basic unit of meaning. I do so for various reasons, chiefly because of the vagueness of the more general forms of semantic holism. What does Wittgenstein mean when he says "To understand a sentence means to understand a language"? The assertion is unclear. For example, most native speakers can be said to understand their particular language. In my case it is English. Consider the Japanese sentence *Mado wa akete imasu*. Assume that I have just taken my first lesson in Japanese and the instructor has translated this sentence for me. According to the teacher, it means the same as "The window is open." Do I understand it even though I do not know which window, if any, is being referred to? Suppose we opt for "yes" as an answer. But if we do, one could not truthfully say that I know Japanese. So I understand the sentence without knowing Japanese.

Does Wittgenstein mean instead that a person can understand *any* sentence as long as he or she knows *some* language? Well, possibly, but he would surely have to expand this concept to include translation into a home language, and possibly also have to indicate in the translation who or what is being referred to, if anyone or anything is. Accurate word by word translation does not always result in communication and understanding, so understanding a sentence may involve more than comprehending the literal meanings of the words it contains. And there is the greater difficulty of what is it to understand a language. There are many words of English that any native speaker does not know. There will thus be some sentences of English that he or she will not understand. Shall we say in such cases that the native speaker knows or does not know English? Consider the following sentence, which I read this morning in a periodical called *ComputerEdge*.

Particularly popular with the Unix crowd, it's actually a bunch of standards including the "thick net" that uses heavy-duty coaxial cable and funny boxes that top off for each computer node, "thin net" that uses inexpensive RG-58 cable and simple BNC connectors to tap off, and "twisted pair," which is just a pair of wires twisted together to keep the signals in.

There is no doubt from the passages preceding and following it, and from the words composing it, that this sentence is in English and that its author was intending to communicate a message to a reader. But neither it nor the immediately preceding collection of words made any sense to me at all. Still, it is true that I know English. How much of any language does one have to know to be said to know a language? When can we say that a child knows English? Does an infant who can understand some words and sentences but is not capable of uttering comprehensible sentences or words know English? These questions do not have general answers. The case by case method I have been advocating throughout this study is further bolstered by such considerations. Therefore, Wittgenstein's apothegm does not provide a useful basis for the analysis of holism.

We find similar difficulties in Quine's position. What exactly is the "corporate body" he mentions? His most dedicated students and colleagues disagree about what he means, and Quine almost without exception disagrees with them. In the volume of the *Library of Living Philosophers* devoted to him, Quine has distanced himself from nearly every interpretation given to his holism. In that volume Putnam, for instance, has provided a lucid and sympathetic exposition of Quine's views, and yet in his response Quine has this to say:

Still I must caution [Putnam] against over-stating my holism. . . . Ironically, even so, the objection to extreme holism that Putnam cites will not stand. He cites the objection himself as "pure legalism," but it is worse. What it says is that any sentence "is confirmed by each experience which confirms at least one total body of theory which contains the sentence." An extreme holist could reply that in this sense every sentence is confirmed by every experience, since any one sentence can be safeguarded by changing others. For my own part, however, as appears from the preceding paragraph, I see extreme holism itself as "pure legalism."[4]

We can see that because of their vagueness and susceptibility to various interpretations, one should tread warily in dealing with these general forms of holism. There is, in addition, another reason for viewing them with suspicion. In many of the most distinguished proponents of the nonsentential forms of holism we find a distinct ambivalence. They wish to take a given proposition in two incompatible ways—an urge that is impossible to satisfy. Something like that is found, inter alia, in Quine and Putnam as well.

In chapter 2, "Reflections on Water," we saw that Putnam's Twin Earth argument led to the conclusion that what "water" means is independent of the thoughts or beliefs of any native speaker. The moral of his argument is "Cut the pie any way you like, 'meanings' just ain't in the *head!*" ("Meaning and Reference," p. 124). According to his argument, though scientists *determine* that water is identical with H_2O, the *truth* of that determination is not a function of their beliefs or psychological attitudes. What any natural-kind word means is determined by what that natural kind is, and since (according to Putnam) water is identical with H_2O, "water" simply means H_2O. The conclusion is that "water" has meaning *independent* of any sentential or belief context.

Yet in other places in his writings Putnam espouses a form of holism similar to Quine's. For instance, he writes,

I have described Quine's argument in the form which I myself find most convincing. In the sequel I shall make use of a distinction Quine did not himself introduce: the distinction between holism with respect to meaning and holism with respect to belief fixation. In this essay I shall not attempt to say when my arguments reproduce Quine's, when they merely parallel Quine's and when they are completely my own.[5]

As the issue has been formulated historically, the holist-nonholist alternatives are taken to be at least exclusive, so no one can rationally hold both positions. Yet the textual evidence makes it plain that Putnam adopts both alternatives. Quine does much the same thing. In his reply to Putnam he says,

Observation sentences do have their empirical content individually and other sentences are biased individually to particular empirical content in varying degrees.[6]

This passage seems flatly to contradict what in that same essay he stated to be his canonical view, specifically, as I quoted above, the following:

The dogma of reductionism survives in the supposition that each statement, taken in isolation from its fellows, can admit of confirmation or infirmation at all. My countersuggestion . . . is that our statements about the external world face the tribunal of sense experience not individually but only as a corporate body.[7]

As these citations indicate, Putnam and Quine wish to have it both ways: statements about the external world have empirical content individually, and they do not. These thinkers thus support, *per impossibile,* both holism and antiholism. For reasons such as these, I shall avoid such antisentential forms of holism.

We can find in the less general form of semantic holism views that are prima facie clearer and are supported by compelling arguments. As mentioned at the beginning of the chapter, I shall consider one of these, Russell's theory of descriptions, using it as a test case for the merit of any form of holism.

I also intend to restrict my focus to views that, at least for some sentences, presuppose that the meaning of a whole sentence is a function of the meaning of its constituent elements. Frege also held such a compositional view, though I shall be discussing Russell's view here, not Frege's. Both are ingenious and have strange, often paradoxical features. Russell's is more paradoxical and (to my way of thinking) more ingenious.

Here is the kind of strangeness we find in Frege. He asserted, as is well known, that a declarative sentence is a name—a genuine oddity when looked at from the standpoint of ordinary language or conventional grammar. It has the oddity that unlike most locutions that he calls "names," sentences are names one cannot find in a dictionary. He also held that as a complex name, a sentence is composed of simpler units that are also names. Even the sorts of *phrases* that Russell called "definite descriptions," such as "the child I am now holding," Frege labeled as names. No ordinary person would call that phrase "a proper name," let alone think of it as the name of the child I am holding.

It is the less paradoxical features of his theory that are relevant to our inquiry. These are, of course, so familiar they need no extensive description. But I will mention them because of their immediate reference to holism. Frege held that each name expresses a *Sinn*—a notion that is given different renderings, such as "sense," "meaning," "concept," or "intension." He also held that many names have a *Bedeutung*—translated generally as "reference" or "extension"—but that some do not. The *Bedeutung* of "the evening star" is the planet Venus. "The greatest natural number" has no *Bedeutung* in a natural language, though it can be given an artificial denotatum in regimented languages.

Even these seemingly benign principles are laden with paradox, for Frege also maintained that sense determines reference—a thesis that Kripke and Putnam strongly object to, as I noted in chapter 2. Independently of their particular cavils, the thesis has several paradoxical consequences. It follows from it, for example, that an indexical term such as "I," which has a unique *Sinn*, should pick out exactly one and only one individual. But, of course, in normal use it picks out diverse individuals—the multifarious speakers who use it to refer to themselves in statement-making contexts. But since Russell, not Frege, is my target I will not pursue such difficulties further here.

Nevertheless, Frege's form of holism is important because he claimed that the sense (meaning) expressed by a declarative sentence is a function of the senses (or meanings) of the names composing the sentence. His compositional thesis thus implied that the meaning of a sentential name is identical with the aggregated meanings (senses) expressed by its nonsentential names. This holistic meaning he called a *proposition*. Propositions differ from sentences, since different sentences may express the same proposition and different propositions may be expressed by the same sentence.

Frege also, independently of Russell, developed a version of the theory of descriptions. It differs from Russell's in important ways, notably in holding that a sentence that contains a name that lacks a *Bedeutung* is not false but meaningless. Russell's version of the theory does not hold that sentences are names or that all sentential constituents are names, but it does presuppose that for sentences *logically* in subject-predicate form—i.e., whose subject terms are proper names—the meaning of the whole sentence is a direct function of the meanings expressed by its sentential parts. Thus it does incorporate Frege's compositional principle but limits its application to a specific class of sentences. For sentences *grammatically* but not *logically* in subject-predicate form (specifically, those containing descriptions in the subject position), it gives noncompositional holistic analysis. I will be discussing this point in detail later, since it is a key to the theory. Russell's holism thus goes beyond Frege's, exhibiting a greater sensitivity to the difference between ordinary names and phrases. As I mentioned earlier, it also holds that proper names are independently meaningful. As with every ingenious theory, it has its share of paradoxes.

It is one of those paradoxical features, connected with holism, to which I shall now turn. Russell explicitly asserts that linguistic units that have no meaning outside of a sentential context contribute to the meaning of the sentential context in which they occur. The doctrine thus implies that an expression that lacks meaning outside of a sentential context somehow acquires meaning in such a context. Unless it did acquire meaning in context, it would be impossible to explain how it could contribute to the meaning of the whole context. In a view of this sort we are immediately confronted with paradox. How can something meaningless contribute meaning to the broader context in which it occurs? Russell's theory seems to violate the old adage *Ex nihilo nihil fit* (From nothing, nothing comes).

The problem that both Frege's and Russell's forms of holism raise is thus something like that of the classical dilemma about the chicken and the egg, namely, Which came first? If there were no egg to begin with, how could something become a chicken? If there were no chicken to begin with, how could something become an egg? Either horn of the dilemma seems impossible, and yet, as experience makes plain, both eggs and chickens do exist.

Likewise, if terms have no independent meaning, how can they contribute to the meaning of a larger semantic unit? Yet according to Russell they do, and in support of this assertion he gave a number of what he declared to be decisive arguments (often writing "Q.E.D." after their conclusions). We shall consider some of these below. Yet an antiholist could argue that if any semantic whole has a meaning, it can only be because it is an aggregate of the meanings of its constituent expressions. And if this is so, each such constituent must have independent meaning. The objection would thus apply to the views of Wittgenstein and Frege as well as to those of Russell. (As a logical objection, it would also apply to the more general forms of holism advanced by Putnam and Quine.) We thus have a dilemma.

It is like the puzzle about the chicken and the egg. Experience suggests both that sentential subunits have independent meaning and that they don't. The argument for each point of view might run—indeed, has run—as follows. According to the antiholist, the meaning of individual words can be looked up in dictionaries. Hence, they must have independent meaning. One can also understand what they mean without knowing every word in the language. Therefore, they are not language-dependent. Moreover, if there were no basic set of words, how could one construct sentences to begin with—what, for example, would be the correct sentential order if one did not know what the constituent words meant? This is the view that advocates primacy of the egg. In a different terminology it is found in Locke and Hume, who wished to show that all knowledge derives from experience. They contended that complex specimens of knowledge are constructed from simple ideas originating in sensory experience. The logical positivists were twentieth-century proponents of this form of empiricism.

Yet a holist, like the later Wittgenstein, insisted that words acquire their meanings only through their use in sentences, thus derivatively. We cannot know a priori or in general what they mean apart from particular contexts of use. In this sense, they are language/context-dependent and have no inherent significance. Here we have a defender of the primacy of the chicken. To him the antiholist might respond by asking, "How can we possibly know what sentences mean (or how to use them correctly) unless we know what their constituent words mean?" The debate seems endless. So which is the egg and which the chicken? Is it the word or the sentence? Who is right in this debate?

THREE

Russell's theory of descriptions is perhaps the most widely discussed semantic theory of the twentieth century. I will show in what follows that this theory, which strikes one as paradoxical and yet as interesting and important, is not really paradoxical and is less interesting and important than it initially seems. Since this is a controversial opinion, I wish to begin by establishing that I am not flogging a straw man. Some quotations will dispel that possibility.

What Russell is advocating certainly *sounds* paradoxical. From his earliest discussion of the theory of descriptions in the *Principles of Mathematics* of 1903 to such late works as *My Philosophical Development* of 1959, he repeated the same seemingly startling thesis. In "On Denoting" of 1905, for example, he states,

According to the view which I advocate, a denoting phrase is essentially *part* of a sentence, and does not, like most single words, have any significance on its own account.[8]

In the *Philosophy of Logical Atomism* of 1918 he expresses the point this way:

These things, like "the author of *Waverley*," which I call incomplete symbols, are things that have absolutely no meaning whatsoever in isolation but merely acquire a meaning in a context. "Scott" taken as a name has a meaning all by itself. It stands for a certain person, and there it is. But "*the author of Waverley*" is not a name, and does not all by itself mean anything at all, because when it is rightly used in propositions, those propositions do not contain any constituent corresponding to it.[9]

And then a late citation:

The central point of the theory of descriptions was that a phrase may contribute to the meaning of a sentence without having any meaning at all in isolation. Of this, in the case of descriptions, there is precise proof.[10]

These passages speak about *denoting phrases, incomplete symbols,* and *descriptions.* As Russell explains, these terms are to be distinguished from what he calls *names* (i.e., what would ordinarily be called *proper* names).

Take the proposition, "Scott is the author of *Waverley.*" We have here a name "Scott," and a description "the author of *Waverley*" which are asserted to apply to the same person.

A name is a simple symbol whose meaning is something that can only occur as subject, i.e., something of the kind that we defined as an "individual" or a "particular." And a "simple" symbol is one which has no parts that are symbols. Thus "Scott" is a simple symbol, because, though it has parts (namely separate letters), these parts are not symbols. On the other hand, "the author of *Waverley*" is not a simple symbol, because the separate words that compose the phrase are parts which are symbols.

. . . We have then, two things to compare: (1) a *name,* which is a simple symbol, directly designating an individual which is its meaning, and having this meaning in its own right, independently of the meanings of all other words; (2) a *description,* which consists of several words, whose meanings are already fixed, and from which results whatever is to be taken as the "meaning" of the description.[11]

Russell not only asserts that names are different from descriptions but also that descriptions have no meaning in isolation. In asserting the latter, he seems to differ from direct-reference theorists, who claim that descriptions have meaning and that many theorists have mistakenly assumed that it is via the meaning of a description that one fixes its reference. As I have mentioned, Russell offers proofs of both claims. Here is an argument that speaks to the first.

A proposition containing a description is not identical with what that proposition becomes when a name is substituted, even if the name names the same object as the description describes. "Scott is the author of *Waverley*" is obviously a different proposition from "Scott is Scott": the first is a fact in literary history, the second a trivial truism. And if we put anyone other than Scott in place of "the author of *Waverley*" our proposition would become false, and would therefore certainly no longer be the same proposition.[12]

Now let us look at an argument of the second sort. It attempts to demonstrate that descriptive (or denoting) phrases lack meaning in isolation. Note that it presupposes that the sentences in which such phrases occur are meaningful, i.e., it presupposes the sentential form of holism.

If "the author of *Waverley*" meant anything other than "Scott," "Scott is the author of *Waverley*" would be false, which it is not. If "the author of *Waverley*" meant "Scott," "Scott is the author of *Waverley*" would be a tautology, which it is not. Therefore, "the author of *Waverley*" means neither "Scott" nor anything else, i.e., "the author of *Waverley*" means nothing. Q.E.D. (Russell, *My Philosophical Development,* p. 85)

Like all reference theorists, from Mill to Marcus, Russell assumes that sentences containing proper names and/or descriptions are meaningful. With this assumption in mind, one can isolate three distinct claims in the preceding passages:

(1) Names are to be distinguished from descriptions.

(2) Names but not descriptions have independent meaning.

(3) Descriptions that have no meaning "in isolation" (or which mean "nothing") contribute to the meaning of the sentence in which they occur.

It is this last claim that expresses the paradoxical form of Russell's holism. On the assumption that a whole sentence is meaningful, Russell obviously thinks that these three theses are connected, i.e., that (1) and (2) imply (3). Each of these claims has a complicated status: (1) and (2) are supported by arguments, but (3) is not. In both cases the supporting arguments are fallacious. Nonetheless, a given statement may be true even if an argument in its support lacks cogency. How shall we assess (1) and (2) then? Depending on how it is understood, (1) can be said true, or it can be said to be false. Claim (2) is a technical one, and understood as Russell advances it, it is false. Claim (3) is very complicated as it works through the intricate fabric of Russell's writings. Understood in one way—as Russell intended it—it is false. Understood in another, it is true. But when understood in this way, it is neither paradoxical nor philosophically significant.

FOUR

Let us examine with some care (1) and (2) and their supporting arguments. Before doing so, I wish to emphasize the point just mentioned, namely that these arguments do not prove what Russell takes them to prove, namely (3). They not only do not prove his seemingly paradoxical holistic thesis; they are not even relevant to it. Instead, they bear upon and attempt to prove (1) and (2), namely that descriptions differ from names and that descriptions lack meaning in isolation. Russell makes a conceptual (and indefensible) leap from (1) and (2) to (3), i.e., to the holistic conclusion he wishes to reach.

How does he in fact establish that descriptions contribute meaning to the sentential contexts in question? He does it not by argument but by *analysis*. That is, he gives a *paraphrase* of the meaning of the English sentences in which such expressions occur. An analysis of this sort is not an argument. His analysis is, of course, famous. According

206

to Russell "Scott is the author of Waverley" means the same as "Exactly one thing wrote *Waverley* and that thing is identical with Scott." The grammatically singular sentence "Scott is the author of *Waverley*" is thus transformed via the analysis into a *general* sentence containing, inter alia, indefinite pronouns and predicates.

I will have more to say about the significance of this move below, since it is critical for my ultimate assessment of Russell's holism. For now, however, I merely wish to emphasize that Russell does not anywhere proffer an argument in support of his holistic thesis. Insofar as he argues for any case, it is that the original singular sentence and the subsequent general sentence are synonymous. But an additional argument would be required to prove that they are synonymous *because of the semantic contribution made by the descriptive phrase.* I will show that there is a reasonable explanation for this lapse. It is that no argument would do the job. This will be demonstrated at the end of this chapter.

Let us now look at (1) and (2), beginning with the former. Claim (1) holds, of course, that names differ from descriptions. Is this claim true or false? How good is the argument in its support? The status of (1) is peculiar in Russell's text, since Russell begins by *defining* names and descriptions as different. He says a name is a simple symbol having no parts that are symbols. A name designates an individual person or thing and has meaning independently of the meanings of all other words. It does so because its meaning is the individual it designates. In contrast, a description is a complex symbol, whose parts are themselves symbols. Descriptions do not have independent meaning. And so forth.

Several issues arise at this point. First, if Russell has distinguished these notions by *definition,* why does he need an argument at all to *prove* that they differ? Clearly, an argument, or at least the kind of argument he gives, is otiose. One could imagine his giving a Moore-type argument. Moore says in "Proof of an External World" (*Philosophical Papers*), "Here is one hand, here is another, and therefore two material objects exist." Russell could argue similarly: "Here is a simple symbol, 'Scott,' and here is a complex symbol, 'The author of *Waverley.*' Therefore, names and descriptions exist and are different from one another." Nevertheless, he does give an independent argument, which—as I shall show in a moment—does not prove what he takes it to prove. But at best it is not necessary.

Returning to the definition for a moment, we can ask, "Is it any good?" Does it mark out an exclusive distinction between names and descriptions? Is every expression that satisfies his definition either a name or a description, and not both? The answer is "no." According to Russell, *The Wine Advocate* and *The Wine Spectator* are both descriptions. They use "the" in the singular and are complex symbols. Yet neither describes anything, let alone a particular individual who is a wine advocate or another who is a wine spectator. Instead, they are the *names* of two wine periodicals. Russell's definition does not give us a sharp distinction. If (1) is interpreted to mean that names and descriptions are *always* distinguishable according to his criteria, (1) is clearly false. But if (1) means that *some* expressions, such as "the child I am now holding," are not names and that some names, such as "John," are not descriptions, that is surely true. But this latter construal is clearly not what Russell means. He means (1), and that is not true.

Does the argument from *Introduction to Mathematical Philosophy* that Russell gives (and that I quoted above) prove that names are different from descriptions? Let me quote him again.

A proposition containing a description is not identical with what that proposition becomes when a name is substituted, even if the name names the same object as the description describes. "Scott is the author of *Waverley*" is obviously a different proposition from "Scott is Scott": the first is a fact in literary history, the second a trivial truism. And if we put anyone other than Scott in place of "the author of *Waverley*" our proposition would become false, and would therefore certainly no longer be the same proposition.[13]

It should be noted at the outset that Russell's formulation of the argument turns on a use-mention confusion. He says, "If we put anyone other than Scott in place of 'the author of *Waverley*' our proposition would become false and would therefore no longer be the same proposition." Scott is, of course, a person and is not the sort of thing that can be substituted for a linguistic expression in a sentence. Russell is thus confusing talk about a name, i.e., about "Scott," with talk about the person so named. But let us ignore this complication and follow his formulation in posing our objection, since the point I wish to make does not turn on it. His argument can then be formulated in the following three steps.

(i) "Scott is Scott" is a trivial truism.

(ii) "Scott is the author of *Waverley*" is a fact in literary history.

(iii) If we put anyone other than Scott in place of "the author of Waverley," (ii) would become false.

Russell infers from this conjunction of premises that the difference in significance between (i) and (ii) is to be accounted for in terms of the difference between names and descriptions, since (i) and (ii) are exactly alike except that in (ii) a description replaces a name. But this inference is invalid. Consider the following "mirror image" of the argument:

(i.a) "The author of *Waverley* is the author of *Waverley*" is a trivial truism.

209

(ii.a) "The author of *Waverley* is the author of *Ivanhoe*" is a fact in literary history.

(iii.a) If we put anyone other than the author of *Waverley* in place of the "author of *Ivanhoe*," ii.a) would become false.

But the difference between (i.a) and (ii.a) cannot now be accounted for in terms of the distinction between names and descriptions, since all the terms involved are descriptions. I do not think Russell's argument can be saved by insisting that "The author of *Waverley* is the author of *Waverley*" is not an instance of the law of identity and is therefore not a trivial truism at all. To make this move is to beg the question at issue by *assuming* the correctness of the theory of descriptions. (As I pointed out in the previous chapter, it is one of the consequences of Russell's theory of descriptions that true sentences with descriptions flanking the identity sign are not instances of the Law of Identity.) The whole point of the argument in *Introduction to Mathematical Philosophy* (and in "The Philosophy of Logical Atomism") is to establish the correctness of the theory of descriptions by proving that there is a difference between descriptions and names. Since the above objection shows that Russell fails to establish this difference *by the argument he uses,* he cannot get the theory off the ground at all.

FIVE

I shall now turn to (2), the claim that descriptions, unlike names, lack meaning in isolation. As I have mentioned, Russell's argument to this effect (though with some variations) occurs in a large number of places in his writings. I have already quoted it in section 3 above. Let me set it forth again and then show why it fails.

If "the author of *Waverley*" meant anything other than "Scott," "Scott is the author of *Waverley*" would be false, which it is not. If "the author of *Waverley*" meant "Scott," "Scott is the author of *Waverley*" would be a tautology, which it is not. Therefore, "the author of *Waverley*" means neither "Scott" nor anything else, i.e., "the author of *Waverley*" means nothing. Q.E.D.[14]

Russell, of course, wishes to prove that definite descriptive phrases are meaningless in isolation and thus differ from proper names in this respect. But the conclusion the argument arrives at is that they mean nothing at all. If the conclusion were true, the "central point" of the theory of descriptions would be even more remarkable than Russell presents it as being. For now a phrase that has no meaning at all will "contribute meaning to the sentence in which it occurs."

We can develop a counterargument by substituting "Scott" for "the author of *Waverley*," and vice versa. The outcome of this process, which gives us a mirror image of the original argument, is that "Scott" has no meaning.

If "Scott" meant anything other than "the author of *Waverley*," "The author of *Waverley* is Scott" would be false, which it is not. If "Scott" meant "the author of *Waverley*," "The author of *Waverley* is Scott" would be a tautology, which it is not. Therefore, "Scott" means neither "the author of *Waverley*" nor anything else, i.e., "Scott" means nothing. Q.E.D.

If this duplicate version of Russell's argument is sound (and being structurally identical with the original, there is no reason why it should be less sound), it establishes too much. Instead of helping us to see the distinction between names and descriptions, it serves to obliterate it. For now, not only "the author of *Waverley*" but also "Scott" has no meaning. And if, *à la* Russell, we are allowed to generalize beyond this formal argument, then we can infer that no description and no proper name has any meaning. The supposed difference between names and descriptions has vanished.

This counterargument thus establishes that there is no difference in status between proper names and descriptions. For either it shows that proper names and descriptions alike mean nothing, or if one regards the above result as a *reductio,* it shows that if proper names are meaningful, then descriptions are too. Neither it nor Russell's original argument shows that there is a difference between names and descriptions with respect to their significance, but this, as we have seen, was the overall point that Russell's "proof" was designed to establish. There is thus no reason to believe that (2) is true.

SIX

As I have indicated, though Russell frequently explains what he means by a name and even gives an account of what it means to say that names have meaning in isolation, he never provides an explicit argument in support of this claim anywhere in his logical works. Why did he not hold, as his predecessor Mill did, or as Ruth Marcus later seems to have argued, that proper names are meaningless? There is a good argument in support of this suggestion. If one holds that the meanings of words can be looked up in dictionaries and that proper names are not susceptible to this process, one can plausibly hold that they are meaningless. After all, what do "John" and "Russell" mean? Marcus has, in fact, used this argument in her work. She writes as follows:

On this account, "proper name" is a semantical, not a merely syntactical, notion. Reference is supposed. We may mistakenly believe of some syntactically proper name, say "Homer," that it has an actual singular referent and is a genuine proper name, but if its use does not finally link it to a singular object, it is not a genuine name at all.

It is for such reasons that linguists exclude proper names from the lexicon altogether. P. Ziff, *Semantic Analysis* (Ithaca: Cornell University Press, 1960) and elsewhere, adopts the linguists' view. Proper names are not "part of the language" in the sense of being lexical items in a dictionary. Qua proper names, they don't have meanings as ordinarily viewed. In the case of names of persons, for example, biographical dictionaries, "dictionaries" of proper names, help, through description, to tell us what or who is being referred to, but that is not given as the "sense." The referent of a proper name remains fixed, even where attributions claimed by narrative are in error.[15]

It seems that Russell decided to let the point rest at the definitional level. It is as if he assumes that it is *obvious* that names have meaning and that the meaning they have is independent of the meaning of all other words, and assumes equally that what is not obvious and is in need of explanation is that descriptions do not. Hence the panoply of arguments in the latter case and the absence of arguments in the former. The entire thrust of his work is directed toward showing that though descriptions seem to function like names, in fact they don't, a thrust that issues in the celebrated distinction between grammatical and logical form.

If Russell did assume, rather than argue for, the position that names are meaningful independently of all other words, it is interesting to speculate on what might have given rise to this assumption. No doubt the distinction he draws between knowledge by acquaintance and knowledge by description plays a role here, especially in its application to one of the essential principles in the philosophy of logical atomism, namely that simples cannot be described but only named. But I think that these doctrines themselves may rest on a deeper assumption, one insufficiently noted in the literature.

Without arguing the point in extenso, I feel it sufficient to call attention to the importance of the theory of propositional functions in Russell's logical writings. Simplifying radically, one can say that in Russell's thinking, propositional functions stand in a kind of opposition to propositions. For him, they are matrices, incomplete symbols or expressions, or open sentences (as distinct from complete sentences). There are two ways in which such open sentences can be converted into complete sentences (or alternatively, propositions).

Either one can bind the variables by quantifying over them, or one can replace them with constants. In the former case, the results are always general sentences (or propositions). But a wholly general logic would be insufficient for Russell. It would fail completely to describe the world, and moreover, unless some values of such general sentences were true, general sentences could not be true either. Singular sentences, he says, are the values that render such general sentences true. General sentences are thus tied to the world via singular sentences. But the only way to convert propositional functions into singular sentences is to replace the variables in them with constants, i.e., with proper names. The effect of such a replacement is to turn a meaningless matrix, "X is bald," into a meaningful sentence, such as "Socrates is bald." The need to use names is thus essential in producing the singular sentences that are basic to logic.

Russell might well have reasoned that if "Socrates" or any other proper name were meaningless, no substitution of a proper name could have converted a meaningless expression into a meaningful one. But since replacing a variable by a proper name produces a meaningful sentence, this must be because the proper name is meaningful. The further step that Russell took, that of saying that proper names have no *Sinn* but merely mean the individuals they denoted, is immediately suggested by this line of reasoning. For if a proper name had meaning in the intensional, Fregean sense, this could be captured in a descriptive phrase, and then the proper name could be eliminated from the sentential context in which it occurred.

This was in fact the line Quine was later to take. But the resulting sentences or propositions would be *general* sentences or propositions. Thus Russell's feeling (unlike Quine's) that logic must be grounded in singular sentences and his view that such sentences are only derivable from propositional functions through the substitution of names for variables are perhaps one way of explaining why he held proper names to be meaningful independently of all other words, i.e., to mean the individuals they denoted. This account would also explain why Russell's holism is restricted to a specific class of sentences, those containing descriptions, and never reaches the full generality we find in Quine and Saussure.

SEVEN

These remarks allow us to pinpoint a profound difficulty with (3)—the proposition that descriptions, which have no meaning in isolation, contribute to the meaning of the sentence in which they occur. As I asserted above, Russell does not anywhere provide a direct argument in support of (3), and instead he substitutes an analysis in which sentences containing descriptions can be transformed into sentences that do not contain them. As the previous account indicates, the results are always general sentences.

But the procedure gives rise to a fatal flaw in his holism. According to (3), expressions that are meaningless outside of sentential contexts contribute meaning to the sentences in which they occur. As he explicitly says, "The central point of the theory of descriptions was that a phrase may contribute to the meaning of a sentence without having any meaning in isolation" (*My Philosophical Development,* p. 85).

And now the difficulty. According to Russell's account, an original English sentence containing a description, such as "Scott is the author of *Waverley*" really means "Exactly one thing wrote *Waverley,* and that thing is identical with Scott." But to which sentence does the description contribute its meaning: to the original singular sentence or to the new general sentence? We must choose one or the other. Which shall it be?

Suppose that it is the general sentence. But this will not do. For the whole point of the analysis is to show that descriptions are incomplete symbols, and this entails that when the analysandum containing them is correctly analyzed, they will have disappeared from the analysans. This is just the difference, according to Russell, between "Scott" and "the author of *Waverley.*" "Scott" cannot be made to disappear by means of analysis; it will appear in the analysans as well as in the analysandum. But "the author of *Waverley*" has been eliminated from the analysans. The new sentence (i.e., the analysans) substitutes for it quantifiers and predicates (or their English analogues). So if the general sentence does not contain the description at all, how can that phrase contribute to its meaning? Indeed, it cannot, because it does not occur there.

The other horn of the dilemma is equally unacceptable. In section 3 above I quoted a passage from *Introduction to Mathematical Philosophy* where Russell is contrasting names and descriptions. In speaking there of descriptions, he says, "A description . . . consists of several words, whose meanings are already fixed, and from [them] results whatever is to be taken as the "meaning" of the description" (p. 174). What does he mean when he says that a description consists of several words whose "meanings are fixed"? The answer, I believe, is this. Consider the descriptive phrase "the pen on the floor." It might occur in a sentence like "The pen on the floor is blue." The phrase consists of five words, two occurrences of "the," two common nouns, "pen" and "floor," and a single occurrence of the preposition "on." Each of these words, like all adjectives, common nouns, and prepositions, can be found in any good English dictionary.

More that that, the meaning for each such word is given in the dictionary. It follows that the description contains words whose meanings—as Russell says—"are already fixed," and from them results "what is to be taken as the 'meaning' of the description." The meanings of the words are fixed in the sense that they are lexical items that belong to the English language and can be looked up in any dictionary. Proper names, such as "John" and "Russell," are not fixed in this sense. From such facts it is plausible, as Ruth Marcus has pointed out, to infer that proper names do not belong to natural languages.

How do these considerations bear upon (3)? The answer is that there is a sense in which a whole descriptive phrase, such as "the pen on the floor," might be said not to have *independent* meaning. This would be the sense in which the whole phrase is taken as a unit and is contrasted with its constituents, words such as "the," "pen," and "on." One cannot look up the meaning of the *whole* phrase as one can look up the meanings of its constituent words. In this sense the phrase does not have independent meaning. Nonetheless, it has meaning as a unit. Its meaning is a function of the meanings of its constituent lexical items.

There is thus a sense in which it can be understood outside of any sentential context. Provided that one understands the meaning of its constituent words, one will understand it. So though one cannot look up its meaning in a dictionary, it will have meaning as a unit. We might call this "a secondary sense of independent meaning."

Note that on this last interpretation, the descriptive phrase as a unit would contribute meaning to the sentence in which it occurs. The sentence "The pen is on the floor" is perfectly meaningful. We thus have a case in which an expression that, under one interpretation, has no independent meaning contributes to the meaning of the sentence in which it occurs. But under a different interpretation, a phrase that has independent meaning will contribute exactly that meaning to the sentential context in which it occurs.

On either interpretation Russell's holistic thesis is in trouble.

Russell thinks of (3) as making the point that a phrase like "the pen on the floor" is not a name and therefore, unlike names, has no meaning in isolation. But from the fact that the phrase is not a name, it does not follow that it has no meaning in isolation, as the preceding comments make clear. As a unit, it has, under either interpretation, *at least* the meanings contributed to it by the meanings of its constituent words. When the phrase occurs in a sentence like "The pen on the floor is blue," it contributes those "fixed meanings" to the whole sentence. It does not become a naming expression in context, and yet it contributes lexical meaning to the context.

Russell's account subtly suggests the opposite. It implies that somehow "the author of *Waverley*" contributes a kind of meaning in context that it does not possess in isolation. But this is either a sheer mistake or is highly misleading. What "the author of *Waverley*" contributes to the whole sentence is just the lexical meaning it has whether "in isolation" or not.

There is, accordingly, no change in the status of its "meaning," whether it occurs in a sentential context or not. The notion that there is such a change is due to Russell's conflating or confusing two different senses of "independent meaning," and in this sense there is a subtle kind of equivocation involved in the remarkable "central point" of the theory. But the theory is much less striking or paradoxical if it is rewritten to say that a descriptive phrase that has a certain kind of lexical meaning contributes just that meaning, and no other, to the sentence of which it is a part. The central point of that "remarkable" theory is thus philosophically trivial. It reduces to the notion that whatever lexical meaning a descriptive phrase has is just the meaning, and no other, that it will contribute to the sentential context in which it occurs.

If this analysis is correct, what shall we say about holism, at least in Russell's form? The regrettable answer is that this version of the problem about the chicken and the egg remains just as unanswerable as it was before.

EIGHT

I end this chapter with two concluding notes.

First, direct-reference theorists have argued that proper names are rigid designators that pick out or tag individuals without the intercession of senses or meanings. In contrast, descriptions pick out particulars indirectly via such meanings. I disagree, but obviously I cannot argue the point in the detail it deserves at the end of this long study. Let me just flatly assert that there is no difference in the referring powers between descriptive phrases and names. If I cannot remember the name of the Hungarian dentist who has just moved in next door, I can refer to him with a phrase like "the Hungarian dentist who moved in next door." If I later remember that his name is *Matthias Pince* and refer to him via that expression, my reference is no more direct than it was before.

Why, then, do we have both names and descriptions if either category of expressions will do the same job? At least one answer is that most things we refer to are not important enough to have names. "The pen on the floor" is a good example. Neither the pen nor the floor has a name because neither, from our personal perspective, is worth naming. The dog I own is different. For me, it is important, and hence I call it "Corrie." But for Matthias Pince, it may just be "the dog next door." Names and descriptions do not have different referring powers. Rather, names single out things that are especially meaningful to some humans beings.

Second, it is a fact that as persons age, they have more trouble remembering names. But oddly enough—unless they suffer from such serious illnesses as Pick's disease or Alzheimer's—they have no difficulty in using descriptive phrases. For most of us, then, "The Hungarian dentist next door" may be the wave of the future.

ONE

One of the distinctive differences between science and philosophy is that scientific problems are susceptible to definite solutions in a way that philosophical problems are not. Since time immemorial ordinary folk have noted that children often closely resemble their parents in size, weight, hair coloring, and modes of speech, but despite all sorts of speculative guesses about why this was so, there was no real understanding of the nature of hereditary transmission until the work of Mendel. With the development of gene theory and the subsequent discovery of DNA in this century, the problem was solved. To that issue one can now write "Q.E.D."

Many other scientific problems have a similar history. A celebrated case is that of the discovery of the planet Neptune. On July 3, 1841, John Adams, a twenty-two-year-old British astronomer, wrote the following in his journal:

Formed a design in the beginning of this week of investigating, as soon as possible after taking my degree, the irregularities in the motion of Uranus . . . in order to find out whether they may be attributed to the action of an undiscovered planet beyond it.

Four years later he predicted the existence of such a planet and where it could be found, and in 1846, on the basis of an independent calculation by Leverrier, Neptune was observed by Johann Galle of the Berlin Observatory. Not only was Neptune's orbit as predicted by Adams and Leverrier, but it was subsequently learned from stellar occultation profiles that the planet is seventeen times as massive as the earth. The case is a beautiful instance of how a scientific conjecture can be investigated and then signed, sealed and delivered.

Compare these examples with the most celebrated of all epistemological puzzles: our knowledge of the external world. This is a problem whose modern formulations can be traced to Descartes, though its antecedents are much older and exist in classical Greek philosophy. Yet despite "solutions" by Berkeley, Hume, Kant, and a myriad of twentieth-century philosophers, it is still with us. As Benson Mates points out,

The External World problem, as would be expected, has many variant formulations and begets a number of derivative problems that are troublesome enough in their own right. . . . It has of course been turned on all sides by its analyzers and would-be solvers and dissolvers; every joint in every form of it has been pronounced a nonsequitur by somebody; every crucial term that appears in it has been declared stretched or in some other way abused or misused; and a criterion of meaning has been invented according to which the central question and its possible answers turn out to be nonsensical or at least "devoid of cognitive content." Yet, despite all the attacks, death notices, and even obituaries, the problem is still with us.[1]

But why is it still with us? No doubt the question is complex—in its full complexity, too difficult to be explored in detail here. In this chapter I wish to suggest one reason (surely not the only one) that it is still present in the twentieth century. The reason is simple. It is that many philosophers, psychologists, and scientists, including those whose specialty is perception, now think of it as a scientific problem. They feel it is merely a question of time until it can be wrapped up, just as Adams and his colleagues settled the matter of the hypothesized existence of Neptune. The prevailing attitude is expressed by J. R. Smythies, a distinguished neuropsychiatrist, whose recent study of the relationship between mental activity and perception begins with these words:

This book presents an attempt to scale an unconquered peak in science—the discovery of how the mind, in particular consciousness, is related to its brain. I hold that this problem is essentially a scientific one, that will be solved by the scientific method of observation, speculative hypothesis and experiment.[2]

I will argue in this chapter that as these scholars formulate the problem, it contains conceptual infusions of which they are unaware and that cannot be resolved by science. There may well be elements of the problem that are purely scientific, and I shall indicate what these are. But there are others that are not, and these are crucial in preventing a scientific solution. Among them are the distinctions between the inner and the outer and between direct and indirect perception. These are key notions in the Cartesian model of the mind, which exercises a significant influence on what purport to be strictly scientific investigations. In this chapter my focus will not be on the mind per se (though reference to the mind is crucial to any statement of the problem) but on what supposedly exists outside of the human mind, the so-called external world.

The problem in these contemporary formulations, as in its Cartesian precursors, turns on taking the mind to be something inner. Its contents are called "perceptions" (representations, ideas, qualia, sense data, etc.), many of which are believed to originate from external sources. Each of us is said to have direct access to his or her own perceptions and only indirect access to their external progenitors. If one accepts the Cartesian model, the classical problem of our knowledge of the external world immediately arises. This is how Mates formulates the difficulty:

> Ultimately the only basis I can have for a claim to know that there exists something other than my own perceptions is the nature of those very perceptions. But they could be just as they are even if there did not exist anything else. Ergo, I have no basis for the knowledge-claim in question.[3]

As the title of his book indicates, Mates wishes to defend a form of scepticism, namely that there is no way of proving whether or not we have knowledge of external objects. I have already discussed scepticism in the first chapter and will say nothing further about it here. Rather, my focus is on views that either assert or presuppose that there is an external world and that we have perceptual access to its objects. Such views are traditionally called "realistic."

Realism exhibits two main features: one ontological, the other epistemological. The ontological aspect asserts that the world contains mind-independent, public objects; the epistemological aspect affirms that human beings have epistemic access to these objects. Both aspects come in all sorts of colors, for example, that the kind of epistemic access human have is so strong as to qualify as knowledge or certitude, or that it is limited and is at best probable only, and so forth. I shall ignore these finer-grained, though important, differences here.

The basic watershed that divides realists—and this is the feature I shall concentrate on in this chapter—is whether such access is direct or indirect. The issue is thus different from what Mates is describing, since on his account of the problem, it is possible that no external objects exist at all, or that we may have no epistemic access to them. In a recent paper by Robert Oakes, who uses the terms "representationalism" and "indirect realism" interchangeably, there is a better description of the issue we shall be discussing.[4] He puts the matter this way:

Consider, for example, some object which is before our sense-organs, such as the lamp on the table next to the sofa. The issue between the representationalist and the direct realist can be brought into sharp relief by way of the following question: what is it that a percipient apprehends *directly* when focusing perceptual attention on the lamp in question? At the heart of the representationalist thesis is that the object before our percipient's sense-organs, *the lamp,* is perceivable only by virtue of *attentive direct perception* of an entity which is effected by the relevant lamp and is interior to consciousness. Attentive perception of this entity, of the "lamp-sensum," requires the attentive perception of nothing else: it is absolutely direct. According to Direct Realism, of course, the perception of the lamp does *not* occur by virtue of the perception of anything interior to consciousness. Rather, the direct realist maintains that perceptual apprehension of objects before our sense-organs in no way proceeds by indirection; in other words, such perception is accomplished without being mediated in any way by the perception of something interior to consciousness. Hence, the view of the direct realist is that, since there *are* no such entities as sensa, the perception of objects before our sense-organs is absolutely direct.[5]

On the whole, Oakes's formulation of the issue between direct and indirect realists is neutral, and I can use it as a starting point for my discussion, but it does contain two mistakes that require correction before I can proceed. He asserts that direct realists claim that there are no such entities as sensa, and he infers from this statement that their view is that the perception of objects "before our sense organs is absolutely direct." Of course, the term "sensa" is sometimes used in a technical way that might induce some direct realists to deny that there are sensa. But the examples he gives of sensa include such common phenomena as mirror images, and surely no direct realist has ever denied that there are such things. Beyond this they acknowledge that persons are subject to hallucinations, illusions, and other sorts of visual aberrations. What they do deny is that in seeing a lamp one is *always* seeing two things: a mental picture of a lamp and a lamp.

These examples illustrate the second mistake that Oakes's account contains. The mistake arises from a confusion about quantifiers. For Oakes the issue is whether on *every* perceptual occasion one's visual access to the external world is mediated by mental representations. He implies that direct realists hold that in *every* perceptual act one is seeing a physical object directly. But this assertion is a distortion of the tradition. Direct realists hold a much more limited thesis, namely that on *some* occasions human beings see physical objects without the intermediation of such mental representations as images, ideas, sense data, etc. The issue should thus be understood in this way. If we keep these emendations in mind, we can accept Oakes's characterization of the issue between indirect and direct realists.

TWO

What kinds of considerations, then, prevent the problem of the external world as so construed from attaining a scientific solution? I can identify three factors: (1) a failure to recognize that some key issues in the problem are not straightforwardly empirical and thus are not resolvable by scientific investigation, (2) a failure to supply a sufficiently large range of examples, and/or to produce clear, relevant, and applicable examples, in support of claims, and (3) a failure to notice that in formulations of and proposed solutions to the problem, ordinary discourse is often so distorted as to result in conceptual incoherence. These liabilities occur in both direct and indirect forms of realism and are usually submerged in complex argumentation. In consequence, proponents of these views do not recognize that their philosophical intrusions jam up the works in all sorts of complicated ways. One of the most important of these intrusions is how the so-called "causal" story is to be understood. We shall see in what follows how both sides interpret that story.

THREE

Let us begin with a direct realist. In chapter 9 of his celebrated book *The Ecological Approach to Visual Perception,* J. J. Gibson says the following:

Direct perception is what one gets from seeing Niagara Falls, say, as distinguished from seeing a picture of it. The latter kind of perception is *mediated.* So when I assert that perception of the environment is direct, I mean that it is not mediated by *retinal* pictures, *neural* pictures, or *mental* pictures. *Direct perception* is the activity of getting information from the ambient array of light. I call this a process of *information pickup* that involves the exploratory activity of looking around, getting around, and looking at things. This is quite different from the supposed activity of getting information from the inputs of the optic nerves, whatever they may prove to be.[6]

In what follows, I shall focus on Gibson's claim that "direct perception is what one gets from seeing Niagara Falls, as distinguished from seeing a picture of it." As we explore this remark, uncovering the sorts of conceptual liabilities mentioned above, we shall find that Gibson is wrong in holding that a case of seeing Niagara Falls is to be characterized as a case of direct perception and that seeing a picture of Niagara Falls is to be described as an instance of mediated (indirect) perception. Here we find a good illustration of how a theory depends on poorly selected examples. The way these cases should be characterized is an interesting and difficult question that I shall address later.

At the outset it is essential to realize that we are in the world of theory. In using the phrase "direct perception" Gibson believes he is opposing one theoretical outlook to another. As he tells us,

There are experiments, of course, that seem to go against the theory of a direct perception of layout and to support the opposite theory of a *mediated* perception of layout. The latter theory is more familiar. It asserts that perception is mediated by assumptions, preconceptions, expectations, mental images, or any of a dozen other hypothetical mediators.[7]

As the quotation indicates, Gibson thinks of the issue between him and his opponents as an *experimental* issue: he speaks of "experiments that seem to go against his theory." Later on in his book, and especially in chapters 9 through 11, he describes the experimental evidence that supports his view. So his way of formulating the issue suggests that the dispute is wholly scientific in character. As I have indicated above, I agree that it is partly scientific but deny that it is wholly so. In my opinion, the deepest issues between him and his opponents are not scientific but philosophical. To see why, let's begin by looking at the opposite theory in some detail.

As Gibson indicates, "the opposite theory" may take many forms. But all of them have two things in common. First, they hold that the observer is apprehending something, say a mental representation or a picture, that stands in a certain relationship to the perceived object but is itself not identical with the perceived object. Moreover, according to Robert Oakes, "Attentive perception of this entity, of the 'lamp-sensum,' requires the attentive perception of nothing else: it is absolutely direct."[8] The theory thus makes use of the notion of direct perception; only it holds that it is a mental representation rather than the physical object that is directly perceived. Second, theories of mediated perception hold that the representation intervenes, as it were, between the observer and the object and, in so doing, mediates the observer's apprehension of the object. Accordingly, the observer's apprehension of the object is both indirect and conditioned by the nature of the mediator.

Let us look at a sophisticated, contemporary example of such a theory. The author is the distinguished cognitive scientist Richard L. Gregory. He is commenting specifically on Gibson.

Science's hypotheses have a kind of life of their own. This is just how I see perceptions. This notion is essentially different from the views of proponents of direct theories of perception, such as J. J. Gibson's (1950) account, in which perceptions are supposed to be "direct-pick-up" samples of reality. However enticing as promising certain knowledge from the senses, this claim cannot be supported given the indirectness imposed by the many physiological steps or stages of visual and other sensory perception. And it cannot account for "perception's power" to predict into the immediate future; so, as we have said, although there is an irreducible physiological delay of neural signals to the brain there is usually no reaction time, and behavior continues through extensive losses of signals. For these and other reasons (Gregory, 1978) we may safely abandon direct accounts of perception, in favor of indirectly related and never certain (what I suggest might be called) *hypotheses* of reality. It is the evident indirectness of perception, together with its power to predict unsensed properties of objects, and into the immediate future that makes it appropriate to call perceptions 'perceptual hypotheses' (cf. Gregory, 1968, 1970). How far they depend on explicit knowledge of science and (largely implicit) brain models, many of which we may have inherited, is an open question.[9]

In this passage we find the thesis of indirect perception defended on causal grounds. Such grounds, he indicates, are "imposed by the many physiological steps or stages of visual and other sensory perception." But there is also the striking statement that perceptions are hypotheses, akin to scientific hypotheses in that they have predictive power. In making this statement, Gregory thinks he is giving a straightforward scientific account of perception. Yet I can show, as follows, that it embodies one of those philosophical intrusions, with ineffectual examples, that I mentioned above.

In considering the objection that if perceptions are themselves hypotheses, they cannot be evoked to confirm or disconfirm other hypotheses, he states, "This, however, is no objection, for it is common experience that a perception can confirm or disconfirm other perceptions. And one scientific hypothesis may (it is usually held) confirm or disconfirm other hypotheses in science."[10] But contrary to what he says, perceptions and hypotheses are radically different from one another. It is a mistake to choose a hypothesis as an example of a confirming instance. On the contrary, hypotheses are conjectures that await and need confirmation or disconfirmation. Observations based on perceptual experience may provide evidence pro or con. But no hypothesis itself provides evidence; rather, hypotheses are suppositions requiring evidence. And because this is so, one hypothesis cannot confirm or disconfirm another. This distinction is embedded both in technical and ordinary discourse. A hypothesis can be published, presented for consideration in written or oral form, argued for or against. None of these things can be said about perceptions. Here, despite Mates's sarcastic comment that every crucial term in the external-world problem has been "declared to be stretched or in some other way abused or misused," we find a scientist doing just those things. By speaking of perceptions as if they could be hypotheses, and of hypotheses as if they could confirm or disconfirm other hypotheses, Gregory's "scientific" account has drifted into conceptual incoherence. I will not dwell on the point here, however, since it is the causal story that is my real target.

FOUR

In reflecting on these quotations, one is immediately struck by the pronounced philosophical character of the terminology that Gregory and Gibson are using to characterize a debate supposedly taking place within experimental science. Both describe themselves as experimentalists, and both adduce experimental data in support of their views. Yet they also use a terminology that belongs to the classical epistemological tradition that derives from Descartes, for whom the opposition between directly and nondirectly seeing is fundamental. Even the somewhat twisted terminology that Gibson employs—using "mediately" in contrast to "directly"—is part and parcel of that tradition (we find it, for example, in Berkeley's *Three Dialogues*). Such usage supports the suspicion that both Gibson and his opponents are more philosophical in their approaches than they purport, or even realize themselves, to be. That they speak in these ways is, as we shall see, a matter of considerable importance in trying to understand the nature of their disagreement.

That disagreement turns less on whether mental representations are images or pictures and more on how they understand what I am calling the "causal theory." I can bring this point out as follows. With respect to images and pictures, Gibson is surely right in thinking that there is a difference between seeing Niagara Falls and seeing a picture of it. It is true, of course, that there are special circumstances in which it is in order to say things like "Today I saw Niagara Falls," when what you saw was a picture of Niagara Falls. This might happen if you were describing a slide show you had attended dedicated to the world's most famous waterfalls. Nobody who knew what the circumstances were would take you to mean that today you had actually been on the Canadian-American border and had seen the falls from that site. So when such ambiguities are eliminated, nobody would think that seeing Niagara Falls is the same as seeing a picture of Niagara Falls. If this is all that Gibson means, it would seem that he is beating a dead horse.

One could grant him this obvious fact while arguing that such a concession does not entail that the perception of Niagara Falls is unmediated. Indeed, a majority of contemporary philosophers, psychologists, and cognitive scientists whose speciality is vision believe that all perception of objects is mediated. According to these critics of Gibson (Gregory, Smythies, French, inter alios) human beings process stimulus inputs, creating mental structures for interpreting other stimuli. These structures, connected by grammarlike sets of rules and not produced by experienced associations, they call *mental representations*. It is these that organize preperceptual sensory data into what common folk would ordinarily call perceptions. Thus the mediating factors are not pictures or sense data or mental images, as Gibson supposes, but various types of rulelike structures that intervene between an observer and the object and condition that individual's perception of the object. What is at stake, as they see the issue, is the nature of such intermediation, i.e., how it works and how it affects the reliability of the observer's apprehension of the object. The answers to these questions, they believe, will depend on future developments in the cognitive sciences.

The general position of Gibson's opponents that no perception is unmediated is, like Gibson's itself, very familiar, being a variant of a causal argument that we find in the literature from the seventeenth century to the present. Gregory has produced the most detailed version of that argument. He breaks perception down into four steps or stages, the latter three of which describe what happens to external stimuli when they are absorbed into and processed by the human visual system, including the brain.[11]

Given its detail, I would need more space than I have to describe his version of the argument. Instead, I will offer the simpler version, consistent with his characterization, that twentieth-century philosophers from Bertrand Russell to Robert French have advanced in one form or another. Here is French's version:

> I shall assume at the outset that visual perception is indirect, and thus that we are never immediately aware of even the surfaces of physical objects. Instead, I will hold that our immediate visual awareness consists of a phenomenal field of colors, visual space, whose geometrical and qualitative features are determined by causal connections with the physical objects being "seen"; that is by light rays reflected from these objects being focussed on the retina, and the various subsequent neural events which take place in the brain.[12]

The causal account typically begins with a description of an optical fact, namely that according to well-known physical laws, light is reflected off an opaque object, traverses the space between the object and an observer, and then, if certain standard conditions are operative, is picked up by the observer's visual system. This system includes the eye (and its various features, such as the rods, cones, and retina), the optic nerve, and the brain, which processes the informational "inputs" received from these various systems. The events in this sequence are causally related, i.e., light strikes the eye, which causes an image to be formed on the retina, which in turn causes a reaction in the optic nerve, and so on. The last event in this causal sequence is called "seeing." This is the first half of the causal argument, and I propose to dub it the "scientific story." Both Gibson and his opponents would accept the scientific story.

So far, nothing in the causal argument speaks about mediation. The account does say that the events described stand in certain sorts of causal relationships to one another, but to say that A causes B is not to say that B mediates A. This requires a new step. Let us call this second step the "conceptual story." It carries the causal argument into the domain of the conceptual and philosophical. Gibson's opponents contend that it is not merely that light causes an image to form on the retina. They also wish to add that light is affected in various ways as it traverses space. Reflected off objects and passing through a series of filters, such as clouds and particulate matter in the air, it is bent, diffracted, and in other ways distorted. Further distortion is added by the eye, whose capacity for acuity is affected by a variety of factors, some of them having to do with the physical condition of the observer.

According to proponents of such theories of mediated perception, similar remarks can be made about the optic nerve and especially about the brain. Each of these systems conditions the information that ultimately leads to the event or state called "seeing." What the brain is processing, as is obvious, is not the object itself but a complex series of highly mediated events that, along with stored knowledge, give rise to a mental representation, and the nature and properties of the object are inferred from that representation. Mediation thus occurs all along the causal chain; the notion that we see things unmediated is tantamount, on this account, to saying that these various intervening events, processes, and representations have no effect upon the character of human perception—a conclusion that Gibson's critics find incredible.

CHAPTER SEVEN

This is what Gregory means when he says that direct realism cannot be supported, "given the indirectness imposed by the many physiological steps or stages of visual and other sensory perception."[13] The correct inference to be drawn from this train of reasoning, he argues, is that perception is never unmediated and therefore is never direct in Gibson's sense. He asserts that Gibson's theory, which claims the opposite, is patently inconsistent with the findings of contemporary science.

The important point to note here, in reflecting on the conceptual story, is how its scientific and philosophical components are inextricably intertwined. Yet we can distinguish these components. One can interpret the statement that light bounces off objects in at least two different ways: first, that unless these causal antecedents were present, vision would not occur, and second, that what is called "seeing" is mediated by the events occurring in the causal sequence. The first claim is neutral; it is the scientific story. The second claim is not neutral; it is a conceptual/philosophical story. That it is not neutral can be seen from its paradoxical implications, for example, that we are never immediately aware of the surface of any opaque object. G. E. Moore also advanced such a view, without any scientific backing. Like Moore's, French's assertion glosses the scientific story in a nonscientific way. It speaks not only of causality but of mediation. One can accept the scientific story without accepting the conceptual story. That is what Gibson does.

FIVE

In particular, what is it in the preceding account that Gibson rejects? Gibson's theory can also be divided into two parts, a scientific story and a conceptual story, but it does not purport to be a causal theory in the way that the opposing account does. The first half of his theory is identical with that of the opposing view. That is, he accepts the scientific story. But the second part is strikingly different. It makes almost no use of what his opponents declare to be mediators. Gibson relegates these to a different category. Let us call them "facilitators." They extend and amplify the knowledge we obtain through direct perception but do not alter it.[14]

For Gibson, most objects in an ecological environment have objective properties: a more or less definable shape, as determined by "surface layout," surfaces with diverse sorts of textures, edges in various configurations, a certain size, etc. When Gibson speaks about "information" contained *in* light, he means that light accurately reflects these properties. Here his view is very close to the commonsense idea that when you turn on the light in a darkened room, it illuminates the objects so that an individual can see them. The commonsense idea is that turning on a light does not distort one's perception of the objects in a room but facilitates it, and this is similar to Gibson's conception.

I should say a bit more about the concept of being a facilitator. What Gibson is asserting in using this notion, and its analogues, is that the events in the causal chain as described in the scientific story are *not* mediators. They do not intervene or stand between the human observer and the external object. Let's consider two examples of mediation and contrast them with a case where theory might incline one mistakenly to speak of mediation. In the first case a referee who separates two angry hockey players functions as a mediator. He stands between the athletes and keeps them apart. In the second case a lawyer functions as a mediator between two parties seeking a divorce. He stands between them, but not to separate them. Instead, he tries to bring them together to resolve their disagreement.

Now consider a young woman who decides to eat dinner in a perfectly normal way. She wishes to eat some steak, which she cuts with a knife. With a fork she picks up the meat and inserts it into her mouth. She could, of course, less elegantly have picked up the meat with her fingers. Is the fork a mediator between her and the meat? In such a case what distinction would one be drawing in distinguishing between picking up the meat with her fingers and picking it up with a fork? But then why not say her fingers were a mediator? After all, she might have just leaned over and picked up the meat with her mouth. What counts as a mediator in this situation? The answer is not obvious. In each of these cases we *are describing a causal sequence,* beginning with her desire to eat the meat and ending with the meat disappearing into her mouth. Yet none of the events in that sequence—her fingers picking up the meat, her arms lifting it to her mouth, her mouth chewing the meat, and so forth—could uncontentiously be described as a mediator.

Each of those events, and the objects in them, made it possible for her to eat the meat. They were thus facilitators in Gibson's sense. This is how he thinks of the visual scientific story, even through to its last event, the seeing of an object. His notion is that the human visual system normally allows the observer to see objects as they really are. The role of the eye or the optic nerve, etc., is to transmit information. Just as a fork allows one to pick up food, but does not "mediate," "condition," or "distort" it, so the eyes, the optic nerve, and the brain facilitate, but do not mediate, one's seeing of the ambient environment. Human visual access to external objects is thus normally direct, just as the fork provides direct, not indirect, access to food. In the light of this brief summary, we can say that the second part of Gibson's theory is not part of the causal story. Instead, it adds something noncausal—the verdict "direct"—to the scientific account that both he and his opponents accept.

In reflecting on the passage in which Gibson describes seeing Niagara Falls as a case of direct perception, we can see that there are two distinct issues embedded in it and that Gibson does not distinguish between them. The first is the question of whether, when we see Niagara Falls, we are seeing something akin to a picture or an image. (And even this issue could be subdivided, because as Wittgenstein points out, "An image is not a picture, but a picture can correspond to it.")[15]

That these are two different issues can be inferred from the fact that Gibson's "cognitivist" critics, as mentioned above, deny that we see images or pictures in normal cases of perception but nonetheless assert that in all such cases one's perception is mediated via mental representations. In particular, they do not think of representations as what the older tradition called "sense data," that is, as thin, decal-like entities that, at least in some cases, are copies or duplicates of the external object. Instead, a mental representation "reproduces" the object via a complicated set of projection rules, so that it may not look like the object at all. As Robert French has written, "While there may be various structural resemblances between portions of visual space and the corresponding physical objects being 'seen,' many of which being given by the laws of projective geometry, it remains possible that both the topological and metric structure of visual space is quite different from that of physical space."[16]

Suppose that Gibson were to accept their statement that we do not see pictures or their imagistic congeners. Would he then be willing to concede that we see Niagara Falls not directly but only as mediated by mental representations or phenomenal visual space? The answer would be "No." He surely would not deny this part of the causal argument. Indeed, he has stated that his theory is consistent with the known facts of optics and neurobiology. Thus the issue for him is not whether such causally intervening events are pictures or images but whether or not they are mediators as well.

We have now reached the stage where we can see that in saying that there is a difference between seeing Niagara Falls and seeing a picture of it, Gibson is saying two things at once: first, that the scientific story, what I have labeled the first part of the causal argument, does not entail that one is apprehending pictures or images, and second, that it does not entail that normal perception is always mediated. It is this second claim that represents the point of deepest disagreement between him and his opponents. The sticking point is thus, what counts as a mediator?

It is clear that Gibson's critics do not fully understand that this is so. They continue to insist that there are such things as mental representations and that they function as information processors and also that such information processors are mediators. But the arguments they give support the thesis that mental representations exist, rather than the thesis that they are mediators. On this second point they often assume, rather than argue, that this is so, as the quotation from French indicates. But, as we have seen in the passage from Gibson, whether there are mental images or mental representations is only part of the issue for him, a lesser part. His emphasis, instead, is upon mediation—upon those "hypothetical mediators," as he calls them. In speaking of such mediators as "hypothetical," he does not wish to deny that retinal, mental, and visual images exist, but only that they come into play *every time* a human being sees an external object.

In seeing that mediation and not representation is the central issue, Gibson is more perceptive than his cognitivist critics. But like them, he does not comprehend that the question of what counts as a mediator is a philosophical issue, requiring the clarification of the concept of mediation. As such it cannot be resolved by an appeal to the facts. Thus neither Gibson nor his opposition understands that the second half of the causal story is a nonexperimental, conceptual gloss imposed upon the scientific story. As Wittgenstein could have informed them, the idea that the scientific story itself *entails* the notion of mediation is simply mistaken.

Thus in referring to the "opposite theory," Gibson is not opposing one scientific story with another, as his language would suggest, but rather and unwittingly, one philosophical interpretation of that story with another philosophical interpretation of it. The issue between Gibson and his critics is thus only superficially an empirical one, for they both accept the scientific story. What divides them is a conceptual matter: how the scientific story is to be interpreted—an issue that turns on the question of whether the events in the causal sequence are mediators.

In effect, then, I am emphasizing the neutrality of the scientific story. By "neutrality" I mean that the scientific account, including its references to brain functions, does not entail any verdict about the mediated or nonmediated character of what is seen. To say, as Gregory and French do, that the object is seen indirectly is such a verdict; it goes beyond the scientific story, adding a new element to it. Of course, the scientific story itself might be disputed, but that would be a dispute *strictly within* science. At the present time, there is very little scientific disagreement about what happens to light after it bounces off an object and is picked up by the visual system, whereas there is considerable debate about how the brain processes the information it ultimately receives. Much of the literature about perception today, including the philosophical literature, is concerned with this debate. An example of such a dispute is the so-called "binding problem," i.e., how the brain works to bring together colors, shapes, and sizes into a coherent perceptual whole.

But the issue of mediation stands outside of that debate. Even if it should turn out that there are mental representations, that fact would not affect the neutrality of the scientific story. In particular, it would not allow one to infer, without further argumentation of a *nonscientific sort*, that the perception of objects is always mediated.

SIX

If I am right, there is submerged in this debate an important thesis of which neither side is fully aware, namely that the scientific part of the causal story in perception is philosophically neutral. The thesis is not only important in the case of perception, but generalizing, one can see that it has significant implications wherever causal theories are appealed to. Though, as far as I know, the point has never been explicitly formulated in this way, some contemporary positions with respect to human action could be so expressed, for instance. A defender of the doctrine of freedom of the will, holding a compatibilist position, might argue that the scientific part of the causal story is neutral and therefore does not entail the verdict "unfree." Such a compatibilist could also insist that the scientific story does not entail the opposite conclusion either. The point, he might insist, is that no inference about human freedom follows from that story.

This contention parallels the argument I have developed above, and likewise its scope goes beyond the particular case under discussion. Accordingly, given the importance of the thesis of the neutrality of the scientific story, it is imperative that one ask whether it is true or not.

I propose in this section to generate two arguments in its support. I will do this by considering two contrary positions. If it turns out that these positions are both mistaken, one will have good reasons for believing that the scientific story is neutral.

The first argument is directed against the cognitivist contention that the perception of external objects is always indirect (e.g., Gregory, French, Smythies), and the second against the contention that it is generally direct (e.g., Gibson). I will show that both sides have boxed themselves into conceptually untenable positions that sometimes depend on bad examples and sometimes depend on radical and incoherent deviations from ordinary speech.

The first is a classical argument frequently posed as an objection to any theory of representative perception. A number of writers (e.g., Jonathan Harrison, J. B. Maund, Robert Oakes, and J. R. Smythies[17]) have recently tried to meet this objection, but I believe unsuccessfully. Their view is that the final event in the causal series not only represents, but also conditions, the observer's perception of the object. But how, *at least on the basis of what they themselves perceive,* could they possibly know this, unless they knew what the object looked like *unconditioned?*

Since they claim that all perception of external objects is mediated, they must concede that the unconditioned perception of such an object is impossible. But if so, one could never compare the representation with the unconditioned object via any observational act to ascertain that the representation did not faithfully reproduce the object. This objection does not show that perception is not mediated, but it does demonstrate that no mediationist could know on observational grounds that it is, and this surely affects the credibility of their claim.

The difficulty is equally acute for those who explicitly hold that the mental representation is not a copy of the object, for they have no way of proving that their projection rules reproduce the object as it is in itself. Though I have put this point in epistemological terms, the basic difficulty is conceptual. We have here an instance of the monistic fallacy. It is analogous to arguing that everything is made of water and then defining putative countercases (sand, say) in such a way that they no longer count as countercases. To assert that all perception of the external is mediated is to preempt the very possibility that any such perceptual act could be unmediated. Thus if the claim were correct, there would be no describable circumstances in which one could perceive a physical object directly. But if so, the negation of this claim, namely that all perception is mediated, would lack empirical content, since no relevant test could be devised to falsify it. The argument I am advancing is not a version of verificationism. Instead, I am saying that mediationists wish to support their views on empirical grounds while at the same time advancing views that cannot be tested scientifically. Their position is thus incoherent. I do not see any way out of this dilemma for a mediationist.

The second objection is directed against Gibson. It points out that Gibson has committed a mistake similar to the monistic fallacy of his opponents. The cognitivists say we see representations directly and external objects indirectly. Gibson says the opposite. His view is thus a mirror image of theirs, only the terms are converted. He arrives at his position via a contrast between seeing Niagara Falls and seeing a picture of Niagara Falls. His mistake arises from misunderstanding the role that pictures play in human communication. The clue to his mistake is to be found in a passage from Wittgenstein: "Of course, if water boils in a pot, steam comes out of the pot and also pictured steam comes out of the pictured pot. But what if one insisted on saying that there must also be something boiling in the picture of the pot?"[18] Now no sane person who looks at a picture of a pot would say that real steam is emerging from the pictured pot. Wittgenstein's example is well chosen to illustrate that we must distinguish talk about real objects from talk about pictures, icons, photographs, etc., of those objects. Of course, there can be elliptical ways of speaking that, in some contexts, create misunderstandings, that cause another to think that one is seeing the real thing rather than a picture of it. Compare "I saw the Super Bowl today" with "I saw the Super Bowl on TV today," or again, "I saw President Clinton last night" with "I saw Clinton last night on TV." Talk about seeing things in pictures or in the movies or on TV is similar to and yet different from talk about seeing things in dreams. There are thus additional possibilities for misunderstanding in such cases. To say that I saw President Roosevelt in a dream last night is not to say that on a certain occasion in 1996 I actually saw someone who died a half century ago, which suggests that Roosevelt had been resurrected intact in 1996. Rather, it is to say that last night *I dreamt* that I saw Roosevelt. No one would think that in speaking about seeing the Super Bowl on TV, I was speaking about something that had taken place a half century ago. All these cases resonate with different overtones and must be distinguished, as I have been urging throughout this book.

Gibson, of course, understands that one who is looking at a picture or photograph of Niagara Falls is not literally seeing the falls. To say that one is not "literally" seeing the falls, means that one is not standing at a site on the Canadian-American border looking at that famous waterfall. So Gibson wishes to expand the context to minimize misunderstanding. It is thus conceptual, rather than scientific considerations, that motivate him. But his way of expanding the context, by invoking the notion of seeing indirectly, not only does not help, it creates new misapprehensions.

His intuition for wishing to speak about seeing indirectly is complex. Let me try to reconstruct what he is thinking. He believes that in looking at a picture of Niagara Falls, one is not literally seeing Niagara Falls, which is perfectly correct. But he wishes to explain this fact by saying that one is not *directly* seeing Niagara Falls, and this addition is a mistake. Yet it is also true that in seeing a picture, one is in some sense seeing Niagara Falls. So Gibson concludes that if one is not seeing Niagara Falls directly, one must be seeing it *indirectly.* This last inference compounds the earlier mistake.

What is the monistic fallacy that has been created by these moves? The difficulty is that for the terms "directly" and "indirectly" to express a significant contrast, they must apply to the *same* thing. Here is where getting the examples right is crucial. We can and do say "I heard about Smith's promotion directly; she told me so herself." In this use a contrast is being drawn between hearing about something at first hand and hearing about it second or third hand, or reading it in the newspapers. If one had heard about it from another, one could have said "I heard about it indirectly." Again, if one says "I was directly responsible for recruiting Jones," an opposition is being presupposed between one's playing a major versus a lesser role in Jones's recruitment. In the latter case one could have said "I was indirectly responsible." The point is that all such uses of the direct/indirect distinction (and its adverbial counterparts) *apply to the same event:* in the preceding examples, to Smith's promotion and to Jones's recruitment.

Therefore, if Gibson were developing a sensible contrast between seeing x directly and seeing x indirectly "x" would have to refer to the same thing. But that is not the case he gives us. Instead, in describing indirect seeing, he speaks about seeing a *picture of the object,* not the object itself. A picture of Niagara Falls is not Niagara Falls. In the literal sense of the term, one is not seeing Niagara Falls when one sees a picture of it.

Hence, insofar as the terms "direct" and "indirect" have a sensible use, they must apply to the same thing. The monistic fallacy arises because Gibson does not allow for the same object, in different contextual situations, to be seen either directly or indirectly. There is thus no possible way to see Niagara Falls itself indirectly. And there is no possible way to see a picture of Niagara Falls directly. His theory has thus preempted the formation of counterexamples. It is thus a mirror image of the cognitivist thesis, with the terms reversed. As a result, he does not draw a genuine distinction between seeing a particular *x* directly and seeing the same *x* indirectly. In seeing a picture of Niagara Falls, we are seeing Niagara Falls neither indirectly or directly, because we are not literally seeing Niagara Falls at all. So the account fails.

In the theories of Gibson and his opponents, seemingly straightforward scientific accounts of perception are replete with such conceptual confusion. We see in their work how poorly selected examples and radical deviations from common sense and ordinary discourse can generate philosophical paradox. All this strongly supports the thesis that the scientific story is free of philosophical intrusions.

SEVEN

Is there an antidote to the confusions generated by the theorizing on both sides? I think there are two. The first applies primarily to Gibson. It would consist in a detailed description of the many things human beings call "pictures." The outcome of such an endeavor would show that the relationships between pictures and what they depict are complex, and that though some pictures may represent features of reality, some may distort those features or fail to represent them at all. In this context it is thus crucial to examine a wide range of examples. Many different sorts of things are called "pictures." The category includes pictograms, drawings, engravings, photographs, and even verbal or literary descriptions of a vivid sort, such as Gibbon's depiction of imperial Rome.

Some of these items may bear a likeness to the object being depicted, such as a good portrait. But a likeness, even sheer likeness, is not a sufficient condition for something's being a picture: a statue having this characteristic would not be called a picture. In general, pictures are artifacts, i.e., the products of human skill and workmanship, and not natural objects, such as trees or bushes. But even here language is highly nuanced: we hear it said that the child is a perfect picture of the parent.

The relationship between an actual object and the object pictured is complex and depends on the particular case. It can range from an isomorphism between the pictured object and the real object, as in a Canaletto painting and a certain portion of eighteenth-century Venice, to looser correspondences. Icons would be an example of such a looser correspondence. Of course, some icons are not pictures. A chemical diagram of a molecule, for instance, is an icon that is not a picture, even though there are structural and other similarities between the features in the diagram and features in the object. In the case of very tight correspondences, as in a good photograph or portrait, we can say that what is depicted in the photograph or portrait "looks like" the thing depicted.

But it would not in general be correct to say that what is depicted in everything we call a picture must look like the depicted object. A twelfth-century icon of the Virgin

Mary, can be said to be a picture of the Virgin Mary but one could not plausibly claim that the figure in it looks like the Virgin Mary, since there is no way that the painter, or anyone alive today, could have known or could now know what Mary looked like. The example is important. It shows that we cannot sensibly say that we are indirectly seeing the Virgin Mary, since we are not seeing the Virgin Mary at all. The depicted entity is simply a figment of the artist's creative imagination. This case is different from that of a picture of Niagara Falls and from that of a Canaletto painting. Though it is sensible to say that one is obtaining information about the appearance of eighteenth-century Venice from a Canaletto painting, it is not sensible to say that one is obtaining information about the appearance of the Virgin Mary from the picture in question.

These remarks apply to Gibson in the following way. Gibson's theory is essentially a theory about information "pickup," as he calls it. He means that if we look at a real object, such as Niagara Falls, we obtain an enormous amount of information from what we see. We see an expanse of water, see the water fall from a height, hear various sounds the water makes, see various colors and shades as the light plays on the water, and so forth. When we obtain such maximal amounts of information, Gibson wishes to say that we are seeing the object directly. In contrast, a picture gives us a limited selection of information, say about Niagara Falls. If it is in black and white, information about the colors of the water is diminished or lost. A picture generally cannot give the kind of information one obtains when one looks around and scans the ambient environment. But at least the picture tells us something about Niagara Falls, only less than what we would obtain by seeing the falls itself. In such a case Gibson wishes to say that we see the falls indirectly.

But the idea that pictures provide indirect information about the objects or events they depict cannot in general be true. A picture of the Virgin Mary does not give us any information about the Virgin Mary. So we cannot say that we are indirectly seeing the Virgin Mary in such a case. Gibson's theory can thus be rejected on the ground of overgeneralization. If it has any plausibility as a theory of information pickup, it would apply only to a carefully selected and limited set of examples.

The second antidote is stronger. It denies that in speaking of real objects or depictions of them, we can always sensibly use the modifiers "directly" and "indirectly." Here is how the objection goes: Ordinary persons have the pretheoretical conceptual categories for distinguishing a representation, such as a picture or an image, from the object the representation represents. One can hold a picture of a child in his hand and compare it to the child herself. In such a case, no confusion will arise as to which is which. The picture is here in one's hand, and it depicts a child. The child is over there and is not in one's hand. The difference is obvious. The varied resources ordinary persons have for making such discriminations are multifarious, and they include verbal capacities.

Ordinary persons employ "direct" and "indirect" (and their adverbial forms) to make discriminations, but always in a limited and selective way. In those cases a distinction between the unmediated and the mediated is generally being drawn. But in speaking about seeing Niagara Falls, ordinary persons do not use the language of mediation at all. If they are holding a photograph rather than seeing Niagara Falls itself, they will talk about a good or bad likeness, an interesting perspective, and so forth. But they never use the idioms "direct" and "indirect" in such a case. To hold, as French does, that we should speak of seeing representations when we are literally seeing Niagara Falls is simply wrong. The mediationist gloss put on the scientific story cannot be a correct description of what it is to see Niagara Falls, and no ordinary person would accept it. To say, as Gibson does, that in looking at a picture we are seeing the falls indirectly thus suffers from the same liability.

This objection—the second antidote as I have called it—tells us in effect that in common speech we have all the verbal resources we need for accurately characterizing what we see, so that if we wish on some occasion to qualify or modify what we see, various idioms of modification are readily available to us. If one is looking at Niagara Falls and it is covered with heavy fog, one can say "I can't see it clearly" or "I can barely see it" or "I just can't see it at all," and so forth. Now according to Gibson, "directly" is one such modifier. As indicated, he thought that in an ordinary case of seeing something, say Niagara Falls, we make it still plainer that it is an *ordinary case* of seeing by adding the term "directly." But in fact if one were to say in any circumstances whatever that one was seeing Niagara Falls directly, the addition of the modifier would be a sure indication that the situation was not ordinary. The auditor would be puzzled and want to know what the speaker intended by using such a term. Communication would be blocked and not enhanced. What Gibson, as an information theorist, may have wished to communicate by his mixed vocabulary of technical and ordinary speech would have been defeated by the very idiom he employed.

I said at the beginning of this chapter that Gibson was wrong in holding that a case of seeing Niagara Falls is to be characterized as a case of direct perception, and I added that how it should be characterized is an interesting and difficult question. Among these difficulties would be those alluded to above, namely, to give an accurate account of how the things called pictures differ from one another in important respects. The matter is indeed too difficult to be explored here. Still, whatever Gibson and his cognitive opponents wish to say cannot be said by using the contrast between seeing directly and seeing indirectly. To rest their technical views on such a distinction, with its deep resonances from ordinary speech, is to compound, and not to dispel, confusion. For as we have observed, if ordinary persons wish to modify the statement that today they had seen Niagara Falls, they would always have at hand the conceptual and verbal resources to do so. The fact that the modifier "directly" is never used in such a case is a sure indication that it is never needed. Contrary to what Gibson thought, there is no ordinary perceptual situation that "directly" would help us characterize.

Wittgenstein tells us that ordinary language is all right just as it is, and that in philosophy the hard thing is to see what is obvious in the obsessive, theory-driven search for the hidden. If we had seen Niagara Falls today and wished to describe what we had seen, we couldn't do better than to say that we saw Niagara Falls today. But if instead what we saw was a picture of Niagara Falls today, we couldn't do better than to say that we saw a picture of Niagara Falls today. To add "directly" or "indirectly" to what we said would not have made what we said more clear, more informative, more accurate, or more correct.

Notes

CHAPTER ONE

1
Richard H. Popkin, *The History of Scepticism from Erasmus to Spinoza.*

2
Benson Mates, *The Skeptic Way,* p. 4.

3
Saul A. Kripke, *Wittgenstein on Rules and Private Language.*

4
Edmund L. Gettier, "Is Justified True Belief Knowledge?" pp. 121–123.

5
Robert P. Amico, *The Problem of the Criterion,* p. 1.

6
Roderick M. Chisholm, *The Foundations of Knowing,* p. 62.

7
See my *Moore and Wittgenstein on Certainty,* pp. 48–54.

8
Ludwig Wittgenstein, *On Certainty,* entry 438.

9
Wittgenstein, *On Certainty,* entry 484.

10
Wittgenstein, *On Certainty,* entry 84.

11
For a careful description and critical discussion of the "deconstructionist" approach to be found in Austin and Stroll, and especially how it differs from the deconstructionism of such writers as Derrida, see A. P. Martinich, "Analytic Phenomenological Deconstruction."

12
Barry Stroud, *The Significance of Philosophical Scepticism.*

13
Quoted in Stroud, *The Significance of Philosophical Scepticism,* p. 11.

14
Quoted in Stroud, *The Significance of Philosophical Scepticism,* p. 11.

15
Benson Mates, *Skeptical Essays,* pp. 106–108.

CHAPTER TWO

1
Saul A. Kripke, *Naming and Necessity,* p. 116.

2
Hilary Putnam, "Meaning and Reference," p. 130.

3
J. J. C. Smart, "Sensations and Brain Processes," pp. 163–165.

4
Hilary Putnam, "Meaning and Reference," p. 129.

5
Throughout this essay I do not challenge the assumptions that there are natural kinds and that we can distinguish them from nonnatural kinds, such as chairs. The issue is too complex to be discussed here. Paul M. Churchland has challenged both assumptions in his "Conceptual Progress and Word/World Relations: In Search of the Essence of Natural Kinds."

6
Saul A. Kripke, *Naming and Necessity,* pp. 120–121.

7
Hilary Putnam, "Meaning and Reference," p. 127.

8
Hilary Putnam, "Meaning and Reference," p. 129.

9
Ludwig Wittgenstein, *On Certainty,* p. 62e, entry 476.

CHAPTER THREE

1
W. V. O. Quine, "Two Dogmas of Empiricism," p. 37.

2
Quine, "Two Dogmas of Empiricism," p. 39.

3
Quine, "Two Dogmas of Empiricism," p. 37.

4
Quine, "Two Dogmas of Empiricism," p. 38.

5
Georgios Anagnostopoulos, "Plato on the Sciences."

6
Patricia S. Churchland, *Neurophilosophy*, p. 249.

7
Hilary Putnam, *Representation and Reality*, p. 107.

8
Ludwig Wittgenstein, *Philosophical Investigations*, entry 92.

9
Wittgenstein, *Philosophical Investigations*, entry 126.

10
Hilary Putnam, *Mind, Language, and Reality*, p. 235.

11
Hilary Putnam, *Representation and Reality*, p. 4.

12
Putnam, *Representation and Reality*, p. 32.

13
Putnam, *Representation and Reality*, p. 109.

14
Saul A. Kripke, *Naming and Necessity*, p. 138.

15
See Sisler, VanderWerf, and Davidson, *College Chemistry*, p. 256.

16
See Sisler, VanderWerf, and Davidson, *College Chemistry*, pp. 256–258, for a detailed, scientific discussion of the properties of water and ice.

17
Hilary Putnam, "Meaning and Reference," pp. 124.

18
See, for example, my "Primordial Knowledge and Rationality," "Some Different Ways That Things Stand Fast for Us," "Foundationalism and Common Sense," "Wittgenstein and Folk Psychology," and "How I See Philosophy: Common Sense and the Common Sense View of the World."

19
Avrum Stroll, *Moore and Wittgenstein on Certainty*, esp. chaps. 9–10.

1

David Pears, "Wittgenstein's Naturalism," p. 411.

2

Howard Wettstein, "Terra Firma," p. 426.

3

David Hume, *Dialogues Concerning Natural Religion*, part 2.

4

Aristotle's third-man argument in the *Metaphysics* (bk. 11., chap. 1) can be regarded as a criticism of the *mimesis* interpretation of the relationship.

5

Quoted in *Webster's Third New International Dictionary*, s.v. "example." In this essay I do not discuss how evaluative words work with "copy," "example," "sample," etc. This is a major task in its own right. But it is worth mentioning that "*x* is a bad example" may sometimes imply that *x* is not an example at all, or it may imply that *x* is an example but is somehow morally inferior and is therefore not to be followed or emulated. The former use applies more frequently when "example" works like an "instance" word, and the latter when "example" is used in the sense described above.

6

The argument is fallacious since the "is" in the premises is not used in the same sense as the "is" in the conclusion: in effect, Plato has confused something like a predicative sense of "is" with an identity sense of "is." As I have argued in previous chapters, the mistake is similar to that made by Putnam and Kripke when they interpret the "is" in "Water is H_2O" to be the "is" of identity rather than the "is" of composition.

CHAPTER FIVE

1

Saul A. Kripke, "Identity and Necessity," pp. 78–79, and *Naming and Necessity*, p. 5.

2

Kripke, "Identity and Necessity," p. 79.

3

The paper, with the accompanying discussion, has been reprinted in Ruth B. Marcus, *Modalities: Philosophical Essays*, pp. 3–38.

4
Marcus, *Modalities: Philosophical Essays*, pp. xiii–xiv.

5
In *Lingua Franca*, Jan./Feb. 1996, 29–39.

6
Interestingly enough, in two still later works, *An Inquiry into Meaning and Truth* and *Human Knowledge: Its Scope and Limits*, Russell reverts to his earlier views that proper names are to be distinguished from descriptions. See Marcus, *Modalities*, pp. 185 ff., where Marcus says that Russell's views in these works "are striking in their closeness to contemporary theories of direct reference."

7
Marcus, *Modalities*, p. 203.

8
Marcus, *Modalities*, p. 207.

9
Marcus, *Modalities*, p. 204.

10
Kripke, "Identity and Necessity," p. 81.

11
Kripke, *Naming and Necessity*, p. 21 n.

12
Keith Donnellan, "Speaking of Nothing," p. 218.

13
Zeno Vendler, *The Matter of Minds*, chap. 4.

14
W. V. O. Quine, "On What There Is."

15
Quine, "On What There Is," p. 200.

16
Barry Smith, *Austrian Philosophy: The Legacy of Franz Brentano*, p. 128.

17
Bertrand Russell, *Introduction to Mathematical Philosophy*, p. 170.

18
Herbert Feigl, "Logical Empiricism," p. 7.

19
P. F. Strawson, "On Referring," in A. Flew, ed., *Essays in Conceptual Analysis*, pp. 35–36.

1
Ruth Marcus, *Modalities*, p. 212.

2
W. V. Quine, "Reply to Jules Vuillemin," in *The Philosophy of W. V. Quine,* ed. by Hahn and Schilpp, p. 619.

3
W. V. Quine, "Two Dogmas of Empiricism," p. 41. Quine, in a footnote to this passage, mentions that the doctrine was "well argued by Duhem."

4
W. V. Quine, "Reply to Hilary Putnam," in *The Philosophy of W. V. Quine,* ed. by Hahn and Schilpp, p. 427.

5
Hilary Putnam, "Meaning Holism," p. 406.

6
W. V. Quine, "Reply to Hilary Putnam," in *The Philosophy of W. V. Quine,* ed. by Hahn and Schilpp, p. 427.

7
W. V. Quine, "Two Dogmas of Empiricism," p. 41.

8
Bertrand Russell, "On Denoting," p. 110.

9
Bertrand Russell, "The Philosophy of Logical Atomism," p. 253.

10
Bertrand Russell, *My Philosophical Development,* p. 85.

11
Bertrand Russell, *Introduction to Mathematical Philosophy,* p. 174.

12
Russell, *Introduction to Mathematical Philosophy,* p. 174.

13
Russell, *Introduction to Mathematical Philosophy,* p. 174.

14
Russell, *My Philosophical Development,* p. 85.

15
Marcus, *Modalities,* pp. 203–204.

1
Benson Mates, *Skeptical Essays,* pp. 99–100.

2
John R. Smythies, *The Walls of Plato's Cave,* p. 1.

3
Smythies, *The Walls of Plato's Cave,* p. 104.

4
Robert Oakes, "Representational Sensing: What's the Problem?"
Oakes states that he is using the expressions "representationalism" and "indirect realism" interchangeably in this
paper (p. 85).

5
Oakes, "Representational Sensing: What's the Problem?" p. 73.

6
J. J. Gibson, *The Ecological Approach to Visual Perception,*
p. 147.

7
Gibson, *The Ecological Approach to Visual Perception,* p. 166.

8
Oakes, "Representational Sensing: What's the Problem?" p. 73.

9
Richard L. Gregory, "Hypothesis and Illusion: Explorations in
Perception and Science," pp. 239–240.

10
Gregory, "Hypothesis and Illusion: Explorations in Perception
and Science," p. 242.

11
Gregory, "Hypothesis and Illusion: Explorations in Perception
and Science," pp. 240–243.

12
Robert French, "The Geometry of Visual Space," p. 115.

13
Gregory, "Hypothesis and Illusion: Explorations in Perception
and Science," pp. 240–241.

14
For an excellent discussion of this aspect of Gibson's work, see
E. S. Reed, "James Gibson's Ecological Approach to Cognition."

15
Ludwig Wittgenstein, *Philosophical Investigations,* entry 301.

260 16
French, "The Geometry of Visual Space," p. 115.
17
See their essays in E. Wright, ed., *New Representationalisms: Essays in the Philosophy of Perception,* 1993.
18
Wittgenstein, *Philosophical Investigations,* entry 297.

References

Alexander, Henry A. "Comments on Saying and Believing." In A. Stroll, ed., *Epistemology: New Essays in the Theory of Knowledge,* 1994, 159–178.

Alexander, Henry A. "Surface Knowledge." In A. P. Martinich and M. J. White, eds., *Certainty and Surface in Epistemology and Philosophical Method,* 1991, 67–86.

Allison, Henry E. *Idealism and Freedom.* Cambridge: Cambridge University Press, 1996.

Amico, Robert P. *The Problem of the Criterion.* Lanham, Md.: Rowman and Littlefield, 1993.

Anagnostopoulos, Georgios. *Aristotle on the Goals and Exactness of Ethics.* Berkeley: University of California Press, 1994.

Anagnostopoulos, Georgios. "Plato on the Sciences." *Inquiry* 26 (1983): 237–246.

Austin, John L. *Sense and Sensibilia.* Oxford: Clarendon, 1962.

Baccillieri, Cristina. *L'Erba È Veramente Verde? Wittgenstein e le Modalita della Certezza.* Rome: Donzelli, 1993.

Baker, G. P., and P. M. S. Hacker. *Scepticism, Rules, and Language.* Oxford: Blackwell, 1984.

Barnes, J. *The Toils of Scepticism.* Cambridge: Cambridge University Press, 1990.

Bornet, Gerard. *Die Bedeutung von "Sinn" und der Sinn von "Bedeutung."* Bern: Haupt, 1996.

Bornet, Gerard. "George Boole's Linguistic Turn and the Origins of Analytical Philosophy." In J. Hintikka and K. Puhl, eds., *The British Tradition in 20th Century Philosophy,* 1995, 236–248.

Casati, Roberto. "Notes on Phenomenology and Visual Space." In R. Egidi, ed., *Wittgenstein: Mind and Language,* 1995, 185–194.

Casati, Roberto, and Achille C. Varzi. *Holes and Other Superficialities.* Cambridge: MIT Press, 1994.

Chisholm, Roderick M. *The Foundations of Knowing.* Minneapolis: University of Minnesota Press, 1982.

Chisholm, Roderick M. *The Problem of the Criterion.* Milwaukee: Marquette University Press, 1972.

Chisholm, Roderick M. *Theory of Knowledge.* 3rd ed. Englewood Cliffs, N.J.: Prentice-Hall, 1989.

Churchland, Patricia S. *Neurophilosophy.* Cambridge: MIT Press, 1986.

Churchland, Paul M. "Conceptual Progress and Word/World Relations: In Search of the Essence of Natural Kinds." *Canadian Journal of Philosophy* 15 (1985) no. 1: 1–17.

Clay, Marjorie, and Keith Lehrer, eds. *Knowledge and Skepticism.* Boulder, Colo.: Westview Press, 1989.

Conway, Gertrude D. *Wittgenstein on Foundations.* Atlantic Highlands, N.J.: Humanities Press, 1989.

Davidson, Donald. "A Nice Derangement of Epithaphs." In A. P. Martinich, ed., *Philosophy of Language,* 1996, 465–475.

Diamond, Cora. *The Realistic Spirit.* Cambridge: Harvard University Press, 1991.

Donnellan, Keith. "Reference and Definite Descriptions." In A. P. Martinich, ed., *Philosophy of Language,* 1996, 231–243.

Donnellan, Keith. "Speaking of Nothing." In S. P. Schwartz, ed., *Naming, Necessity, and Natural Kinds,* 1977, 216–244.

Egidi, Rosaria. "Meaning and Actions in Wittgenstein's Late Perspective." *Grazer Philosophische Studien* 42 (1992): 161–179.

Egidi, Rosaria. "Wittgenstein between Philosophical Grammar and Psychology." In R. Egidi, ed., *Wittgenstein: Mind and Language,* 1995, 171–184.

Egidi, Rosaria, ed. *Wittgenstein: Mind and Language.* Dordrecht: Kluwer, 1995.

Feigl, Herbert. "Logical Empiricism." In H. Feigl and W. Sellars, eds., *Readings in Philosophical Analysis.* New York: Appleton-Century-Crofts, 1949.

Ferry, Luc, and Alain Renaut. *French Philosophy of the Sixties: An Essay on Antihumanism.* Amherst, Mass.: University of Massachusetts Press, 1990.

French, Robert. "The Geometry of Visual Space." *Noûs* 21 (1987): 115.

Frongia, Guido. "Wittgenstein and Memory." In R. Egidi, ed., *Wittgenstein: Mind and Language,* 1995, 263–278.

Frongia, Guido. "Wittgenstein and the Diversity of Animals." *Monist* 78, no. 4 (Oct. 1995): 534–552.

Frongia, Guido. *Wittgenstein: Regole E Sistema.* Milano: Angeli, 1983.

Garver, Newton. "McGuiness on the *Tractatus.*" In J. Hintikka and K. Puhl, eds., *The British Tradition in 20th Century Philosophy,* 1995, 85–99.

Garver, Newton. *This Complicated Form of Life.* Chicago: Open Court, 1994.

Garver, Newton, and Seung-Chong Lee. *Derrida and Wittgenstein.* Philadelphia: Temple University Press, 1994.

Gettier, Edmund. "Is Justified True Belief Knowledge?" *Analysis* 23 (1963): 121–123.

Gibson, J. J. *The Ecological Approach to Visual Perception.* Boston: Houghton-Mifflin, 1979.

Gregory, Richard L., "Hypothesis and Illusion: Explorations in Perception and Science." In E. Wright, ed., *New Representationalisms: Essays in the Philosophy of Perception,* 1993.

Gregory, Richard L. *Mind in Science: A History of Explanations of Psychology and Physics.* London: Weidenfeld and Nicolson, 1981.

Hacker, P. M. S. "Wittgenstein and Post-War Philosophy at Oxford." In J. Hintikka and K. Puhl, eds., *The British Tradition in 20th Century Philosophy,* 1995, 100–121.

Hahn, L. E., and P. A. Schilpp, eds. *The Philosophy of W. V. Quine.* La Salle: Open Court, 1986.

Haller, Rudolf. "Justification and Praxeological Foundationalism." *Inquiry* 31 (1988), no. 3: 335–345.

Haller, Rudolf. *Questions on Wittgenstein.* Lincoln, Nebraska: University of Nebraska Press, 1988.

Hannay, Alastair. "Conscious Episodes and *Ceteris Paribus.*" *Monist* 78, no. 4 (Oct. 1995): 447–463.

Hannay, Alastair. *Human Consciousness*. London: Routledge, 1990.

Hannay, Alastair. "New Foundations and Philosophers." In A. P. Martinich and M. J. White, eds., *Certainty and Surface in Epistemology and Philosophical Method*, 1991, 25–40.

Hilmy, Stephen S. *The Later Wittgenstein: The Emergence of a New Philosophical Method*. Oxford: Blackwell, 1987.

Hilmy, Stephen S. "Wittgenstein on Language, Mind, and Mythology." In R. Egidi, ed., *Wittgenstein: Mind and Language*, 1995, 235–248.

Hintikka, Jaako, and Klaus Puhl, eds., *The British Tradition in 20th Century Philosophy*. Vienna: Holder-Pichler-Tempsky, 1995.

Hintikka, Jaakko. "The Longest Philosophical Journey." In J. Hintikka and K. Puhl, eds., *The British Tradition in 20th Century Philosophy*, 1995, 11–26.

Holt, Jim. "Whose Idea Is It, Anyway?" *Lingua Franca* 6, no. 2 (Jan./Feb. 1996): 29–39.

Hume, David. *Dialogues Concerning Natural Religion*. New York: Hafner, 1977.

Hume, David. *A Treatise of Human Nature*. 2d ed. Oxford: Clarendon Press, 1985.

Hylton, Peter. "The British Origins of Analytic Philosophy." In J. Hintikka and K. Puhl, eds., *The British Tradition in 20th Century Philosophy*, 1995, 341–352.

Hylton, Peter. *Russell, Idealism, and the Emergence of Analytic Philosophy*. Oxford: Oxford University Press, 1990.

Johannessen, Kjell S., Rolf Larsen, and Knut O. Amas, eds. *Wittgenstein and Norway*. Oslo: Solun Forlag, 1994.

Kenny, Anthony. "Wittgenstein on Mind and Metaphysics." In R. Egidi, ed., *Wittgenstein: Mind and Language*, 1995, 37–46.

Klein, Peter D. *Certainty: A Refutation of Scepticism*. Minneapolis: University of Minnesota Press, 1981.

Kripke, Saul A. "Identity and Necessity." In S. P. Schwartz, ed., *Naming, Necessity, and Natural Kinds*, 1977, 66–101.

Kripke, Saul A. *Naming and Necessity*. Cambridge: Harvard University Press, 1980.

Kripke, Saul A. *Wittgenstein on Rules and Private Language*. Oxford: Blackwell, 1982.

265   Malcolm, Norman. "Disentangling Moore's Paradox." In R. Egidi, ed., *Wittgenstein: Mind and Language*, 1995, 195–206.

Malcolm, Norman. *Nothing Is Hidden*. Oxford: Blackwell, 1986.

Marcus, Ruth B. *Modalities: Philosophical Essays*. New York: Oxford University Press, 1993.

Martinich, A. J. "Analytic Phenomenological Deconstruction." In A. J. Martinich and M. J. White, eds., *Certainty and Surface in Epistemology and Philosophical Method*, 1991, 165–184.

Martinich, A. J. *Communication and Reference*. New York: de Gruyter, 1984.

Martinich, A. J., ed. *Philosophy of Language*. 3rd ed. New York: Oxford University Press, 1996.

Martinich, A. J., and Michael J. White, eds. *Certainty and Surface in Epistemology and Philosophical Method*. Lewiston: Edwin Mellen Press, 1991.

Mates, Benson. *The Skeptic Way*. New York: Oxford University Press, 1996.

Mates, Benson. *Skeptical Essays*. Chicago: University of Chicago Press, 1981.

Matson, Wallace I. "Certainty Made Simple." In A. P. Martinich and M. J. White, eds., *Certainty and Surface in Epistemology and Philosophical Method*, 1991, 7–24.

McGinn, Marie. *Sense and Certainty*. Oxford: Blackwell, 1989.

McGuinness, Brian. *Wittgenstein, a Life: Young Ludwig, 1889–1921*. Berkeley: University of California Press, 1988.

Monk, Ray. *Ludwig Wittgenstein: The Duty of Genius*. New York: Free Press, 1990.

Moore, George E. *Philosophical Papers*. London: Allen and Unwin, 1959.

Naess, Arne. *Scepticism*. New York: Humanities Press, 1968.

Nagel, Thomas. *The View from Nowhere*. New York: Oxford University Press, 1986.

Oakes, Robert. "Representational Sensing: What's the Problem?" In E. Wright, ed., *New Representationalisms: Essays in the Philosophy of Perception*, 1993, 70–87.

Pears, David. *The False Prison*. 2 vols. Cambridge: Harvard University Press, 1987.

Pears, David. "Russell and Wittgenstein: Holism and Atomism." In J. Hintikka and K. Puhl, eds., *The British Tradition in 20th Century Philosophy*, 1995, 138–149.

Pears, David. "Wittgenstein on Philosophy and Science." In R. Egidi, ed., *Wittgenstein: Mind and Language*, 1995, 23–36.

Pears, David. "Wittgenstein's Naturalism." *Monist* 78, no. 4 (Oct. 1995): 411–424.

Phillips, D. Z. *Introducing Philosophy*. Oxford: Blackwell, 1996.

Popkin, Richard H. *The High Road to Pyrrhonism*. San Diego: Austin Hill Press, 1980.

Popkin, Richard H. *The History of Scepticism from Erasmus to Spinoza*. Berkeley: University of California Press, 1979.

Popkin, Richard H. "Prophecy and Scepticism in the Sixteenth and Seventeenth Century." *British Journal for the History of Philosophy* 4 (1996), no. 1: 1–20.

Popper, Karl. *Conjectures and Refutations*. New York: Basic Books, 1962.

Putnam, Hilary. "Meaning and Reference." In S. P. Schwartz, ed., *Naming, Necessity, and Natural Kinds*, 1977, 119–132.

Putnam, Hilary. "Meaning Holism." In L. E. Hahn and P. A. Schilpp, eds., *The Philosophy of W. V. Quine*, 1986.

Putnam, Hilary. *Mind, Language, and Reality*. Cambridge: Cambridge University Press, 1975.

Putnam, Hilary. *Representation and Reality*. Cambridge: MIT Press, 1989.

Quine, W. V. O. *From a Logical Point of View*. 2nd ed. Cambridge: Harvard University Press, 1961.

Quine, W. V. O. "Meaning." In A. P. Martinich, ed., *Philosophy of Language*, 1996, 446–455.

Quine, W. V. O. "On What There Is." In L. Linsky, ed., *Semantics and the Philosophy of Language*, 2nd ed., 189–206. Urbana: University of Illinois Press, 1972.

Quine, W. V. O. "Two Dogmas of Empiricism." In *From a Logical Point of View*, 2nd ed., 20–46. New York: Harper and Row, 1961. First published in 1950.

Quine, W. V. O. *"The Ways of Paradox" and Other Essays*. New York: Random House, 1966.

Reed, E. S. "James Gibson's Ecological Approach to Cognition." In A. Costall and A. Still, *Against Cognitivism: Alternative Foun-*

267   *dations for Cognitive Psychology.* New York: Harvester Press, 1986.

Rescher, Nicholas. *Scepticism.* Totowa, N.J.: Rowman and Littlefield, 1980.

Russell, Bertrand. *Human Knowledge: Its Scope and Limits.* London: G. Allen and Unwin, 1948.

Russell, Bertrand. *An Inquiry into Meaning and Truth.* Baltimore: Penguin Books, 1940.

Russell, Bertrand. *Introduction to Mathematical Philosophy.* London: Allen and Unwin, 1919.

Russell, Bertrand. *My Philosophical Development.* London: Allen and Unwin, 1959.

Russell, Bertrand. "On Denoting." In H. Feigl and W. Sellars, eds., *Readings in Philosophical Analysis.* New York: Appleton-Century-Crofts, 1949.

Russell, Bertrand. "The Philosophy of Logical Atomism." In R. C. Marsh, ed., *Logic and Knowledge.* London: Allen and Unwin, 1956.

Saussure, Ferdinand de. *Course in General Linguistics.* New York: Philosophical Library, 1959.

Schwartz, Stephen P., ed. *Naming, Necessity, and Natural Kinds.* Ithaca: Cornell University Press, 1977.

Searle, John R. "Proper Names." In A. P. Martinich, ed., *Philosophy of Language,* 1996, 249–254.

Searle, John R. *The Structure of Social Reality.* New York: Free Press, 1995.

Sher, Gila. *The Bounds of Logic.* Cambridge: MIT Press, 1991.

Simons, Peter M. "Faces, Boundaries, and Thin Layers." In A. P. Martinich and M. J. White, eds., *Certainty and Surface in Epistemology and Philosophical Method,* 1991, 87–100.

Simons, Peter M. *Parts: An Essay in Ontology.* Oxford: Oxford University Press, 1987.

Simons, Peter M. *Philosophy and Logic in Central Europe from Bolzano to Tarski.* Dordrecht: Kluwer, 1992.

Sisler, Harry H., Calvin A. VanderWerf, and Arthur W. Davidson. *College Chemistry.* 3rd ed. New York: Macmillan, 1967.

Smart, J. J. C. "Sensations and Brain Processes." In V. C. Chappell, ed., *The Philosophy of Mind,* 160–172. Englewood Cliffs, N.J.: Prentice-Hall, 1962.

Smith, Barry. *Austrian Philosophy: The Legacy of Franz Brentano.* Chicago: Open Court, 1994.

Smith, Barry. "Towards an Ontology of Common Sense." In J. Hintikka and K. Puhl, eds., *The British Tradition in 20th Century Philosophy,* 1995, 300–308.

Smythies, John R. *The Walls of Plato's Cave.* Aldershot, England: Avebury, 1994.

Stough, Charlotte L. *Greek Skepticism.* Berkeley: University of California Press, 1969.

Strawson, Peter F. "On Referring." *Mind* 59 (1950): 320–344. Also in A. Flew, ed., *Essays in Conceptual Analysis.* London: Macmillan and Co., 1960. And in A. P. Martinich, ed., *Philosophy of Language,* 1996, 215–230.

Strawson, Peter F. *Scepticism and Naturalism: Some Varieties.* New York: Columbia University Press, 1985.

Stroll, Avrum, ed. *Epistemology: New Essays in the Theory of Knowledge.* Aldershot, England: Ipswich, 1994.

Stroll, Avrum. "Foundationalism and Common Sense." *Philosophical Investigations* 10 (1987), no. 4: 279–298.

Stroll, Avrum. "How I See Philosophy: Common Sense and the Common Sense View of the World." In A. P. Martinich and M. J. White, eds., *Certainty and Surface in Epistemology and Philosophical Method,* 1991.

Stroll, Avrum. *Moore and Wittgenstein on Certainty.* New York: Oxford University Press, 1994.

Stroll, Avrum. "On Following a Rule." In R. Egidi, ed., *Wittgenstein: Mind and Language,* 1995, 93–106.

Stroll, Avrum. "Primordial Knowledge and Rationality." *Dialectica* 36, no. 2–3 (1982): 179–201.

Stroll, Avrum. "Some Different Ways That Things Stand Fast for Us." *Grazer Philosophische Studien* 22 (1984): 69–89.

Stroll, Avrum. *Surfaces.* Minneapolis: University of Minnesota Press, 1988.

Stroll, Avrum. "Wittgenstein and Folk Psychology." In *Philosophy, Law, Politics, and Society: Proceedings of the 12th International Wittgenstein Symposium, August 1987,* 264–270. Vienna: Holder-Pichler-Tempsky, 1988.

Stroud, Barry. *The Significance of Philosophical Scepticism.* Oxford: Clarendon, 1984.

269

Suter, Ronald. *Interpreting Wittgenstein*. Philadelphia: Temple University Press, 1989.

Tully, Robert E. "Recasting Russell's Problems." In J. Hintikka and K. Puhl, eds., *The British Tradition in 20th Century Philosophy*, 1995, 367–382.

Vendler, Zeno. "Epiphenomena." In A. P. Martinich and M. J. White, eds., *Certainty and Surface in Epistemology and Philosophical Method*, 1991, 101–116.

Vendler, Zeno. "Goethe, Wittgenstein, and the Essence of Color." *Monist* 78, no. 4 (Oct. 1995): 391–410.

Vendler, Zeno. *The Matter of Minds*. Oxford: Clarendon, 1984.

Von Wright, George H. "Wittgenstein and the Twentieth Century." In R. Egidi, ed., *Wittgenstein: Mind and Language*, 1995, 1–19.

Von Wright, George H. "Wittgenstein in Relation to His Times." In E. Leinfellner et al., eds., *Wittgenstein and His Impact on Contemporary Thought*, 73–78. Vienna: Holder-Pichler-Tempsky, 1978.

Wettstein, Howard. *"Has Semantics Rested on a Mistake?" and Other Essays*. Palo Alto: Stanford University Press, 1991.

Wettstein, Howard. "Terra Firma." *Monist* 78 (1995): 425–443.

White, M. J. *The Continuous and the Discrete*. Oxford: Oxford University Press, 1992.

White, M. J. "Folk Theories and Physical Metrics." In A. P. Martinich and M. J. White, eds., *Certainty and Surface in Epistemology and Philosophical Method*, 1991, 135–164.

Wittgenstein, Ludwig. *Last Writings on the Philosophy of Psychology*. Vol. 2. Oxford: Blackwell, 1993.

Wittgenstein, Ludwig. *On Certainty*. Oxford: Blackwell, 1969.

Wittgenstein, Ludwig. *Philosophical Investigations*. Oxford: Blackwell, 1958.

Wittgenstein, Ludwig. *Tractatus Logico-philosophicus*. Trans. by D. F. Pears and B. F. McGuinness. London: Routledge and Kegan Paul, 1961.

Wright, Edmond, ed. *New Representationalisms: Essays in the Philosophy of Perception*. Aldershot, England: Avebury, 1993.

Index

272